Pragmatic Aspects of Reported Speech

STUDIES IN ENGLISH MEDIEVAL LANGUAGE AND LITERATURE

Edited by Jacek Fisiak

Advisory Board:
John Anderson (Methoni, Greece), Norman Blake (Sheffield),
Ulrich Busse (Halle), Olga Fischer (Amsterdam),
Richard Hogg (Manchester), Dieter Kastovsky (Vienna),
Marcin Krygier (Poznań), Roger Lass (Cape Town),
Peter Lucas (Cambridge), Donka Minkova (Los Angeles),
Ruta Nagucka (Cracow), Akio Oizumi (Kyoto),
Katherine O'Brien O'Keeffe (Notre Dame, USA),
Matti Rissanen (Helsinki), Hans Sauer (Munich),
Liliana Sikorska (Poznań), Jeremy Smith (Glasgow)

Vol. 17

PETER LANG
Frankfurt am Main · Berlin · Bern · Bruxelles · New York · Oxford · Wien

Matylda Włodarczyk

Pragmatic Aspects of Reported Speech

The Case of Early Modern English
Courtroom Discourse

PETER LANG
Europäischer Verlag der Wissenschaften

Bibliographic Information published by the Deutsche Nationalbibliothek
The Deutsche Nationalbibliothek lists this publication in the Deutsche Nationalbibliografie; detailed bibliographic data is available in the internet at <http://www.d-nb.de>.

Printed with the financial support of the
Adam Mickiewicz University.

ISSN 1436-7521
ISBN-10: 3-631-55344-7
ISBN-13: 978-3-631-55344-2
US-ISBN 0-8204-9945-5

© Peter Lang GmbH
Europäischer Verlag der Wissenschaften
Frankfurt am Main 2007
All rights reserved.

All parts of this publication are protected by copyright. Any utilisation outside the strict limits of the copyright law, without the permission of the publisher, is forbidden and liable to prosecution. This applies in particular to reproductions, translations, microfilming, and storage and processing in electronic retrieval systems.

Printed in Germany 1 2 3 4 5   7

www.peterlang.de

Rodzicom

ACKNOWLEDGEMENTS

This thesis and the publication have been prepared as a PhD project under the supervision of prof. dr hab. Marcin Krygier and have been supported by the Polish Research Committee (Komitet Badań Naukowych), grant no H01D 006 26, which is hereby gratefully acknowledged. The author wishes to express her gratitude to the supervisor of the thesis, prof. dr hab. Marcin Krygier for his continuous support and to prof. dr hab. Jacek Fisiak for his constant encouragement and invaluable suggestions. Finally, my great thanks go to prof. dr hab. Roman Kalisz.

Contents

List of tables and figures ix
Abbreviations xi
Introduction.. 1

Chapter One: The 'bad-data problem' in historical pragmatics................. 5

1.1 The 'bad-data problem' – a definition... 5
1.2 The emerging new discipline and its focus on spoken language............ 6
    1.2.1 Historical pragmatics – a more in-depth account....................... 7
    1.2.2 English vs. German.. 9
    1.2.3 Speech-based vs. non-speech-based genres............................. 9
    1.2.4 Literary material in use and early criticism............................ 11
    1.2.5 Pragmaphilology: written texts as communicative acts.............. 12
1.3 The 'bad-data problem' in the major areas of historical pragmatics...... 13
    1.3.1 Summary.. 14
    1.3.2.1 Summary of the approaches to the 'bad-data problem'........... 14
    1.3.2.2 Summary of the approaches to primary sources.................... 17
    1.3.2.2.1 General remarks... 19
    1.3.2.2.2 A model approach to primary sources............................. 19
    1.3.2.2.3 Arguments for source text selection: Conclusions.............. 22
1.4 Conclusions for the present work.. 22
    1.4.1 Arguments for a rigorous methodological procedure................. 23
    1.4.1.2 Medium transmission... 23
    1.4.1.3 Textual transmission.. 25
    1.4.2 A methodological compromise.. 26

Chapter Two: Aspects of reported speech analysis..................................... 27

2.1 Aims and directions of the present research into reported speech........... 27
2.2 Reported speech studies – an introduction...................................... 28
    2.2.1 The interdisciplinary nature of reported speech studies............. 29
    2.2.2 Terminology... 30
    2.2.2.1 Speech and thought (re)presentation................................... 32
2.3 Definition.. 34
    2.3.1 Studies outside historical pragmatics..................................... 34
    2.3.1.1 Volosinov's definition... 35
    2.3.1.2 Problematic definitions... 36

vi

    2.3.2.2.1 What is speech event?... 36
    2.3.2.2.2 Anterior speech event.. 36
    2.3.2.2.3 Syntax versus pragmatics: the pragmatic nature of reported
    speech... 39
    2.3.2.2.3.1 Boundaries and marking.. 40
    2.3.2.2.3.1.1 Prosodic marking of reported speech................................. 41
    2.3.2.2.3.2 Communicative versus syntactic subordination.................. 41
    2.3.2.2.3.3 Intention and mediation... 43
    2.3.2.4 The source... 46
    2.3.2.4.1 Evidentiality... 47
    2.3.2.4.2 Implications of 'source' for the definition of reported
    speech... 48
    2.3.2.5 Text, utterance, thought – the medium problem........................ 48
    2.3.2.6 The context.. 50
    2.3.2 Studies outside historical pragmatics – implications for the
    definition.. 53
2.4 Categorisation.. 54
    2.4.1 Categorisation criteria.. 55
    2.4.1.1 Perspective/point of view... 56
    2.4.1.2 Other anterior utterance-biased criteria..................................... 56
    2.4.1.2.1 Dimensions of reporter's choice.. 57
    2.4.1.2.2 Singleness of deictic center.. 59
    2.4.1.3 Narrator/reporter control.. 60
    2.4.2 Implications of categorisation proposals for the present study..... 64
2.5 Implications from historical dialogue analysis... 64
2.6 Dominant theoretical approaches in the studies of reported speech........... 65
    2.6.1 The Bakhtinian legacy... 66
    2.6.1.1 Through voicing and speech interference to the hearer............ 67
    2.6.2 Goffman's legacy... 68
2.7 In conclusion: the definition.. 71

Chapter Three: A historical sketch and preliminaries.................................... 73

3.1 Introduction: source texts... 73
    3.1.1 The *State Trials* and ecclesiastical records................................ 75
3.2 The *State Trials* – description of the source... 77
    3.2.1 Trial of Sir Nicholas Throckmorton... 78
    3.2.1.1 Throckmorton, the defendant... 80
    3.2.2 Trial of Thomas Howard, Duke of Norfolk................................. 81
    3.2.2.1 Norfolk, the defendant... 83
    3.2.3 Acquittal and death sentence: towards a pragmatic explanation 85
3.3 Furnival (1897) – description of the source... 85

3.4 Recent studies into historical courtroom discourse.................................. 86
3.5 Some methodological preliminaries... 88
    3.5.1 Size and representativeness of the samples........................... 89
    3.5.2 Between the turn and the report – basic description units.......... 90
    3.5.3 Annotation of the data.. 91
3.6 Concluding remarks.. 92

Chapter Four: Reported speech as a marker of stance – pragmatic aspects of categorisation.. 93
    4.1.1 Accounts of reported speech in Early Modern English............... 93
    4.1.2 Extensions and emendations of Leech and Short's model (1981)... 94
4.2 Preliminary verification of Leech and Short's (1981) categories and further aspects of reported speech analysis... 95
    4.2.1 Thought presentation in institutional discourse........................... 97
    4.2.2 The status of reporting clauses in speech and thought presentation.. 99
4.3 Pragmatic aspects of the verb in reported speech....................................... 101
    4.3.1 Reported speech as a marker of stance – a working assumption... 103
    4.3.1.1 Formulas and fixed phrases – some statistics......................... 107
    4.3.1.2 Pragmatic aspects of formulas and fixed phrase..................... 111
    4.3.1.2.1 *that is to say*... 112
    4.3.1.2.2 *how say you*.. 113
    4.3.1.2.3 *may it please you*... 115
    4.3.1.3 Verb semantics vs. discourse markers..................................... 117
    4.3.1.3.1 Parentheticals... 119
    4.3.1.3.2 *I pray you*... 121
    4.3.1.3.3 *I beseech you*... 126
    4.3.1.3.4 Parentheticals – some statistics... 127
    4.3.1.4 KNOW-verbs – a model of evidentiality................................. 129
    4.3.1.5 KNOW-verbs – epistemic modality or thought presentation.... 130
    4.3.1.5.1 Epistemic modals and hedges... 132
    4.3.1.5.2 KNOW-verbs – a semantic classification............................ 133
    4.3.1.5.3 *Doubt not* and *doubt*... 134
    4.3.1.5.4 *I know, you know, it is well known* etc............................. 135
    4.3.1.5.5 *I think, methinke* and *think*... 139
    4.3.1.5.6 *Appear* – functions of non-factive verbs........................... 143
    4.3.1.5.7 *Hear* – perception verb... 147
    4.3.1.5.8 Evidentials – some statistics.. 149
    4.3.1.5.9 Hedges – a brief summary.. 152
    4.3.2 Concluding remarks... 154

Chapter Five: Pragmatic aspects of individual reported speech categories...... 155

5.1 Introduction: embedding levels... 155
5.2 Pragmatic aspects of reports and dialogue – the textual level................... 155
    5.2.1 Institutional roles... 158
    5.2.1.1 Aspects of defendants' direct speech... 159
    5.2.2 Possible directions of reported speech analysis – the textual
    level.. 163
5.3 Features of reported speech on the interaction level................................. 163
    5.3.1 Pragmatic aspects of selected grammatical features of reported
    speech categories.. 164
    5.3.2 RSA – the dominant strategy and control.. 167
    5.3.3 Indirect speech – hierarchy of information prominence................... 168
    5.3.4 Direct speech – heteroglossic information....................................... 170
    5.3.5 Indirect thought.. 171
    5.3.6 Reports of thought acts... 172
    5.3.7 Free categories and slipping.. 172
5.4 State trials and court records – a comparison.. 174
5.5 Concluding remarks... 176

Conclusions... 177

Appendix... 181

Bibliography... 183

LIST OF TABLES

Table 1: Summary of the approaches to the 'bad-data problem'
Table 2: Overall presentation of the quality of primary sources
Table 3: Model applications of primary sources
Table 4: Indicators of the reproduction of words for the five uses of reported speech (after Vincent and Dubois 1996: 367)
Table 5: Functional options for language reports (after Thompson 1996: 524)
Table 6: Structural options for language reports (after Thompson 1996: 524)
Table 7: Categories in the SW&TP Written corpus and their equivalents in the Spoken Corpus (after McIntyre et al. 2004 57)
Table 8: Categories outside the discourse presentation clines (after McIntyre et al. 2004: 57)
Table 9: A selection of recent studies into trials and depositions as speech-based genres
Table 10: Reported speech instances in the data
Table 11: Distribution of tags: grammatical categories
Table 12: Most frequent verbal tags and percentages in <TH> and <N>
Table 13: The distribution and classification of fixed phrases in <TH>
Table 14: Distribution and classification of fixed phrases in <N>
Table 15: A comparison of the distribution and tag categories of fixed phrases in both trials
Table 16: Problematic fixed verbal phrases in <TH> and <N>
Table 17: Features of *I pray you* parenthetical
Table 18: Distribution of parenthetical verbs in the trial of Throckmorton
Table 19: Distribution of parenthetical verbs in the trial of Norfolk
Table 20: Comparison of parentheticals' distribution in two trials
Table 21: Distribution of evidential verbs in the trial of Throckmorton
Table 22: Evidential verbs in <TH>: a classification
Table 23: Distribution of evidential verbs in the trial of Norfolk
Table 24: Evidential verbs in <N>: a classification
Table 25: Comparison of evidentials' distribution in two trials
Table 26: Word count of reports vs. dialogue – textual level
Table 27: Dialogue in <TH> and <N>
Table 28: Type-to-token ratio in tags
Table 29: Comparison of the most frequent tags' in defendants' speech
Table 30: Comparison of the distribution of reported speech categories in <TH> and <N>
Table 31: Correlation between selected grammatical features and reported speech categories
Table 32: Comparison of the distribution of reported speech categories in the speech of the defendants

Table 33: Comparison of selected grammatical features of IS in <TH> and <N>
Table 34: Comparison of RS count in the two sources
Table 35: Comparison of frequencies of individual RS categories in two sources
Table 36: Comparison of most frequent tags in the two sources
Table 37: Strategies of RS in the speech of the defendants

LIST OF FIGURES

Figure 1: The semantic domain of evidentiality (based on Willet (1988); after Dendale and Tasmowsky (2001: 343))
Figure 2: Reported speech categories; based on Short – Semino – Culpeper (1996: 115)
Figure 3: Embedded discourse levels in the Lancaster Witches (after Culpeper and Kytö 1999b: 175)
Figure 4: A sample from Furnivall (1987)
Figure 5: Complete list of verbs occurring in the analysis of stance (adapted from Biber 2004: 133-135)
Figure 6: Model of epistemological stance adoption (adapted from Mushin 2001b: 59)
Figure 7: Palmer's model of epistemic modality (adapted from Mushin 2001b: 25)
Figure 8: A semantic categorisation of mental verbs

ABBREVIATIONS

AP	Adjectival phrase or verb-adjective combination
DA	Direct address
DO SUP	*Do*-periphrasis in affirmative clauses
DR	Distinctiveness ratio
DS	Direct speech
EV	Evidential expressions
F	Fixed expression or formula
FADE IN	Slipping – one category of RS 'fading into' another
FDS	Free direct speech
FDT	Free direct thought
FIS	Free indirect speech
FIT	Free indirect thought
GERUND	Gerundival construction
HEDGE	Non-propositional attitude-marking expression
IMP	Imperative construction
INF	Infinitival construction
INTERPOSED	Tag position inside the clause
INV	Affirmative clauses with inversion
IS	Indirect speech
IT	Indirect thought
N	Noun
<N>	Trial of Thomas Howard, Duke of Norfolk
NRS	Narrator's report of speech
NRSA	Narrator's report of speech act
NRTA	Narrator's report of thought act
Q	Question
PAR	Parenthetical
PASS	Passive construction
POSTPOSED	Tag position following the clause
PP	Past participle without the copula
PROGR	Progressive passive construction or passive gerund
RS	Reported speech
RSA	Report of speech act
RTA	Report of thought act
THAT-DEL	*That*-deletion
<TH>	Trial of Nicholas Throckmorton

Introduction

The scope and foci of interest in this study can be delineated with a reference to the title of the latest major publication in the field of reported speech studies: *Reported discourse. A meeting ground for different linguistic domains* (Güldemann and Roncador 2002). The subtitle is particularly telling, and can be seen as more than an apt metaphor. A meeting ground for different linguistic domains, reported speech studies is open to all kinds of theoretical perspectives, and invites the linguist to construct and arrange it from the elements of essentially individual choice. No-one but a student in the field is in a position to provide a montage of his/her own linguistic interests and to choose his/her research interests relatively freely. What is more, the resulting montage is best to remain in a state of constant flux, not only allowing in new, but also continuously revising existing, components. In this study the following research areas are included in the common ground mentioned above:
- studies into the history of the English language
- a pragmatic perspective on reported speech
- studies of Early Modern English courtroom discourse

The interests of the present research evolved out of a need to fill a gap in the area of reported speech studies. As Culpeper and Kytö (1999) maintain "very few studies have ventured further back in time than the eighteenth century and even fewer historical studies have examined the full range of speech presentation categories" (Culpeper and Kytö 1999: 179). Indeed, despite an immense body of research (the latest comprehensive reported speech bibliography contains over a 1000 entries; cf. Güldemann – Roncador – Van der Wurff 2002), historical studies of reported speech have not attracted consistent attention either on the part of investigations into English, or other languages. Hence a general aim of this work is to contribute – through a synchronic description – some analytic tools and linguistic insights relevant for a historical description of reported speech in the English language. The phenomenon under consideration is viewed from a pragmatic perspective, which has so far not been systematically applied to the history of English in this respect. The pragmatic perspective does not entail, nor limit the scope of attention to, any specific pragmatic theory of language or communication, but rather endeavours to utilise elements of different approaches and a wide range of interdisciplinary insights serving auxiliary explanatory purposes in the analysis of reported speech.

The incentive for adopting a historical pragmatic framework comes from Collins (2001), a monograph on mediaeval Russian. The material studied here is drawn from Hargrave[1] (1776), with additional data as grounds for comparison obtained from Furnivall (1897), the two sources containing courtroom records and witness depositions from the Early Modern English[2] state and church courts respectively. It is proposed that the selected sources are indeed acceptable provided that the authenticity of events underlying instances of reported speech is not the central concern of the investigation. Still, the two sources differ in the degree to which they depart from the authentic interaction due to the differences in their institutional background. Actually, reported speech instances in the courtroom data pertaining to state trials are similar in nature to *imagined speech* (Rissanen 1986), or "simulated spoken interaction" (Bax 2001: 37). On the other hand, the data recording the ecclesiastical procedure are closer to the actual interaction, which is reflected in certain respects in the features of reported speech. A comparison of two kinds of data demonstrates the pragmatic nature of the phenomenon in question as its characteristics are clearly determined by the context of interaction. Furthermore, an institutional setting and some (genre) conventions, combined with the general intention of the court reporter (be it his own or externally imposed), provide a context for the creative application of reported speech strategies at their disposal, though the institutional conventions of the ecclesiastical records definitely leave less scope for creativity than in the case of state trials. Nevertheless, since edited data have recently been described as objectionable (e.g., Kytö and Walker 2003, Hiltunen and Skaffari 2003, Lass 2004), a comprehensive justification of a methodological compromise made in this study is presented in chapter one. Chapter two is devoted to an overview of recent studies in the area of reported speech and it aims at clarifying the most important problematic issues. The outcome of this part of the discussion is a presentation of the analytic tools applied in the analysis proper. Also, a definition of reported speech is abstracted from the literature on the topic. Particular attention is paid to the categorisation of reported speech, as a crucial aspect of the linguistic analysis. Moreover, the significance of the notion of context, with a variety of relevant approaches, is underlined as constituting the major source of arguments that may be resorted to in an attempt at a pragmatic explanation. Consequently, chapter three concentrates on outlining the historical and institutional context of courtroom discourse in Early Modern England, and it gives a detailed background of the trials subjected to analysis. This also delineates some strictly methodological preliminaries of the analysis. Chapter four focuses on those pragmatic aspects of reported speech which have already surfaced in the course of categorisation procedures, and need to be accounted for prior to its

---

[1] Hargrave's edition has been consulted with the manuscript sources in the British Library.
[2] It is assumed that the time span of Early Modern English is 1500-1700 although the delimitation of the period is not uncontroversial (cf. e.g., Görlach 1991: 9-11).

completion. It is assumed that reported speech may be viewed as one of the markers of *stance*, a widely-discussed multifaceted phenomenon. This is corroborated with some results of a detailed presentation of the verb as the most frequently occurring reported speech *tag*. As an outcome of the discussion, the adopted categorisation model (Leech and Short 1981) is revised and extended in order to accommodate the specific phenomena occurring in courtroom discourse. In chapter five, the results of the analysis are presented with the emphasis on the pragmatic implications of reported speech categories on two embedding levels, textual and interactional. The last step in the analysis attempts to provide some conclusive findings, thereby contributing both to the developing discipline of historical pragmatics and to the field of reported speech studies.

Given the highly theoretical nature of pragmatic studies, considerable attention needs to be devoted to a critical discussion of concepts and analytical tools pertaining to reported speech analysis. Also, seeing the lack of linguistic descriptions of the phenomenon in the period under consideration, it is necessary to develop specific means through which such a description becomes possible. Most importantly, the major outcome of the study is constituted by the deployment of analytic tools, such as the revised categorisation model, which, though developed for this specific period, possesses in itself some potential of being applied to other historical stages of the history of English and other languages. Traditionally viewed as the conclusive description of reported speech, the overall results of the categorisation, given the limitations of the database, are possibly less significant and decisive than the observations accompanying the development of the analytic tools. Therefore, the contribution this study hopes to make to the field of historical linguistics lies first and foremost in the conclusions pertaining to the 'bad-data problem', specifically in the area of historical pragmatics; and, secondly, in providing the analytic means and foci of attention to be applied in a historical study of the phenomenon and verifying their efficacy with a view to their descriptive adequacy. Finally, a supplementary aim of the contribution involves a selective comparison of the state and church records with respect to the ways in which the institutional setting determines the features of reported speech – essentially a pragmatic phenomenon.

Chapter One

The 'bad-data problem' in historical pragmatics

> "We may be justified in making use of every possibility, however troublesome or uncertain to reconstruct spoken language of the past"
> (Rissanen 1986: 98).

This chapter[1] aims to present a discussion of a range of methodological issues pertaining to a linguistic analysis within historical pragmatics. Firstly, the problem of the lack of access to spoken language as an obstacle to all kinds of historical linguistic analyses is taken up and the 'bad-data problem', a term coined by Labov (1972, 1994), is defined. Next, the new sub-discipline of historical linguistics, historical pragmatics, is introduced with a view to the handling of the 'bad-data problem' and to some theoretical approaches working toward its solution. Finally, building on the discussion above, some general methodological considerations are incorporated into the present study.

1.1 The 'bad-data problem' – an introduction

Not unlike most historians, historical linguists have no choice but to rely on mute material, which is, moreover, frequently preserved with no specific social or other context. In the 1950s McIntosh warned, "written texts will always be ransacked for information about spoken language" (1956 [1989]: 7). In the 1990s the issue gained even more far-reaching implications as stated by Labov: "[t]hough we know what was written, we know nothing about what was understood" (1994: 10). Nevertheless, within the span of time separating the former and the latter point of view, a sizeable volume of research appeared claiming to provide a range of (more and less convincing) conclusions about the speech of the past in all aspects of linguistic inquiry.

Along with advances in historical sociolinguistics (Romaine 1982) and the emergence of the variationist paradigm (Labov 1972, Rissanen 1986), the issue of the lack of access to spoken language started to receive attention from linguists in a more systematic way. Major discussions had, however, not appeared before the late 1990s[2], accompanying the emergence of historical pragmatics as a sub-field of historical linguistic studies (cf. 1.2.1 for some remarks on its status). Indeed, in the last decade, few researchers in sociohistorical linguistics or historical

---

[1] An earlier version of this discussion was published as Włodarczyk-Golka (2004).
[2] Naturally, prior to sociolinguistic and pragmatic attempts in historical linguistics, the discipline has dealt with this problem (e.g., McIntosh 1956 [1989]) viewing it from a different angle, though.

pragmatics have failed to air their concern about the lack of adequate data for spoken language analysis, with the exception of the very recent past, when audio recordings had become available.

The general predicament of historical linguistics connected with the nature of sources has been summed up by Labov as the 'bad-data problem'[3] (1972, 1994). For Labov the issue is double-faced at least. Not only does the medium of preservation of older linguistic stages contribute to the methodological intricacy of historical linguistics, but also the lack of information on the social background of the authors of texts seems no less serious, particularly for sociolinguistic research. While the latter aspect of the 'bad-data problem' may indeed be successfully overcome in many cases (Nevalainen 1999: 503, 507-510), the former is an insurmountable difficulty inherent in historical linguistic research.

1.2 The emerging new discipline and its focus on spoken language

The last decade in historical linguistics witnessed a rapidly growing interest in hitherto neglected research questions such as speech act analysis, studies of maxims of conversation, studies of politeness and forms of address, dialogue analysis, and the development of discourse markers or pragmatic investigations into reported speech. Although these themes had occasionally been taken up before the 1990s, it was only then when more systematic research efforts began to appear under the label of historical pragmatics. Nevertheless, even in 1995, when the seminal volume edited by Andreas Jucker was published as a first collection of contributions to the new field, the editor emphasised the unexplored nature of this area: "Few people could fall back on existing research. Most contributors had to start from scratch" (Jucker 1995: ix). At the same time, Jucker was convinced that this line of studies could also be seen as "a new label for a range of research efforts that have existed for a long time" (Jacobs and Jucker 1995: 4).

Contributions intended as historical pragmatic, whether innovative or not, and despite a wide spectrum of approaches and interests, clearly share one basic consideration: they set out to discuss phenomena typical of, or sometimes even confined to, spoken language. Such indeed has been the stance of general

---

[3] "The fundamental methodological fact that historical linguists have to face is that they have no control over their data; texts are produced by a series of historical accidents (...) the great art of the historical linguist is to make the best of this bad data – 'bad' in the sense that it may be fragmentary, corrupted or many times removed from the actual production of native speakers" (Labov 1972: 100; quoted also in Romaine 1982: 122). In his later work Labov repeats the above point of view: "Historical linguistics can then be thought as the art of making the best use of bad data" (1994: 11; quoted also in Nevalainen 1999: 503). The term has been widely accepted and referred to also without references to its real origin – for instance Sell (2001: 2) traces the term back to Nevalainen (1999). Some contributors adopted the term for the titles of their papers e.g., Nevalainen (1999), Kytö and Walker (2003).

pragmatics[4], as Jacobs and Jucker point out: "Pragmatics is predominantly concerned with spoken language" (Jacobs and Jucker 1995: 6). In the end the whole empirical apparatus of pragmatic research is made up of direct data-gathering and observation techniques[5]. Hence, it comes as no surprise that one of the main concerns of historical pragmatics has been the absence of adequate data for historical stages of the language, where the only surviving sources are written texts, often with serious limitations, both generically and in terms of register. Sharing the fate of all historical linguists, pragmatically oriented researchers have had no choice but to provide some solutions to the 'bad-data problem'. Though the range of explanations is very broad, it is still possible to discern some general tendencies embodying common theoretical standpoints. The following discussion provides a review of these standpoints on the basis of the most important literature in the field published over the last decade.

1.2.1 Historical pragmatics[6] – a more in-depth account

Defining historical pragmatics is an increasingly difficult task despite the existence of a range of reasonable attempts at a definition (e.g., Stein 1985, Jacobs and Jucker 1995, Jucker 1998, Mazzon 1997, Arnovick 1999). One of the latest comprehensive overviews of pragmatics[7], *The handbook of pragmatics online* (2003), offers an explanation of this difficulty. In the introduction, Verschueren makes an issue of the interdisciplinary character of general or traditional pragmatics when discussing "the 'waste basket' view of pragmatics" (2003). To an extent, historical pragmatics shares the fate of synchronic pragmatics in the sense that it does not exhibit either methodological or topical unity. Therefore, delimitation both of the traditional line of pragmatics as well as its new offshoot, i.e., historical pragmatics, may never be possible. As Verchueren further claims: "pragmatics can be developed without defining it as a component of a theory of language and without yielding to misplaced ambitions to establish a discipline" (2003). The fact that the *Handbook*, comprehensive as it is, does not devote a separate paper to historical pragmatics, shows that its status as a separate field is indeed fairly questionable. A similar opinion is explicitly aired by the authors of

---

[4] This study does not make an attempt to redefine pragmatics in line with its specific needs and concerns. Its interest is more in a coherent description of historical pragmatics, the area which is different from a simple equation of historical linguistics and linguistic pragmatics. For a discussion of definitions and overviews of approaches to the latter cf. Levinson (1983: 1-51); Kalisz (1993: 9-27); Kopytko (2003: 5-16).

[5] Cf. Jacobs and Jucker's discussion of the data problem (1995: 6-10).

[6] That the term "historical pragmatics" is in circulation beyond any doubt. Thus, opinions like that of Mazzon: "this label does not seem much in use in English-speaking linguistics" (1997) seem unfounded.

[7] Compare Carroll et al. (2003: 10f).

the introduction to one of the latest collections devoted to historical discourse studies (edited by Hiltunen and Skaffari 2003): "The fuzziness characteristic of a new field of research is indicated by the variety of labels used for historical pragmatics: we are evidently not yet dealing with a fixed paradigm" (Carroll et al. 2003: 2).

Not only the interdisciplinary character and methodological variation, but also the confusingly rich inventory of terms describing research efforts in historical linguistics with a pragmatic approach, put into doubt the feasibility of viewing historical pragmatics as a separate discipline. For instance, in one of the very first English-language publications in which the term has occurred, Stein uses the general "sociohistorical linguistics" (1985: 347), as well as more specific "diachronic lexical semantics" (1985: 349) and "Pragmatische Texttheorie" (1985: 351) labels. Kopytko talks about "socio-historical pragmatics" or "historical socio-pragmatics" (1993: 16), placing both terms within socio-historical linguistics. Jacobs and Jucker divide historical pragmatics into "pragmaphilology" and "diachronic pragmatics" (1995: 11-13); the latter term is also applied e.g., by Arnovick (1999: 11-14) as well as in the title of a collection of essays published in Italy (*English diachronic pragmatics* edited by di Martino 2000). Archer provides yet another proposal, namely placing her own work within a "historical sociopragmatic approach" (2002: 3; cf. Archer and Culpeper 2003) or "sociohistorical pragmatics" (2003: 2); she sees the latter as a sub-discipline of historical pragmatics. As if this is not enough, the matter could be complicated even further. For instance, in an ongoing project at the University of Turku, *Discourse Perspectives on Early English,* which is "intended to bring together the history of English and the study of discourse, text, and pragmatics" (*Discourse Perspectives on Early English* 2004), the term "discourse linguistics" is used "incorporating both historical discourse studies and historical pragmatics" (*Discourse Perspectives on Early English* 2004). Similarly in their brief outline of "the field of historical discourse linguistics and pragmatics" (Carroll and Skaffari 2002: 48), different authors talk about *historical discourse linguistics* (University of Turku), *historical discourse pragmatics* (Leslie Arnovick and Jonathan Culpeper) or *discourse-oriented historical linguistics* (Laurel Brinton) as terms circulating among various researchers. Furthermore, what one may also come across at the University of Wuerzburg is "the relatively new field of historical pragmalinguistics" which "focuses on the historical development of the linguistic expression of requests (orders, invitations, suggestions, requests proper)" (*Lehrstuhl fuer Romanische Philologie I* 2004).

In the introduction to the volume edited by the Turku team (Hiltunen and Skaffari 2003), whose approach is text-based and synchronic, the authors explain: "we see ourselves as engaged in historical discourse linguistics specifically rather than any other field of historical pragmatics generally" (Carroll et al. 2003: 1).

Thus, we may be dealing with a tendency to view historical pragmatics as the most general label comprising a range of more specific areas of interest.

Inconclusive as it is, the discussion above underlines the fact that up to this point, historical linguistics has not been able to come to terms with the diversity of pragmatic perspectives on former stages of the language and the growing body of pragmatic attempts which are increasingly difficult to classify. According to Carroll and Skaffari (2002), the efforts that could possibly be unified under one label and that are directed at text, discourse and pragmatics in a historical perspective, share the "emphasis on *context* and speakers/writers – on language as it was actually used rather than as an idealised system" (2002: 48; original emphasis).

1.2.2 English vs. German

As mentioned above, though 1995 is an important caesura in the field of historical pragmatics, one cannot deny the existence of related contributions prior to this date. Particularly visible in this area in the late seventies and in the eighties is the crude dividing line between German (and German-speaking) and English scholarship, with the former showing much more robust efforts in the direction of historical pragmatics (an overview is given in Stein 1985[8]; cf. also Jacobs and Jucker 1995; Jucker – Fritz – Lebsanft 1999). What might strike a reader familiar with recent developments in the English line of historical pragmatics is the comprehensiveness of the German historical pragmatic research as summarised in Stein (1985; e.g. Schlieben-Lange 1983). The range of problems taken up by the German-speaking scholarship has up to this point hardly been matched by the intensely growing body of English-language research. The reasons for this discrepancy can be seen, according to Stein (1985: 347), as ideological, i.e., the "pragmatische Wende" of German linguistics may by and large be a part of the reaction against generative theory in the seventies and eighties. To give justice to the English historical pragmatics, the beginning of the 1990s is marked by an upsurge of interest for this field also within the English scholarly community. What remains a cause for regret is that up to this day the English line has been developing largely independent of the German one.

1.2.3 Speech-based vs. non-speech-based genres

Within historical pragmatics the ideas employed when dealing with the data problem go back to the Helsinki school in its 'pre-corpus' era (Kytö and Rissanen

---

[8] The paper was presented at the *Sixth International Conference on Historical Linguistics* organised by Adam Mickiewicz University on August 20th 1983 in Poznań, Poland.

1983, Rissanen 1986[9]). The question frequently asked of late about the distance of written sources from spoken language has been central to the developing variationist approach since the 1980s. Not only the questions but also some basic answers provided by research into historical pragmatics hark back to this source. For instance, the division of texts into speech-based and non-speech-based introduced by Rissanen and Kytö in the 1980s (Rissanen 1986, Kytö and Rissanen 1983: 477) is still accepted. Moreover, the notion of *imagined speech* i.e., "dialogue in drama, narration or even other kinds of text" (Rissanen 1986: 99) as another source suited for the purpose of spoken language reconstruction also originates from the Helsinki school. In drawing a line of distinction between data drawn from speech-based genres and imagined speech of literature, Rissanen and Kytö provided foundations for the two separate lines of research within historical pragmatics.

As far as the former approach is concerned, the major argument put forward by Rissanen was "that texts which record speech for some reason or another, are closer to spoken language than texts which are not based on actual speech" (1986: 98; cf. Kytö and Rissanen 1983: 474). At this point Rissanen enumerated records of meetings[10], sermons, depositions, private diaries as relevant to the study of Early Modern English and early American English. In the 1990s historical pragmatics would go beyond the temporal limitations to include text-types from earlier periods of the English language and to include other genres. Accepting the necessity of utilising speech-based genres, Rissanen and Kytö do not claim at any point that written texts reproduce speech faithfully, bearing in mind the issues of medium interference and the level of formality of recorded situations (Kytö and Rissanen 1983: 474, Rissanen 1986: 108). Rather than regard written texts as reflections of spoken language, the advocated stand is to draw conclusions from a comparison of speech-based against non-speech-based genres.

Selected literary data, too, may serve the purpose of studies into the speech of the past, as they provide imagined speech which "contains a number of features with which an author hopes to create an illusion of spoken idiom" (Rissanen 1986: 99). This intuitive statement finds corroboration in the later work of Biber and Finegan (1989, 1992) on the evolution of selected genres in the history of English. These studies provide a sound theoretical justification for the use of literary material as a reflection of spoken language and offer some selection criteria for future research. By comparing the development of three written

---

[9] The terms speech-based vs. non-speech-based genres have become an integral part of historical pragmatic inquiries to the extent that their origin seems to remain obscure to many.

[10] Compare a study into Hansard reports by Slembrouck (1992) who admits that although the record "masks the spoken nature of the debate" it is still able to provide "clear markers of the spoken, interactive origin of the text" (1992: 110). This empirical argument lies at the core of the speech-based v. non speech-based distinction of texts.

(fiction, essays, letters) and two speech-based genres (dialogue in fiction, dialogue in drama) the authors arrive at distinct patterns of their respective evolutions and feel justified in distinguishing between two independent linguistic systems (Biber and Finegan 1992). The basis of assessment of the degree of orality preserved in writing is exclusively linguistic in these studies: a matrix of empirically discerned features (Biber 1988) is used for a thorough statistical analysis. It is important to emphasise that neither of the arguments in favour of utilising literary material in the studies of spoken language of the past accepts its equivalence to speech, neither do scholars decide to resort to this kind of material facing the lack of more suitable sources. Rather, both Rissanen (1986) and Biber and Finegan (1989, 1992) make a conscious choice in using data from literary texts for the linguistic study of the speech of the past.

1.2.4 Literary material in use and early criticism

With regard to some further studies utilising literary texts as sources for spoken language analysis, Bax (1981) on ritual challenges in Middle Dutch romances and Kopytko (1993) on politeness and forms of address in Shakespeare are relatively early examples. Bax sees literary texts as providing *simulated spoken interaction* (1983, 1991) and accepts that some kinds of verbal interaction in literature "may be taken to reflect a real life situation" (Jacobs and Jucker 1995: 7). Brown and Gilman (1989) take a similar view and, moreover, maintain the inevitability of resorting to literary data (Shakespeare's four tragedies) due to the lack of anything else (at least for the analysis of Early Modern English the authors are interested in), assuming at the same time a one-to-one correspondence between the linguistic usage in drama and real Early Modern English speech. The line of research within politeness theory is continued by Kopytko (1993), who largely accepts the above views on the applicability of dramatic texts not only to the study of Early Modern English spoken language in general but spoken colloquial language in particular (1993: 59).

Jonathan Hope (1994) criticises this standpoint in the study of *thou/you* usage in Early Modern spoken English. Hope challenges Brown and Gilman's (1989) assumptions by proposing court depositions as an alternative source of evidence which comes closer to the spoken language than other written genres (1994: 142-143). Given that depositions are "accounts of conversations which occurred in everyday life, repeated by witnesses for the benefit of the court" (Hope 1994: 143), they are treated as a verbatim record of authentic speech. Hope's study indeed constitutes an important step towards a critical and cautious approach to historical data. Moreover, using a modernised (19th century) edition of the depositions, the author is aware of the possibility of editorial interference and checks his examples against the manuscripts (Hope 1994: 142). Thus, one might get the impression that in this study an ideal solution is found for the predicament of both historical pragmatics and sociolinguistics. Unfortunately, this is not the case. Hope's study avoids some important methodological issues: the problems involved in the transmission of speech into writing are not touched upon. Another major flaw is regarding direct speech occurrences from the perspective of the largely criticised and uncorroborated verbatimness hypothesis (cf. Collins 2001: 49-58). Nevertheless, this study marks the beginning of a new line (cf. Rissanen 1986) in historical research into spoken language. By overtly criticising the validity of statements based exclusively on literary material it constitutes a fruitful application of utilitarian speech-based material to the study of forms of address (cf. Wright 1995 for a similar step in the study of syntax).

1.2.5 Pragmaphilology: written texts as communicative acts

As early as the 1950s, McIntosh pointed out the danger inherent in the excessive interest for spoken language in historical linguistic research:

> "the very fault of the traditional approach to written language – that of concentrating unduly on the task of revealing facts about the spoken language – has had the unfortunate result of tending to inhibit progress in the development of techniques adequate for the description of spoken language" (McIntosh 1956 [1989]: 15).

Similarly, Romaine, when criticising Labov's overstatement of the 'bad-data problem' claimed: "the only way in which they [historical data, MW] can be bad (...) is by invidious or inappropriate comparison with the spoken language" (Romaine 1982: 122). Also within historical pragmatics – despite the fact that the study of speech functions is crucial for it – the issue of direct unavailability of spoken language is not central to those investigations which assume the status of a written text as a communicative act in its own right[11] e.g., Watts (1981) and Sell (1985) on author and reader cooperation on the basis of literature, Danet and Bogoch (1992) on Anglo-Saxon wills, Fritz (1993) on early German newspapers. According to Jacobs and Jucker this approach "includes a careful consideration of the writers of these texts, their communicative intentions and their intended audiences as well as the entire socio-historical context in which these texts were written" (1995: 12). Interestingly enough, these research questions are asked for a range of text-types and in this way the scope of pragmatic investigations is even further expanded to include genres such as foreign language textbooks (Hüllen 1995), grammar books (Watts 1995) or conversation manuals (Fritz 1995). An important aspect of this investigation may be "the similarities and dissimilarities of written and spoken language" (Jacobs and Jucker 1995: 11) as in Hüllen

---

[11] This view to a large extent mirrors Romaine's (1982: 122): "Historical data can be valid in their own right ... (as can other instances of the written language) regardless of the extent to which they reflect or are removed from the productions of native speakers".

(1995), who justifies a pragmatic study of foreign language textbooks with the fact that their orality is determined by the real-life function they performed as a part of the oral language teaching process:

> "the *Dialogues* [Caxton's, MW] are characterised by what could be called their scholastic realism which contains many features of orality, even if we admit that many pragmatic signals would be omitted and stylistic shifts would probably be effected by turning the imagined dialogue into performed speech. But there is no reason to assume that such shifts were particularly drastic" (Hüllen 1995: 107).

In a similar vein, Watts (1999: 216) and Becker (2002: 275) emphasise the communicative goals of the language teaching process.

However suspicious the all-inclusive or even indiscriminate view of data implied in regarding written texts as communicative acts in their own right may be, one cannot deny that pragmaphilological studies contribute an important merit to the discipline: they provide further instances of how utilitarian genres may be employed for the study of linguistic history.

As mentioned above, pragmaphilology as a sub-area of historical pragmatic studies was discerned by Jacobs and Jucker (1995; cf. Leech 1983) and contrasted with "diachronic pragmatics", the latter concentrating on "the linguistic inventory and its communicative use" (Jacobs and Jucker 1995: 13) across time. Nevertheless, at present it is clear that there are many overlaps between the two allegedly different lines, though some researchers do follow this rather arbitrary and short-lived line of division (e.g., Archer 2003: 6-7).

1.3 The 'bad-data problem' in the major areas of historical pragmatics

Above, three major approaches to data in the early contributions to the field of historical pragmatics have been outlined. In the development of the field, these have not only been largely followed but have also been elaborated upon by the latest advances (i.e., post-1995) in the discipline. Considering these advances, some patterns may be traced which allow dividing the post-1995 contributions into the following major areas of interest:
1. Speech act analysis.
2. Syntax, discourse markers, grammaticalisation.
3. Dialogue analysis.
4. Study of politeness and forms of address.
5. Study of ritual behaviour in language.
6. Discourse strategies, semantics.
7. Genre studies.

Obviously, not all the contributions to historical pragmatics allow an easy and unambiguous classification and, moreover, this classification necessarily remains arbitrary. In spite of the vagueness and subjectivity of some classificatory decisions it represents, nevertheless, an advance towards the formulation of some generalisations is essential.

The above-mentioned generalisations result from a thorough investigation into a range of contributions to the field of historical pragmatics. Apart from *Historical pragmatics* (1995), contributions to several other volumes and the leading journal (*Journal of Historical Pragmatics*) were analysed. This choice was, naturally, arbitrary but it took into consideration the milestones of historical pragmatics (*Historical pragmatics. Anglistentag 1997 Giessen,* 1998; *Historical dialogue analysis,* 1999; *Diachronic pragmatics: seven case studies in English illocutionary development,* 1999). The contributions were analysed with the following aspects of data and methodology in mind: the generic and functional dimensions (literary vs. non-literary/utilitarian) as well as the quality of primary sources used (i.e., manuscripts, imprints, contemporaneous editions or modern editions; cf the Appendix). A more detailed discussion of those theoretical approaches to the 'bad-data problem' that have contributed some new selection criteria to the field of historical pragmatics has been presented in Włodarczyk-Golka (2004).

1.3.1 Summary

The approaches to primary sources and the standpoints on the 'bad-data problem' in the seven major sub-fields arbitrarily discerned within historical pragmatic studies published in the last decade, endeavoured to reveal some patterns and point out possible mutual stances. Unfortunately, this aim cannot have been achieved to an equal degree for all areas. Within the well-represented sub-fields (e.g., studies into discourse markers and historical dialogue analysis) it is possible to notice some model approaches. For example, one may notice a preference for electronic resources in the syntactic group of papers, while the opposite is typical for historical dialogue analysis. Other areas were underrepresented (e.g., genre studies) and only the approaches of individual researchers could be referred to. The reason for the unequal representation of individual sub-fields may lie in the choice of material for discussion. It is, however, still my contention that this essentially arbitrary choice makes possible a presentation of the recent status and interest enjoyed by the respective areas. Most probably an analysis of an equal number of papers in each group would have resulted in a clearer picture but, on the other hand, it would have distorted the distribution of the foci of interest within the highly heterogeneous field of historical pragmatics.

1.3.1.1 Summary of approaches to the 'bad-data problem'

Below a table summarising the arguments discussed above – both maintaining and solving the predicament of the 'bad-data problem' – is presented in order to provide a succinct illustration of the wide range of approaches (Table 1). As is clearly shown, rarely does one come across a study in which the possibility of access to speech through written texts is accepted without reservations. Thus, the impossibility of a final solution to the 'bad-data problem' is revealed once again.

AUTHOR	CATEGORY	SOURCES	ARGUMENTS 'Bad' indeed	ARGUMENTS Not so 'bad'	WEAK POINTS
Jucker and Taavitsainen 2000	SA	both		Real-life verbal aggression reported in utilitarian genres	
Schrott 2000	SA	LIT	Literary representations determined by relevant text traditions		
Culpeper and Semino 2000	SA	UTI			No disclaimer as to identicalness of investigated features and speech
Arnovick 1999	SA	LIT		Dialogue and speech events in written texts give access to orality	Random data selection
Bernández and Tejada 1995	DM	both		If generalisations are difficult, determine word order of different text-types	Modest samples
Schwenter and Traugott 1995	DM	both	Nothing more than reconstruction is possible, relevant text-traditions as a filter		Edited punctuation problem mistakenly resolved by the use of corpora
Brinton 1998	DM	both		Oral residue of mediaeval texts	
Fludernik 2000	DM	LIT		Oral substrate of mediaeval and early Modern texts	
Onodera 1995, 2000	DM	LIT		Interactive character of some genres	No info as to the quality of primary sources
Taavitsainen 1995	DM	both		Statistically asses the distance of genres from speech	
Taavitsainen 1999	DA	UTI		Mimetic dialogue	

Fritz 1995	DA	both	As products of intentional action texts do not allow for more than a reconstruction	Use a broad context; dwell from different disciplines; Recent dialogue forms allow research on the basis of reliable material	
Bax 1999	DA	LIT	Authenticity question has to be left out	Mimetic reliability of literary texts cannot be denied completely	
Bax 2001	DA	LIT	Simulated spoken interaction only	Utilitarian sources in particular depict linguistic conventions of the past	
Schrott 1999	DA	LIT		*la rhétorique du conversationnel* is reflected in the early documents of realism	
Lebsanft 1999	DA	both	Exclusively elements of spontaneous orality may be found; no real interaction but an intentional representation	The difference between spoken and written was much smaller than nowadays	
Culpeper and Kytö 1999a	DA	both	A definitive picture of spoken conversation of the past is not to be achieved	Compare speech-based with non-speech-based genres to assess distance between them	Bibliographic details for primary sources are lacking
Ramge 1999	DA	UTI	Dialogues in utilitarian texts are modelled to fulfil a legal purpose of the document rather than to reflect real spoken conversation	Investigation into details of composition and production of texts may be fruitful	
Oesterrreicher 1999	DA	both	There may occur a range of external factors determining the shape of accounts of real life events	Analyse communicative context	
Koch 1999	DA	both		Communicative immediacy of written texts makes them well-suited for analysis	
Nevalainen and Raumolin-Brunberg 1995	PO	UTI	Spoken language reconstruction should not be overstated	Interactive aspects of society may be helpful	Observer's paradox, particularly valid for letter writing is ignored
Archer 2002	PO	UTI	Note-taking process has to be considered an obstacle	It is possible to find genres providing approximations of speech	

Table 1: Summary of the approaches to the 'bad-data problem'

Some striking similarities may be discerned in the solutions offered with regard to the 'bad-data problem' as applied to a variety of theoretical perspectives and material. A considerable number of researchers support the argument of (a degree of) mimetic reliability of literary (Bax 1999, Schrott 1999, Lebsanft 1999) and utilitarian texts (Jucker and Taavitsainen 2000, Taavitsainen 2001, Bax 2001, Lebsanft 1999). Others point to the elements of orality in written texts as characteristic for different periods in the history of a language (Arnovick 1999, Brinton 1998, Onodera 1995; 1999, Fludernik 2000, Koch 1999). It is, moreover, shown by some that particular speech events reflected in writing contain traces of orality (e.g., Arnovick 1999) or in a similar vein, approximations of speech are to be found in many genres (e.g., Archer 2002). The importance of taking into consideration the broad context of a speech event as well as of seeking explanations in neighbouring disciplines is emphasised by Fritz (1995), Ramge (1999) and Oesterreicher (1999). There is also a whole range of issues which could facilitate a pragmatic insight into speech of the past. These could be described after Gloning as the communicative budget of each period (cf. Knoblauch (2001: 24):

> "One method of applying historical pragmatics is to describe the communicative budget of a period. To describe (parts of) a communicative budget means to describe forms of communication, their organization and their "sense" (function, task) and how they were socially used by different groups" (Gloning 1999: 84).

Nevertheless, neither careful selection of texts on the basis of orality and interactive criteria, nor a careful investigation into the communicative budget of a given period may provide answers to the issues of authenticity of the underlying speech event (Bax 1999) or present a clear picture of the speech of the past (Culpeper and Kytö 1999a). Even the most convincing researchers will agree that a historical pragmatic analysis is unlikely to contribute to historical linguistics more than a reconstruction of the spoken language of the past (e.g., Schwenter and Traugott 1995, Fritz 1995, Nevalainen and Raumolin-Brunberg 1995). As one of the major explanations behind this state of affairs, numerous authors accept the relevant text traditions as a factor determining the representations of speech in both literary and utilitarian written genres (Bach 1998: 100, Fritz 1995: 472, Gloning 1999: 84, Oesterreicher 1999: 444, Ramge 1999: 372, Schrott 2000: 294, Taavitsainen 1999: 244). In connection with the text traditions, one further complicating factor is that texts invariably are products of intentional action (Fritz 1995, Lebsanft 1999), and that unravelling the intentions of their authors may be by far the greatest challenge a historical pragmatist may have to face.

1.3.1.2 Summary of approaches to primary sources

The other major focus of the analysis has been the quality of primary sources used in historical pragmatic research and verification of the degree to which this quality complies with what was postulated by Jacobs and Jucker (1995)[12]. Cases of exemplary (e.g., Schrott 2000) as well as objectionable (e.g., Arnovick 1999) approaches to the source material may be pointed out. A statistical overview clearly demonstrates that the former approach is rarely encountered (Table 2).

		PAPERS	THORETICAL	LITERARY	NON-LITERARY	LITERARY+NO N-LITERARY	CORPUS	CORPUS+MOD. ED.	MOD.ED.	CONT.ED.	MOD.ED.+CON T.ED.	FACISIMILE	FACS.+MOD.ED.	FACS.+CONT.E D.	MOD.ED.+CON T.ED.+CORPUS	FACS.+MOD.ED. + CORPUS
SA	JOHP	5	1	1	1	2	2						1		1	
DM	HP1995	9		5		4	3	1	2							
	HP1998	4		1	2	1	2		2							
	JOHP	7		2	1	4	4	1	2							
	TOTAL	20	1	8	3	9	9	2	6							
DA	HP1995	1				1						1				
	HP1998	2		1	1				1				1			
	HDA 1999	16		5	6	4	1		10	3		1				
	JOHP	3	1	2	1				2	1						
	TOTAL	22	1	8	8	5	1		13	3	1	1	1	1		
PO	HP1995	2		1	1		1		1							
	JOHP	2		1	1				2							
	TOTAL	4		2	2		1		3							
RI	JOHP	9	3	3	3			2	3							
DS	HP1995	1			1											
	HP1998	1		1			1		1							
	JOHP	11	4	3	4		2		4			1				
	TOTAL	13	4	4	5		3		5			1				
GS	HP1998	1			1								1			1
	JOHP	4			4			1	1		1					
	TOTAL	5			5			1	1		1		1		1	

Table 2: Overall presentation of the quality of primary sources

---

[12] Cf. Jacobs and Jucker (1995: 10).

1.3.1.2.1 General remarks

The overall number of papers put under scrutiny was 81, including 10 theoretical ones which did not carry out research on the basis of primary sources and 2 lacking relevant information. This leaves 69 empirical studies, in which 13 use either editions of texts contemporaneous to their composition or facsimiles, or combine contemporaneous editions with facsimiles or modern editions, modern editions with facsimiles and corpora. Thus, only a fraction of studies in question (roughly 18% of the total number of empirical papers) comply with the standards of quality proposed by Jacobs and Jucker (1995). In most cases the failure to consult the most reliable edition is not even touched upon and instances of researchers justifying/substantiating their selection of source texts are rare (e.g., Hüllen 1995[13]).

Extreme ignorance concerning the problems and pitfalls discussed in this chapter can be observed in the papers by Onodera (1995) and Ilieva (2003), both failing even to provide information on the nature of their source material, rendering the papers impossible to classify in the overall presentation. What one has to conclude is that despite the preoccupation of historical pragmatics with the 'bad-data problem' and the space devoted to mitigating its acuteness, source text selection has so far not become an issue of comparable gravity.

1.3.2.2.2 A model approach to primary sources

The observation made in the previous section as to the relative scarcity of papers utilising high quality primary sources i.e., facsimiles or contemporaneous editions, requires further elaboration. The most important reason behind the state of affairs might be methodological complacency on the part of researchers who ignore the fact that the reliability of their findings might be determined by the quality of source material. There may, however, be some other less obvious causes which might be revealed through a careful overview of the minority of studies in which the selection of primary sources was exemplary. The following table (Table 3) presents relevant details.

---

[13] Hüllen gives a practical justification for the reliance on a modern edition: despite "severe criticism" of his source text: "As the facsimile edition is very difficult to read and the Gessler edition is difficult to come by, I will stick to quoting from Bradley" (1995: 114).

	MATERIAL	CATEGORY	LIT	NON LIT	FACS	CONT. ED.	MOD ED.	CORPUS
Culpeper and Semino (2000)	treatises on witchcraft; depositions	SA		√		√	√	√
Schrott (2000)	romance	SA	√		√		√	
Fritz (1995)	a treatise on marriage; romance	DA	√	√		√		√
Gloning 1999	pamphlets	DA		√		√		
Schwitalla 1999	pamphlets	DA		√		√		
Beetz (1999)	politeness manuals	DA		√		√		
Koch (1999)	court records; cartoons	DA	√	√		√		
Fries (1998)	grammar books; manuals	DA		√		√	√	
Becker (2002)	language teaching textbooks	DA		√			√	√
Blake (2002)	tragedy	DS	√		√			
Bach (1998)	pamphlets	GS		√		√	√	
Fritz (2001)	newspapers	GS		√			√	√
Mäkinen (2002)	herbals	GS		√		√		√

Table 3: Model applications of primary sources

The most noticeable preference is for non-literary material (11 papers – including 2 which combine both kinds of material – against only 2 papers relying on literary sources exclusively). Secondly, 7 papers out of 13 fall within historical dialogue analysis and 3 belong to genre studies. The former finding is not as striking as the latter, because dialogue as a speech-based genre is particularly affected in the process of transition to the written medium. Thus, it seems crucial to avoid additional filters[14], such as e.g., editorial interference in its representation. In the case of genre studies, whose major occupation is the investigation of the evolution of text-types regardless of their correspondence to spoken language, the caution applied to the quality of data reveals a degree of methodological rigorousness lacking in the majority of remaining studies.

A key to the explanation of the question why these and not some other papers utilise sources of exemplary quality may also be sought in the text-types under investigation. Three papers study pamphlets (Bach 1998, Schwitalla 1999, Gloning 1999); one paper deals with newspapers (Fritz 2001), one further study researches politeness manuals (Beetz 1999), another a marriage treatise or manual (Fritz 1995). All these text-types circulated in printed format and enjoyed extreme popularity in their day as they were closely connected to major social or historical developments. Therefore, they have been preserved in ample quantities essentially as historical evidence, which naturally facilitates access to them.

As far as the remaining contributions are concerned, Mäkinen (2002) does also profit from the fact that the text-type in his focus – the herbal – used to perform an important function in a society lacking professional medical healthcare, hence its popularity, usefulness and need for transmission and preservation. Similarly, Fries' (1998) investigation into instructional texts and Becker's (2002) study of bargaining dialogues in language teaching textbooks, make use of genres which were an integral part of common social phenomena, therefore widely used and valuable enough to be pursued. Even more interestingly, in the case of language textbooks, it is not unfounded to consider them to be part and parcel of the oral language teaching process, which multiplies their value as sources of information on spoken language of the time. Culpeper and Semino (2000) too, utilise relatively easily accessible material (witchcraft narratives), the origin of which can be linked to the compelling social, religious and legal event of witch-hunt, placed in a certain temporal, local and political reality. The only paper which distinguishes itself as far as the popularity of genres under investigation is concerned, is Koch (1999) who uses facsimiles of frescos which he refers to as 'early cartoons'. The other sources used by Koch (1999), similarly to Culpeper and Semino (2000), are court depositions; these are, however, taken from modern editions.

---

[14] Filter is used here and in the sense of Schneider: "written record functions as a filter, as it were: it provides us with a representation of a speech act that we would have liked to have listened to and recorded acoustically, and that without the written record would have been lost altogether; but at the same time the rendering of the speech event is only indirect and imperfect, affected by the nature of the recording context in certain ways" (2002: 67).

1.3.2.2.3 Arguments for source text selection: Conclusions

The discussion in this chapter has thus far provided quite a wide framework for the presentation of attitudes to data, within which it is possible to sample as many areas of concern as possible in the field of historical pragmatics. The aim of the discussion has been to present a vast spectrum of data which for the greatest part, despite certain limitations, is open to an analysis from a historical pragmatic point of view. Since many of the studies referred to made valuable contributions to linguistics in general and specifically to the discipline in question, it is advisable to pursue some of the approaches, regardless of the difficulty in obtaining primary sources of high quality, such as manuscripts or facsimiles of texts. This postulate does not ignore the importance of methodological issues; on the contrary, it advocates the importance of appreciating the limitations of even the most thoroughly substantiated conclusions and it recommends hedging these conclusions accordingly (Merja Kytö, personal correspondence). Finally, even though this discussion managed to reveal some divergences from what is considered an ideal historical pragmatic inquiry (cf. Jacobs and Jucker 1995) in a number of papers, these shortcomings can only rarely be regarded as disqualifying.

The emphasis placed by historical pragmatics on spoken language should determine the level of rigorousness with regard to primary sources. Contrary to expectation, this discussion has shown that the rigorous selection of material remains by and large a methodological postulate and not a condition rigidly imposed on research. The necessary rigorousness, in a great majority of contributions, turns out to be superficial. Thus, the overview provided above may leave one with the impression that linguists find themselves in a rather underprivileged position when it comes to the availability of data for empirical research in historical pragmatics. Indeed, what other explanation could there be for the methodological complacency apparent in 82% of the contributions, given the indubitable scientific value of the great majority of them? Does this state of affairs not call for a revision of the hitherto only ostensibly accepted standards of the discipline? And does the strictness and relative unattainability of postulates, such as those of Kytö and Walker (2003), not render research into historical pragmatics too exclusive? These questions will provide a background for the discussion in the following section.

1.4 Conclusions for the present work

The incentive for the study carried out above came from the recent publication by Kytö and Walker (2003) dealing with the issue of 'bad data' specifically within the studies of speech-based genres. Since the present work takes speech-based material as the basis of empirical analysis and since its major interest is also in courtroom discourse, the expertise to be found in Kytö and Walker (2003) seemed particularly well suited for its purpose. Indeed, the questions posed by the authors are daring, and their answers are revealing. Therefore, it seemed justifiable to apply some of their findings to the present study. That this task has proved both unattainable and unfeasible is regretful, though by all means justified by the conclusions of this chapter and borne out by the discussion to be presented in the following section.

1.4.1 Arguments for a rigorous methodological procedure

The point of departure of the study by Kytö and Walker is: "The rapidly increasing body of research carried out within the historical pragmatics framework makes it necessary to deepen our knowledge about the philological and textual problems inherent to the material" (Kytö and Walker 2003: 242). In connection with this, they pose two basic questions. The first one is of a general nature and concerns the reliability of written representations of the speech of the past. The second question focuses on "the complications in textual transmission across time" (Kytö and Walker 2003: 222), which determine the value of texts or different versions of texts for a historical linguistic inquiry. Essentially, the latter issue has to be approached as an individual problem unique to every single text.

1.4.1.2 Medium transmission

The following question asked by Kytö and Walker is of particular importance for the present work: "How faithful a record of the spoken language can a trial or deposition text be, considering how difficult it is to take down speech straight form the mouths of the speakers in practice?" (2003: 222). A similar issue, stated though as a general problem of speech representation in writing[15], is raised by Schneider (2002):

> "It is essential for us to know, or to reasonably assess (...) how accurately the original speech event is represented. The level of accuracy may vary from a fairly faithful rendering to a gross distortion, and for the analyst it is essential to determine where on this continuum of faithfulness any given record is positioned, and what consequences this may have" (Schneider 2002: 68).

---

[15] Compare the study by Slembrouck (1992) on a range of factors determining the construction of Hansard reports. Even though the faithfulness to the contents is mostly preserved, despite the access to the spoken word, transcribers do not present the exact wording and they 'filter out' spokenness conforming to an ideology and tradition behind their practice. As the author claims, all this serves the purpose of maintaining "a duality between what is interactionally allowable in the spoken debates and what goes into the record" (1992: 116).

The statements above, though pointing out the intricacy of the medium transmission process, have behind them the same underlying assumption, i.e., that their authors accept that it is indeed possible to render speech in writing. Rather than follow this line of thinking in the present work, it seems more in place to accept a different stance as suggested by Chafe (2001) who convincingly shows – on the basis of a transcript of a contemporary conversation – the impossibility of rendering ephemeral and dynamic spoken interaction in the written medium. As the author comments on the final transcript: "Does it have any validity beyond being a visual representation of a concatenation of utterances that were produced in sequence as the conversation unfolded through time?" (Chafe 2001: 685). Bearing in mind the capability of conversation analysis to graphically show a range of spoken features and the degree of faithfulness to be reached from a live conversation, this statement is indeed a surprising one. A detailed transcript would after all be an ideal for a historical linguist, recording everything that in the transmission from one medium to another is undoubtedly lost, as is emphasised by Kytö and Walker: "Even with the most faithful of records, it is to be expected that certain typical features of speech such as false starts, pauses, slips of the tongue, and the like would be filtered out, yet evidence of such features does remain" (2003: 225). What one has to conclude, is that linguists like Kytö and Walker (2003) – whose view of medium transmission is representative of that of most researchers of speech-based texts – remain under a delusion that speech (though in a way which is far from an ideal representation) can be rendered in writing in a satisfactory manner. Similarly, Schneider (2002) shares this rather inaccurate view when talking about the *Principle of Filter Removal* (2002: 72), which has to be applied for a linguist to be able to reduce the distance of a written text from the original speech event. As he further claims, given the possible intervening filters, direct transcripts are by far the best material for linguistic analysis. Again, what is not taken into consideration here is that even the most perfect of transcripts, regardless of their elaborateness, will never turn written language into spoken language again. Even though Kytö and Walker point out: "we can never claim that the available early speech-related texts are equivalent to actual speech" (2003: 230), they seem to be mistaken: sharing the historian's bias they see language as – to use Chafe's terms (2001: 673) – frozen on paper or turned into a static object of inquiry. In fact, Kytö and Walker (2003) are not isolated in their "written language bias" (Linell 2001: 114), as despite the acclaimed primacy of speech, in general, as Linell goes on to show (2001), linguists for one thing persist in designing models adequate for the analysis of written language but still, even studies of spoken discourse require translating the spoken medium into written texts.

1.4.1.3 Textual transmission

The empirical part of Kytö and Walker's (2003) study is devoted to the verification of source material also with respect to the textual transmission, in connection with which the following warning is issued:

> "There can be striking differences between the versions of speech-related texts available in the various formats. If some of these formats distort either something in the external circumstances of the original speech-event or even the very words supposedly uttered verbatim, those using the evidence for research in historical pragmatics, for instance, may end up drawing erroneous conclusions" (Kytö and Walker 2003: 231).

A similar opinion is found in Fleischman (2002) who talks about 'processed data' as: "data extracted from grammars or edited texts, i.e., at one or more removes from the manuscript sources. Naturally, claims based on such data are only as reliable as the philological foundation on which they rest" (2002: 40-41). What is signalled in the statements above is succinctly summed up by Schneider as "evaluating sources (...) and the role of editing" (2002: 68) as the major preoccupations of a historical linguist.

Before commenting on the quality and reliability of individual versions of original texts, i.e., imprints, facsimiles and editions, Kytö and Walker advocate the use of a manuscript on the condition, however, "that the notes, shorthand or otherwise are unlikely to be available" (2003: 231). Idealistic as the utilising of manuscripts or even original notes would be from the point of view of Kytö and Walker (2003), one has to point out a complete lack of realism in this postulate. First of all, in how many cases would notes have been preserved, particularly for official records of authentic speech events on which the authors focus? Secondly, is the philological, palaeographical, and indeed detective-like effort implied by the need to get hold of notes or shorthand not an exaggeration? Even Schneider (2002), adopting a similar point of view, is at least a bit less radical and more realistic when appreciating research in which: "linguists use unedited, even manuscript sources, which may cause readability problems" (2002: 71). How much work can linguists accomplish within the span of their professional activity if what they should do, in the opinion of Kytö and Walker (2003), is to become simultaneously palaeographers, archive and handwriting experts if not even more than that? Finally, does this radical methodological rigour not look ludicrous in the light of the research into the approach to sources in historical pragmatics carried out above?

Unfortunately, the views presented in the paper under discussion do not contribute to the development of the discipline. On the contrary, what they contribute to is upholding the exclusiveness of idealised historical pragmatic inquiry. This exclusiveness has been demonstrated above whereas methodological rigorousness turned out to be no more than a research postulate. Surprisingly enough, the standards set for the historical pragmatic investigation by Kytö and Walker (2003) do not bear any relationship whatsoever to the reality of the discipline. It would indeed be in place for the authors to at least refer to the existing research, be it in a critical or other way. That such references are lacking is indeed disappointing.

The only way in which the radical statements of the authors could be accounted for is the major aim of their professional activity in the last couple of years, namely the compilation of a specialised corpus which is both an incentive and an aim of the authors in the article under discussion. Therefore their position is that of a corpus compiler who has to bear in mind the needs of the end-user and hence the standards of text selection (or selection of text versions) are set so high. On the other hand, at no point do Kytö and Walker (2003) hedge their postulates in order to make allowances for the reality of historical pragmatics research.

1.4.2 A methodological compromise

This chapter, devoted to the 'bad-data problem', serves as a background to the methodology and source text selection in the present work. Its findings with respect to the reality of methodological standards within historical pragmatics are seen as a justification for the decisions concerning investigated material. Compromising as it may seem, the present work refuses to succumb to the idealistic postulates – addressed at a corpus compiler rather than an individual researcher – in order to follow the majority of historical pragmatic inquiries which rely on edited texts. On the other hand, the awareness of the intricacy of the 'bad-data problem' and the fact that it has become particularly irksome recently, judging by the amount of space devoted to it, the general approach taken in this work is amenable to the implications of source text selection. The assumption is that instead of acting as palaeographers, archive experts, etc., linguists indeed do have the choice to concentrate on their professional activities. Therefore, an edited text[16] should not be rejected without reservations. What is proposed as an alternative in the present work is a careful approach to edited texts and viewing source material essentially as subject to verification as far as its applicability to a historical pragmatic research and the specific focus of interest are concerned.

---

[16] Compare Carroll et al. (2003: 4) for an uncompromising approach.

Chapter Two

Aspects of reported speech analysis

> "... the polyfunctionality of a reported utterance yields a kind of analytical wafer whose layers can coexist but never imply one another"
>
> (Vincent and Perrin 1999: 304).

2.1 Aims and directions of the present research into reported speech

The present work seeks to provide an insight into aspects of reported speech as evidenced in the Early Modern English court records and trial transcripts, i.e., historical sources referring to events that took place in a specific institutional setting. These written records can be placed in a legal context, as they were shaped by the circumstances of their production, reception, generic norms and the functions they were supposed to fulfil. It is assumed that the most fruitful approach to the phenomenon of reported speech preserved in this material has been introduced by historical pragmatics. It has to be borne in mind, however, that within historical pragmatics reported speech has not been studied in an extensive way. An exception is the monograph by Collins (2001) dealing with reported speech in the history of Russian. Notwithstanding its undeniable value, the volume still remains an isolated instance. Some further solutions pertaining to reported speech provided by historical pragmatics are found in its most promising sub-field – historical dialogue analysis.

Despite these contributions, historical pragmatics remains just one among a wide range of linguistic approaches to the issue of reported speech. Hence turning toward the studies outside the discipline is a matter of necessity. Consequently, the assumption as to the advantages of a historical pragmatic approach to the analysed data is tested in the following sections through an overview of studies outside historical pragmatics dealing with reported speech.

The major issue that sets apart historical pragmatic research from studies into contemporary language lies in the so-called data problem which has an important bearing on historical studies (cf. chapter one). It is natural that the historical linguistic data (except for the most recent history) have been preserved in the written form exclusively and, moreover, as their textual transmission can rarely be traced, such data does not allow drawing conclusions about speech and many linguistic aspects that can successfully be researched by means of empirical tools used in the study of contemporary languages, for example in conversation analysis. It is shown, however, that historical pragmatics, which often relies on findings provided by a variety of fields, shares many problematic issues with the studies of present-day languages, and that the two lines not infrequently arrive at parallel solutions.

2.2 Reported speech – an introduction

The phenomenon of reported speech inevitably reaches beyond linguistics. Recently, a comprehensive bibliography[1] of reported speech has been published by Güldemann – Roncador – Van der Wurff (2002), comprising over a 1000 entries, which – despite the authors' claim that it "concentrates on linguistic contributions" (2002: 363) – represents diverse fields and approaches.

The interdisciplinary nature of reported speech studies essentially determines the initial steps taken by anyone getting acquainted with the new discipline. Thus, the overwhelming variety of approaches represented in the field requires setting a clear focus as well as adopting a selective attitude. Such an attitude would find its reflection in the present discussion, whose general aim is to present an outline of the major issues taken up in the studies of reported speech. Furthermore, the following paragraphs mostly dwell on the latest advances within the area, not only to ensure that this contribution is up to date, but also for two further reasons. First of all, the majority of the earlier research into reported speech concentrated on the so-called *free indirect speech*[2] with a clearly literary bias[3] or a 'grammatical bias', as pointed out by Besnier (1993): "linguists have

---

[1] Cf. the bibliography of reported speech published on the web by a French – Belgian – Spanish – Danish – Finnish – Canadian team (http://www.ulb.ac.be/philo/serlifra/ci-dit). While the Güldemann – Roncador – Van der Wurff bibliography (2002) is biased – as the authors claim – towards English, French, Spanish and German publications, this one has a definite preference for contributions in French and Spanish.

[2] McHalle (1978: 249) lists the following terms: *style indirect libre* and *discours direct impropre* (from French scholarship); the list of German names is longer: *verschleierte Rede, erlebte Rede, Rede als Tatsache, peudo-objektive Rede*; in the English research: *represented speech, independent form of indirect discourse, narrated monologue, substitutionary narration*. Coulmas provides the following English terms found in the literature: *veiled speech, quasi-direct speech or discourse, repeated speech, experienced speech, substituted discourse, dependent speech, represented speech* (1986: 8). To this inventory Tomasik adds: *uneigentlich indirecte Rede, le stile direct-indirect, le stile indirect double* (1992:14-15). Cf. McHalle (1978), Coulmas (1986) and Tomasik (1992) for references.

[3] Coulmas discusses "a third kind" of reported speech in which the two basic modes, direct and indirect, are mixed, stating that it occurs in literary narratives and pointing to the focus of the earliest discussion (since 1890s) on French prose (1986: 6). In fact as one reads in Tomasik (1992), earlier discussions (e.g., Bally 1930) analyse *free indirect speech* on the basis of literary or invented examples. Furthermore, the author emphasises the existence of two traditions within the studies into this mode of reporting: a syntactic and a semantic one (Tomasik 1992: 12). None of these approaches is of prime interest for this study, neither is the stylistic function of reported speech in literary works. Therefore, *free indirect speech* and the immense literature relevant to it are omitted in this study (cf. McIntyre et al. 2004).

focused their attention primarily on the grammatical nature of reported speech construction, rather than on the meaning of reported speech in linguistic performance" (1993: 163). Secondly, as has been indicated in the introduction to the latest monograph devoted to the field, one can presently observe "a major shift away from analyzing reported discourse with the help of abstract transformational principles toward embedding it in *functional* and *pragmatic* aspects of language" (Güldemann and Roncador 2002: vii, italics original). Given the pragmatic angle of the present work, it is necessary to concentrate on the more recent advances which are likely to show some affinity of perspective.

2.2.1 The interdisciplinary nature of reported speech studies[4]

In a monograph on reported speech Coulmas states that "reported speech is one of those phenomena whose proper treatment necessarily transcends departmental boundaries" (1986b: 1). Here Coulmas enumerates poetics, logic and the philosophy of language as the fields in which the issue has received some attention. The volume itself, however, shows a uniform comparative approach whose main outcome is a presentation of grammatical features of direct and indirect speech in fourteen typologically diverse languages. An exception to this consistent perspective is Tannen (1986), whose major point is to demonstrate everyday functions of constructed dialogue (as she refers to direct speech) in conversation and story telling rather than contribute to a cross-linguistic overview of the grammar of reported speech.

Another collection of comparative studies whose attention is largely devoted to reported speech is an anthropologically oriented volume on reflexivity in language (Lucy 1993). Reported speech, one of "the most important ... explicitly reflexive activities" (Lucy 1993a: 2), undergoes a linguistic analysis which is supported by insights drawn from folklore, religion, literature, philosophy and social sciences. The heterogeneity of the volume neatly assembles human activities whose functioning may be explained through analyses of reported speech viewed as a political (e.g., Parmentier 1993), rhetorical (e.g., Banfield 1993), cultural (e.g., Moore 1993) and social (e.g., Urban 1993) multifunctional device.

Another monograph on reported speech taking the reflexive functions of language as its starting point is the collection devoted to forms and functions of the verb edited by Janssen and Van der Wurff (1999). The papers in this volume are consistent in their morphological/syntactic/pragmatic focus and, similar to

---

[4] For instance, Holt (1996: 221) notices that the attention devoted to reported speech outside linguistics has come from the researchers in literary criticism, sociology and philosophy. Cf. the report on the *Lancaster Speech, Writing and Thought Presentation* (SW&TP) *Spoken Corpus* project (McIntyre et al. 2004: 50) where the authors also emphasise the interdisciplinary character of reported speech studies.

Coulmas (1986), they place under scrutiny a selection of cross-linguistic material, while the structure of the book is based on the division into language families. Although the interdisciplinary nature of reported speech studies is not explicitly commented on, the authors make use of some contributions from a range of disciplines.

The discourse-oriented, functional perspective has been adopted in the 1999 special issue of *Text,* a collection of articles on the topic of reported speech phenomena within institutional discourse. Not unlike the volumes mentioned above, addressing the lack of a comprehensive and unified "'theory of speech representation' ... the collection represents an interdisciplinary project with contributions drawing in a principled way on pragmatics, literary theory, linguistically informed discourse analysis, social theory, ethnography, conversation analysis, and rhetorical analysis" (Baynham and Slembrouck 1999: 446). The specific orientation of the interdisciplinarity exhibited in this collection is towards the interaction between social worlds and texts with the aim of accounting for the functions of reported speech in real discursive situations[5].

The issue of the interdisciplinarity of reported speech studies is explicitly referred to in the subtitle of the latest monograph *Reported discourse: A meeting ground for different linguistic domains.* Here again, the interdisciplinary vein is of more general character with philosophy, psychology and literary criticism mentioned as the fields within which concern for reported discourse has been substantial (Güldemann and Roncador 2002: vii). This collection, unlike some of the previous ones, is not of a comparative nature; rather it adopts the discourse-oriented approach in tune with its functional and pragmatic standpoint. The organisation of the book reveals the latest foci of interest in the area of reported speech studies.

2.2.2 Terminology

Although general ways of referring to reported speech in the literature exhibit variation (cf. Janssen and Van der Wurff 1996: 3), terminological profusion comparable to that concerning *free indirect speech* (McHalle 1978, Tomasik 1992) – for which some two dozen different terms were coined (cf. footnote 2 above) – has been avoided fortunately. Still, the lack of terminological consistency has characterised, for instance, an early monograph (Coulmas 1986) in which most of the authors use the term *reported speech* for a range of speech-

---

[5] Historical linguistics in particular, cf. Hiltunen and Skaffari (2003) and Hiltunen and Watanabe (2004). Along with the development of corpora and genre studies, a discourse-oriented approach is becoming dominant.

within-speech[6] phenomena, while for others (Rice 1986: 74, Kvavik[7] 1986: 337-338) it is synonymous with *indirect speech*. If over a decade later, editors of another collection decide to prevent terminological confusion by formulating an explicit convention of using "reported speech (or discourse) as a cover term"[8] (Janssen and Van der Wurff 1996: 3), apparently no real consensus had been reached in the literature by that time. Thompson (1996), for instance, uses the term *language reports* "in order to avoid the associations of terms such as 'indirect speech', which are likely to lead to confusion" (Thompson 1996: 502). Similarly, Collins (2001), anticipating possible misunderstandings, makes it clear that in his work the term *reported speech* is "understood as any means of representing spoken and written discourse, not just indirect speech" (Collins 2001: xii). Recently, Huddelston and Pullum (2002: 1023f) have remarked: "[some writers] restrict the term reported speech to the indirect type". An example here might be Doty and Hiltunen (2002) and Hiltunen (2004), who consistently use the *direct* vs. *reported discourse* (not *speech*) opposition in the discussions of Salem witchcraft trials.

No terminological confusion of this sort is apparent in the contributions to Lucy (1993) where the term embraces different ways of quoting, as in Janssen and Van der Wurff (1996) and Collins (2001). The fact that the terms *reported* and *indirect speech* are not confused in the case of Lucy's volume (1993) can be attributed to the wide interdisciplinary perspective adopted by the contributors. The synonymous usage of *reported* and *indirect speech* in more linguistically-oriented monographs (e.g., Coulmas 1986) reflects an applied linguistic perspective or possibly a second language acquisition bias with reported speech viewed as a grammatical structure derived[9] from an authentic, though usually invented, (direct) speech event by a set of rules and shifts. A wider perspective of Lucy (1993) rules out a linguistic prejudice of a similar kind.

Recently, however, a terminological consistency seems to have emerged, since in the most recent monograph there is no instance of terminological confusion despite the primarily linguistic focus of the volume (Güldemann and Roncador 2002: vi). A slight modification of the hitherto widely used term can be

---

[6] Here, the term is used after Janssen and Van der Wurff (1996). The origin is Volosinov (1973 [1929]: 115), the quotation which has been ubiquitous in the literature since the rediscovery of his (Volosinov'/Bakhtin's work; cf. section 2.3.1.1).

[7] The term used by the author is *reported style*, however, at one point he contrasts "direct vs. reported sentence syntax" (Kvavik 1986: 132).

[8] "providing an umbrella term for what most linguists (and non-linguists) intuitively think of as one unitary phenomenon" (Janssen and Van der Wurff 1996: 3). Still, some contributors to the collection (Cate 1996: 190) talk about direct speech vs. reported speech, the latter understood as *indirect speech*.

[9] This derivational or transformational fallacy is accepted within the functional theory, e.g., Halliday (1985: 233-234), Huddleston and Pullum (2003: 1023-30). Cf. the accounts demonstrating that this hypothesis is unfounded (e.g., Baynham and Slembrouck 1999: 452).

observed: *reported discourse* rather than *reported speech* is preferred as a more general notion[10]. The consistency does not exclude the option of applying different terms to the phenomenon, but it definitely does away with the synonymous use of *reported* and *indirect speech*. As in the case of Güldemann and Roncador (2002), and not unlike Janssen and Van der Wurff (1996), Huddleston and Pullum (2002: 1023f) in one of the latest comprehensive grammars of the English language also explicitly opt for the use of *reported speech* as a term covering both *direct* and *indirect speech*.

A certain amount of freedom as to the choice of a general term referring to speech-within-speech has been exercised by some authors, of whom Tannen (1989) has left the most lasting mark. Claiming that "the term 'reported speech' is a misnomer" (Tannen 1986: 311), or that it is "grossly misleading" (Tannen 1989: 101), she proposes the notion of *constructed dialogue* (Tannen 1986) instead. In her understanding, however, the term has a rather narrow application, as it refers exclusively to dialogue in the form of direct speech in conversational narratives. In this sense, one has to admit, statements made by the author about reported speech being a misnomer (Tannen 1986: 311) are defendable. Since it has been coined, the term has been widely accepted and used[11], while its interpretation has by and large remained unchanged.

2.2.2.1 Speech and thought (re)presentation

It has to be emphasised, that the instances of terminological consistency referred to above have serious limitations and cannot be accepted without reservations, even exclusively within the functional/pragmatic line of reported speech studies. As Short – Semino – Wynne (2002) have noticed recently: "Unfortunately, the discussion of discourse presentation has suffered from a number of important terminological and conceptual confusions" (2002: 333). For instance, there are a range of functional/pragmatic studies using terms like *discourse presentation* consistently: Short – Semino – Culpeper (1996), Wynne – Short – Semino (1998), Short –Semino – Wynne (2002), McIntyre et al. (2004). The term *speech and thought presentation* goes back to Leech and Short (1981), but Short – Semino – Wynne (2002: 234-35) provide more detailed comments. More specifically, Wynne – Short – Semino (1998: 233) explicitly choose the term *speech, thought and writing presentation* (ST&WP) for a range of reported discourse phenomena. The term is a continuation of the earlier *Speech and Thought Presentation* (S&TP,

---

[10] Naturally, the polysemy of the term *discourse* may be an incentive for an in-depth consideration of the factors determining the choice between *speech* and *discourse* as in the discussion provided by Short – Semino – Wynne (2002: 333-4).

[11] E.g., Johnstone (1987), Yule and Mathis (1992) and more recently, the study by Koven (2001) lend empirical support to Tannen's position. Cf. Levey (2003), Schiffrin (2002), Sleurs – Jacobs – Waes (2003) and Cukor-Avila (2002: 19).

as in Short – Semino – Culpeper 1996). However, McIntyre et al. (2004), in a review of the extension of the project (*Lancaster Speech, Writing and Thought Presentation Spoken Corpus*) use SW&TP (rather than ST&WP) because of the affinity of presentational categories for speech and writing.

Speech and Thought Presentation (S&TP) has also been used by Marnette (2001), who represents a French line of reported speech studies, mainly based on Oswald Ducrot's[12] *théorie de l'énonciation* (translated by Marnette as 'enunication theory'). Marnette, however, does not make a point of terminological consistency and she also uses *reported discourse* as a synonym for *speech and thought presentation* (e.g., 2001: 244). In a footnote, the author explains: "I am using the generic term 'reported discourse' to refer to both reported speech and reported thought" (Marnette 2001: 260f).

In other frameworks, as, for example, functional and semiotic grammar, Vandelanotte (2003; 2004a; 2004b) uses the term *speech and thought representation* (STR) and *represented speech* justifying the choice, after McGregor (1997: 251) (Vandelanotte 2004a: 490). At the same time, the author does not fail to notice that the term *represented speech and thought* has been widely accepted as standing for indirect speech and thought after Banfield (1982)[13]. Furthermore, Vandelanotte uses the terms *indirect speech or thought* (IST) and *direct speech or thought* (DST) for the two canonical categories.

The term *represented speech* is also used by Baynham and Slembrouck (1999) in a functional study on the basis of institutional discourse. The authors are not, however, too strict about terminology, as they also refer to "quoting", "speech reports" (1999: 441) and "reported speech" (1999: 446). In research on contemporary manifestations of reported speech concentrating on prosodic clues (e.g., Couper-Kuhlen 1998, Klewitz and Couper-Kuhlen 1999) *quoted speech*, not *reported speech*, is used as a cover term. Other scholars studying prosody, use the terms *direct* and *indirect reported speech* (abbreviated as DRS and IRS respectively, Hewlett – Kelsey – Lickley 2003). These terms, but not abbreviations, are used also by Antaki and Leudar (2001) in an article on literal quotation of the official record in the British Parliament.

Although the inventiveness of authors tackling reported speech and related phenomena cannot pass unnoticed, the terminological diversity does not necessarily correspond to a similar diversity of readings and ideas. This short presentation of nomenclature problems indicates that among the terms listed, *reported speech* or *discourse* are the most appropriate ones, and will therefore be used throughout this study.

---

[12] Cf. Marnette (2001) for references.
[13] Banfield, Ann, 1982, *Unspeakable sentences. Narration and representation in the language of fiction.* Routledge & Kegan Paul, Boston

2.3 Definition

The definition of reported speech is constructed with the aim to capture one of the most complex and theoretically diverse concepts applied in the study. The intricacy of the phenomenon is naturally connected with the abundance of theoretical approaches and the unfeasibility of arriving at an all-encompassing designation to the satisfaction of everyone involved in the field. As a universally acknowledged and comprehensive definition is lacking, researchers feel free to contribute their own definitions marked with a specific focus. This, however, does not always result in novel approaches or illuminating ideas, whereas the general concept is becoming more and more blurred. Despite the lingering vagueness of the concept, the benefits of individualised definitions are usually noteworthy for individual researchers or contributions. The following discussion will present a selection of definitions and approaches out of which the individual concept behind *reported speech* in the present work has evolved. Along the way, some recurrent ideas and inconsistencies are pointed out.

2.3.1 Studies outside historical pragmatics

The diversity of approaches to be discerned in the most recent studies outside historical pragmatics is indeed overwhelming and impossible to cover in the brief outline to be presented here. Therefore, a selection of common theoretical standpoints is commented on, while other viewpoints do not receive as much attention and space. Thus, some attention is devoted to the syntactic approaches as a background for the introduction of the pragmatic ones, which are favoured in the present discussion. A certain amount of space is also reserved for studies of reported speech in interaction[14], which have proliferated lately[15]; among these the studies concentrating on prosody will receive a more thorough treatment. Although theoretical affinity is most reasonably sought in the pragmatic/functional studies, the discussion is also informed by semantic, semiotic, philosophical, psychological and anthropological research, bearing in mind the interdisciplinary nature of reported speech studies.

---

[14] Short – Semino – Wynne observe: "a shift of attention in the study of discourse presentation from written to spoken data" (2002: 325).

[15] E.g., Tannen (1989), Mayes (1990), Hickmann (1993), cf. e.g., Tannen (1986), Johnstone (1987), Baynham (1996), Maybin (1996, 1999), Maynard (1996), Vincent and Dubois (1996), Buttny (1998), Couper-Kuhlen (1998), Günthner (1999), Klewitz and Couper-Kuhlen (1999), Myers (1999a), Vincent and Perrin (1999), Golato (2000), Koven (2001), Mushin (2001a), Cukor-Avila (2002), Winter (2002), Levey (2003), Bolden (2004), McIntyre et al. (2004). Compare an overview in Bolden (2004: 1073f).

2.3.1.1 Volosinov's definition

The most suitable start of an overview of reported speech definitions is Volosinov: "Reported speech is speech within speech, utterance within utterance, and at the same time also *speech about speech, utterance about utterance*" (1973 [1929]: 115). This definition has been quoted in all kinds of discussions[16] of the phenomenon. Indeed, if one had to decide upon a definition of reported speech which stands a chance of being universally acknowledged, one would have to admit this one is the most likely candidate. The question to be asked is why this and not some other definition has ever become as popular within a territory of multiple theories, interpretations and approaches. This issue seems particularly intriguing given that Volosinov's formulation does not seem to be favoured by any specific line of reported speech studies.

The first part of the definition, i.e., *speech within speech*, after all, has a very restricted application. What it actually refers to is exclusively the embedding[17] inherent in reports of speech, the feature which is after all not restricted to this phenomenon only. The next part i.e., *utterance within utterance*, consists of is no more than a rhetorical repetition of the first part. The second syntactically parallel chunk in which *within* is substituted for by *about* points to another aspect of reported speech connected with its reflexive nature and the more general reflexive capacity of human language (cf. Lucy 1993a: 2, 11; 1993b: 93). Again the two clauses are syntactically parallel. Thus, as far as what the definition encompasses is concerned, neither embedding nor reflexivity of reported speech, not even both these characteristics together can explain the nature of the phenomenon in a satisfactory manner[18]. Moreover, these features do not even constitute the most notable attributes of reported speech, while operating at a higher level of generalisation instead. Thus, the definition is in fact general and abstract enough to enjoy universal interest and serve manifold functions, hence its popularity. The linguistic structure of the single complex clause undeniably contributes to its appeal (symmetry is most significant here: simple as it is, the sentence sounds and looks fine and articulate; this symmetry is a mnemonic device as well). Safely hidden behind the neat symmetrical design, the lack of explanatory force of Volosinov's definition has somehow passed unnoticed, or at least that is an impression one cannot reject.

These remarks are not aimed at undermining the validity of Volosinov's approach or to diminish his influence on Western thought (cf. section 2.6.1

---

[16] E.g., Caton (1993: 332), Hanks (1993: 132, a paraphrase rather than a quotation), Waugh (1995: 134), Maybin (1996: 463), Baynham (1996: 63), Günthner (1999: 686), Myers (1999a: 393), Holt (2000: 433), Adelmann (2004), Lunde (2004: 56).

[17] At this point embedding does not purport to refer to syntactic relations, cf. Sternberg (1982: 108) and (1991: 88), Dimmendaal (2001: 145), Kammerzell and Peust (2002: 290-1).

[18] This kind of interpretation does not do justice to Volosinov, cf. footnote 29.

below). Volosinov is able to defend himself perfectly well, given that his discussion of reported speech continues as an explanation and elaboration of the definition discussed. What this section points to is the lack of a similar elaboration in many studies of reported speech and the uncritical repetition of a witty and linguistically apt clause designed just as an introduction rather than a summary or thorough analysis.

2.3.1.2 Problematic definitions

Formulating a definition relevant to the present discussion is an exceedingly difficult task. In the face of the multitude of existing approaches a negative selection procedure is proposed. The critical approach adopted does not, however, intend to undermine the discussed standpoints or question their usefulness or explanatory force. As a range of issues are shrouded by inconsistencies in the literature, it is essential to scrutinise the problems, as this may rule out dubious solutions or explanations in the formulation of a definition in accord with the aims of the present work. Therefore, the discussion develops around the controversial issues which demand taking a clear stance.

2.3.2.2.1 What is a *speech event*?

The term speech event has often been used but hardly ever defined in the discussions of reported speech (with the exception of Waugh 1995: 135). What is proposed here is that, unless indicated otherwise, the term could be understood as "activities, or aspects of activities, that are directly governed by rules or norms for the use of speech. An event may consist of a single speech act, but will often comprise several" (Hymes 1967 [1972]: 56). It is, however, important not to limit the notion to the spoken medium, hence a more proper name would be a *language event*[19]. One has to bear in mind, however, as Goodwin and Duranti (1992) point out in their discussion of the model of Hymes[20] that "it represents a major shift in the choice of units of analysis: ... for the first time a non-linguistic unit, the event, becomes the frame of reference for interpreting speech" (1992: 25).

2.3.2.2.2 Anterior/original speech event

Following Halliday (1985), Vandelanotte (2004a) sees reported speech in terms of *projection*[21], as it "involves the setting apart of a represented situation as

---

[19] The term does not have a definite referent, cf. Thompson (1996: 518).
[20] Cf. Gumperz (1972: 16-18) for an elaboration of the notion of speech event based on Hymes.
[21] Projection is defined as "the logical-semantic relationship whereby a clause comes to function not as a direct representation of (non-linguistic) experience but as a representation of a (linguistic) representation" (Halliday 1985: 227-28).

belonging to another, 'semiotic' or 'linguistic' part of reality: the represented situation is then no longer a phenomenon described in the first order reality of things and events experienced, but rather a meta-phenomenon (cf. Halliday 1985 [1994]) in the second order reality of linguistic entities" (2004a: 512). This semiotic approach alludes to the reflexive capacity of language, of which reported speech is one of the most important aspects, and points directly to Lucy's definition: "speech which purportedly re-presents another specific speech event" (1993a: 2). What is central to these approaches is the assumption of the existence of a specific anterior/original speech event which is viewed as an essential condition for an instance of speech reporting to occur in the first place.

This approach[22] is not an uncommon one and it can be found in a range of studies whose general theoretical or disciplinary perspectives are very different from one another. Thus, to give a couple of examples, Coulmas (1986b) in the introductory chapter to the first collection entirely devoted to reported speech states: "Utterances can be made subject of other utterances. They can be criticised, questioned, commented on, or simply be reported. Language can be used to refer to language" (1986: 2). Likewise, Buttny (1998) in a study of conversational reported speech and its context, claims: "Reported speech can be simply characterised as quoting another person's, or one's own, prior words" (1998: 48). Similarly, Golato (2002) who also studies conversational reported speech, claims: "Reported discourse is often defined as a report of something someone else has said before, and it can also be extended in its definition to include internal discourse" (Golato 2002: 49). A similar understanding can be attributed to Maybin (1999) whose view of reported speech[23] is "words or phrases ... grammatically framed as speech of the other" (1999: 460). Also Günthner (1999), who studies the prosody of reported speech and sees its instances as recontextualisations in new contexts, assumes that what speakers do is "reporting past utterances" (1999: 686).

According to Steever (2002), who gives a syntactic study of reported speech in Tamil, this approach stems from the structuralist theory: "Reported speech, as analysed in the structuralist framework formulated in Jakobson (1971), embeds one speech event within another" (2002: 91). Regrettably, the standpoint

---

[22] Referred to as "the 'original utterance' hypothesis" by Baynham and Slembrouck (1999: 443) it has enjoyed a special status in the transformational syntactic accounts of reported speech. Still, next to positions like that of Derleck (1999) who sustains the usefulness of the notion of the 'original utterance' (which he renames as "presumed original utterance" 1999: 84f) and claims that "naturally, you cannot have reported speech (whether DRS or IRS) without there being something that is reported" (1999: 84), there are also syntactic studies in which the hypothesis is not accepted without qualifications (e.g., Salkie and Reed 1997).

[23] Maybin (1999) provides her own classification stating that "in many ways repeated, appropriated, and reported speech can be seen as different points along a dialogic continuum between speech of the self and speech of the other" (Maybin 1999: 461).

instantiated above ignores the functional potential of reported speech, and it may, moreover, even become risky if taken too radically, as it may lead to reducing the functions of the phenomenon to the passing on of messages to speakers who have themselves not witnessed the original speech event (e.g., Bamgbose 1986: 77, Massamba 1986: 99). In this way reported speech might become reduced to an information-carrying[24] device, while its functional dimension evidenced in a range of empirical studies[25] may be ignored. Furthermore, the condition of the anterior speech event obviously rules out numerous instances of hypothetical speech or thought reporting (cf. Myers 1999b). In addition, even if an anterior speech event can be located in time and space, the relationship that reported speech bears to this very event is rarely straightforward but essentially complex in nature[26].

One further instance of the way in which the functional aspects of reported speech may be ignored by those strictly following the anterior/original utterance hypothesis may be found in syntactic studies, whose major weakness lies in the negligence of context and a normative[27] orientation. For instance, one may point to some serious shortcomings of statements like that of Derleck (1999): "one cannot speak of 'reported speech' without there being a 'reported entity'" (1999: 85). This radical formulation may be contradicted by another no less radical point of view advocated by the context-centered approach of Baynham and Slembrouck (1999): "one does not cite another voice unless it serves a purpose in the reporting context" (1999: 451). In the light of this remark, Derleck's (1999) approach comes out as idle and overstated, since it neither convincingly explains motivations of language users employing reported speech or the fact of its occurrence, nor manages to keep a reasonable balance. After all, if the existence of a 'reported entity' indeed determined the occurrence of reported speech, how could one possibly account for the instances of well researched and empirically verified creative functions of direct speech, both in written and spoken narrative (e.g., Tannen 1986, 1989, Johnstone 1987, Koven 2001, Levey 2003)? A syntactic analysis like that of Derleck (1999) is not helpful because it focuses blindly on the anterior/original utterance, disregarding the context of reported speech. A much greater explanatory potential is provided by context-bound approaches acknowledging both the active participation of the person producing reported

---

[24] Compare Matoesian (2000) who sees direct quotes as an implication of a "form of linguistic ideology in which the sole or primary function of language is to refer to things" (2000: 883).

[25] For instance, Mayes (1990), in an empirical study of the authenticity of direct speech finds 50% of cases doubtful. Baynham (1996) who studies classroom discourse is able to disprove the verbatim assumption on the basis of direct speech used by the teacher (1996: 67). Vincent and Dubois (1996) show that the lay perception of reported speech as "the reiteration of words that have already been produced" (1996: 361) cannot be corroborated by the analysis of spoken language.

[26] Cf. Álvarez-Cáccamo (1996: 34f) for references to studies exploring this relationship.

[27] In the sense of providing rules on the basis of which reported speech instances are rendered grammatically acceptable.

speech and the subordination of its form to the immediate aims in a given situation. The roots of this approach can be sought in Bakhtin/Volosinov's[28] work and what they see as the dialogic nature of language[29]. As Baynham and Slembrouck (1999) put it, the basis of this approach is that "all representations count as constructions" (1999: 450). A similar point was elaborated on much earlier in an elegant analysis by Sternberg (1982) who emphasised the communicative subordination of all reported discourse to the context of its production. The influence or even reliance of Western thinking on the Bakhtinian approach cannot be overestimated, neither can one deny the significance of Sternberg's position. Given that, the popularity of the exclusively syntactic approaches is even more unfounded, particularly in the more recent contributions like that of Derleck (1999) discussed above.

2.3.2.2.3 Syntax[30] vs. pragmatics: the pragmatic[31] nature of reported speech

A comprehensive critique of syntactic approaches is beyond the scope of the present discussion and would, moreover, be superfluous when faced with the already existing persuasive critiques, like, for instance the one in Collins (2001: 10-15). To summarise, Collins gives the following reasons for the lack of explanatory force of "syntactic, clause- or sentence-level approaches"[32] (2001: 10): first of all, reported speech is not a category of syntax but of discourse, i.e.,

---

[28] It is accepted here after Collins (2001: xiv) that Bakhtin used the name of his friend Volosinov in his 1929 publication (cf. Collins 2001: 303f for references). This view is supported by Holquist in the introduction to his translation of Bakhtin's *Dialogic imagination* in the note on the authorship of three of his works i.e., *Freudianism, Marxism and the philosophy of language* and *The formal method in literary scholarship*: "ninety percent of the text of the three books in question is indeed the work of Bakhtin himself" (1981: xxvi). A similar opinion is held by Caton (1993: 335f). Compare, however, Maynard (1996: 209f). To find a middle way, follow Goodwin and Duranti (1992: 33f): "Bakhtin's theory recognises any meaning-making process as always cooperative and, therefore, his co-authors and friends deserve from us the credit that his recognises" (Goodwin and Duranti 1992: 33f, quotation in accord with the original).

[29] As pointed out by Collins, the shift from the focus on syntax to the focus pragmatics of reported speech was anticipated by Bakhtin/Volosinov, whom the author also sees as the brilliant pioneer of "[t]he functionalist current of research in reported speech" (2001: xiv).

[30] Baynham (1996) gives an overview of syntactic versus discourse-pragmatic accounts of reported speech (1996: 62-68). In his study, he also provides evidence against the original utterance hypothesis.

[31] According to Recanati (2002), there are three conditions for a pragmatic interpretation of an action: firstly, the rationality of the agent is presupposed; secondly, a pragmatic interpretation is defendable in the light of new evidence; thirdly, there is no limit to the contextual information on which such an interpretation may rely (Recanati 2002: 106).

[32] On a succinct review, rather than another critique, of the sentence-level approaches in the "phenomenological structuralist" tradition cf. Hill and Irvine (1993a: 14).

the boundaries of reported utterances do not coincide with those of syntactic units and their internal relations are not fully explicable by means of syntactic dependencies (cf. Hansen 2000, Vandelanotte 2003); secondly, individual types of reported speech (categories) do not have clear-cut boundaries and they also do not correlate with syntactic units; and thirdly, syntactic approaches are not sensitive to changes in medium. Arguments against sentence-based approaches in general in linguistic analyses are thoroughly reviewed by Goodwin and Duranti (1992) who underline that ignoring the context does not do justice to the reality of language as a human activity and it cannot be overbalanced by the benefits of the analytic clarity secured by the easily detachable unit of description (1992: 12-13). Furthermore, approaching language in ways other than viewing it as a formal system i.e., placing it at the centre of human behaviour, requires devoting special attention to its functioning within the social, cultural and situational context (cf. Goodwin and Duranti 1992: 16-19). Below some aspects of these viewpoints are taken up in order to elaborate on the pragmatic nature of reported speech.

2.3.2.2.3.1 Boundaries and marking

The appropriateness of a pragmatic approach to reported speech is more apparent when contrasted with the remarks above on the shortcomings of syntactic approaches. The following quotation can shed more light on this matter: "Sometimes it is difficult to see whether some utterance is to be interpreted (by the analyzer) as reported speech or not. One cannot always tell from the form of an utterance which is which. This means that reported speech is a pragmatic phenomenon, although it has certain syntactic manifestations" (Haberland 1986: 228). Indeed, the communicative success of language users reporting speech is determined by the receivers' acquaintance with the context and, as maintained by Collins (2001), reported speech cannot be defined without reference to intention and perception (2001: 1-2). In other words, its communicative efficiency depends on the audience's interpretation and their ability to recognise the different 'voices', thereby appreciating the boundaries of reported discourse (cf. Clark and Gerrig 1990: 766). This task can by no means be carried out by relying on syntactic or other formal features (be it graphic, prosodic or extralinguistic, depending on the medium) exclusively, because of their ambiguity, in some instances, and their total absence in the most extreme cases[33].

A different view concerning marking of reported speech is found in Goodwin (2003) who deals with *unattributed imported speech*[34] in which, as he

---

[33] Papers on authoritativeness in Hill and Irvine's (1993b) volume provide empirical cross-linguistic and -cultural instances of the ways in which "speech can come to be seen as reported ... even if it contains no overtly quotative forms" (Hill and Irvine 1993a: 11).
[34] What Goodwin (2003) seems to present as his own 'discovery' or a new category akin to reported speech has been discussed in the literature as *concealed forms of reported speech*

admits, "[s]peakers can import talk from another context into a local telling without explicitly marking this fact for the recipients" (2003: 331). However, the nature of the phenomenon allows – in the opinion of the author – setting it apart from, or even contrasting it with, quotation. This implies that explicit marking is an essential condition in reported speech. That such a conclusion is far-fetched can be inferred also on the basis of instances provided by Goodwin (2003) himself where the lack of explicit marking does not result in communicative difficulties. After all, as Goodwin claims, "in many cases issues of recognition emerge in subsequent talk" (2003: 334). If recipients are able to appreciate the boundaries of different discourse levels, while acknowledging the presence of reported speech, one cannot reasonably maintain that explicit marking is one of the defining features of the phenomenon.

2.3.2.2.3.1.1 Prosodic marking of reported speech

An argument similar to that of Goodwin is conducted by Günthner (1999: 701-704), who discusses instances similar to his *unattributed imported speech* as *concealed forms of reported speech* (the latter term is used after Bakhtin 1981) and aims at substantiating the decisive role of prosodic features in the disambiguation of different discourse levels. Actually, an analysis of some of the author's examples (cf. e.g., 35) reveals that her claim that "[t]he speaker 'borrows' for a moment the words and 'prosodic means' which belong to someone else" (Günthner 1999: 702) cannot be accepted without qualifications. If it is possible for the reader of Günthner (1999) to recognise the introduction of a different 'voice' without the help of prosodic or lexical marking (as in some of her examples), it must definitely be something more than that the speaker resorts to borrowing – to paraphrase the previous statement – since it is clearly possible to sense the embedded voice also in a written representation of the utterance.

2.3.2.2.3.2 Communicative vs. syntactic subordination

The traditional syntactic analysis of reported speech provides a clear-cut distinction between direct reports whose internal relations are paratactic (coordination) and indirect reports analysable as formed on the basis of hypotactic (subordination) relations. That this view may be faulty has been noticed early on by Sternberg (1982) who proposed a discoursal rather than a formal interpretation of the frame – inset relations (as he referred to the reporting and the reported clause, cf. Semino and Short 2004: 36 for other terms used for the two concepts). In his view, a part is essentially subordinated to the whole; in the case of discourse

---

after Bakhtin (1981, cf. Günthner 1999: 701-4) or as *incorporated quotations* after Clark and Gerrig (1990: 689-691).

this relationship is communicative subordination (Sternberg 1982: 108). Almost a decade later, Sternberg (1991) provided a selection of examples on the basis of which the syntactic interpretation of reported speech together with the constraints it imposes on the phenomenon is refuted in its entirety (1991: 82-87). The outcome of the discussion is the detaching of the grammatical (or syntactic) embedding from communicative framing (Sternberg 1991: 88), the former being a variable and the latter a universal of quotation. Sternberg's (1991) argument is a crushing one against the syntactic and in favour of a discoursal/pragmatic view of reported speech. Some support for this view may also be found in Waugh (1995) who in her discussion of journalistic discourse gives a range of hypotactic instances of direct speech and of paratactic relations in indirect speech in Waugh (1995: 141-150).

An interesting extension of this approach has recently been provided by Hansen (2000), whose study conducted in a semiotically-oriented framework surprisingly adds arguments for the pragmatic and against an exclusively syntactic approach to reported speech. In this study, the author discusses the direct vs. indirect speech dichotomy in terms of semiotic and pragmatic difference. Unlike indirect speech, direct speech may be seen as "a fully grammaticalised form of code-switching" (Hansen 2000: 281). As the author goes on to explain, "part of the meaning of the direct-discourse construction is to signal such a switch, thereby showing the reader/hearer that the reporting speaker is abdicating as both author and principal[35] of the quoted material" (Hansen 2000: 312-313). Code-switching (cf. Goffman 1981: 145) here is used broadly, "to cover alternations between more radically different sign systems, such as language and gesture" (Hansen 2000: 312). Viewing directly reported clauses in this way allows accounting for instances which cannot be analysed as direct objects of verbs in the reporting clauses. Thus, where syntax fails to account for instances of reporting of onomatopoeias, noises or gestures, the code-switching hypothesis comes in useful, resolving, in particular, the problem of medium, inexplicable by means of syntactic elucidations.

Hansen's (2000) approach does not, however, reach beyond the sentence level and it has, moreover, received an extensive critique from Vandelanotte (2003) whose semiotic-functional analysis also operates on the level of the sentence. What is demonstrated as unacceptable for Vandelanotte (2003: 27-28f) is not the code-switching proposal but, among others, the syntactic analysis of the relationship between the reporting and reported clause. Hansen (2000) does not abandon the traditional parataxis vs. hypotaxis analysis of the opposition between direct and indirect speech. Within semiotic grammar, these relations are rejected. Vandelanotte (2003: 18-19) presents arguments obtained from McGregor (1990),

---

[35] Author and principal are constitutive elements of the reporter as deconstructed by Goffman (1981: 129, 144-5). Cf. section 2.6.

such as the fact that in parataxis it is unusual for the reordering of elements not to affect the relationship between them, as "the second normally expands on the first" (Vandellanotte 2003: 18). In direct speech such a change of order is not uncommon and does not affect the relationship between the elements. In indirect speech, on the other hand, oddly for hypotaxis, the order of constituents is fixed. In this way, Vandelanotte (2003) contributes another strong argument with regard to the weakness of exclusively syntactic approaches.

2.3.2.2.3.3 Intention and mediation

As has been mentioned already, reported speech is by nature creative and intentional, in that "reports are mediated by mental images of speech events in both the production and the interpretation processes; they do not come directly from the represented speech event" (Collins 2001: 2). This view is akin to the one presented by Sternberg who claims: "to quote is to mediate, to mediate is to frame, and to frame is to interfere and exploit" (1982: 145). According to Günthner (1999), "the quoted utterance is characterised by transformations, modifications, and functionalisations according to the speaker's aims and the new conversational context" (1999: 686). Koven (2001) in an ethnographic study, next to demonstrating that through quotation "speakers perform particular kinds of local, quotable identities" (2001: 514), notices also that reported speech is a "creative performance" (2001: 514). According to Vincent and Perrin (1999) who present a socio-pragmatic study of narrative and non-narrative functions of reported speech, "the discursive competence of speakers includes an intuitive ability to alternate strategies and to vary procedures in such a way that their discourse is more captivating and credible to the interlocutor" (1999: 308). Holt (2000) analyses patterns of reactions to reported speech on the side of the receivers and she concludes on an empirical basis that "both speakers [i.e., the teller and the recipient, MW] appear to be reacting independently but also harmoniously to the reported locution" (2000: 451). This observation on the basis of conversational narratives shows that discourse is a collaborative creation of both the speaker and receiver, also in the case of reported speech. As the author concludes, this collaboration in reaction serves to establish and maintain intersubjectivity (cf. Duranti 1993).

Holt's conclusions (2000), however, need a minor modification concerning the status of the participants in a speech situation. Naturally, instances may be found of asymmetric power relations inhibiting the collaboration on the side of one of the participants (e.g., classroom discourse, cf. Baynham 1996). Thus, Matoesian (2000) demonstrates how during the questioning in court a witness is not given an opportunity of collaboration when it comes to recontextualisations of her earlier speech through electronic media. That is to say, the defence attorney is to a larger extent responsible for the creation of discourse when he plays the tape with prior depositions than the witness who is not in a position to influence even a minor detail of this act (Matoesian 2000: 897). In a similar vein, as Goodwin and Duranti (1992) point out, the traditional speech act analysis[36] allocates an unequal status to speaker and hearer, of whom the latter is "but the projection of the speaker's wants and attitudes" (1992: 18). Though such a configuration is not an uncommon one, power relations are indeed subject to changes and switches; thus, it is more fitting to go beyond the speaker-hearer dyad and accept after Hymes 1967 [1972] the category of a participant (cf. Goodwin and Duranti 1992: 26). Bearing in mind the fluctuations of status and power of participants in discourse as well as the constant switching of places, all participants emerge as potentially active in interaction. Thus, once again, discourse cannot be anything else but a collaborative creation of language users regardless of whether at a given moment they are its producers or recipients.

Except for their mutual relationships, the participants in discourse essentially have to refer to and interact with the surrounding context. Interesting insights in this respect may be provided by the enunciation theory as, for instance, presented by Marnette (2001), in which language is seen in terms of its relations to users and context rather than as an abstract system (2001: 244). Although the theory has not always sought empirical verification in conversational material, it has developed an extensive and heterogeneous model[37] for the study of *speech and thought presentation* (S&TP, as the author refers to reported speech) in narratology, philosophy of language and rhetoric. Like many other recent frameworks designed to deal with the phenomenon of reported speech, enunciation theory has its roots in Bakhtin's notion of polyphony, which assumes the presence of several voices in a single utterance (cf. section 2.6 below). According to this theory "reported discourse deals not only with the subjectivity of the 'locutor', the person responsible for the act of enunciation and referred to as *I*, but also with the subjectivity of other voices which are 'blended' into the utterance ('enunciators')" (Marnette 2001: 244-245). Actually, enunciation theory is one of the sites in which intention and perception as the indispensable aspects of reported speech, emphasised also in other studies, receive a particularly potent place through the "insistence on the polyphonic nature of language" which "emphasises the intricate relationship existing between subjects and discourses – their own and those of the others" (Marnette 2001: 258).

---

[36] For further references, cf. Hill and Irvine (1993a: 7-9) on a critique of the intentionalist models, such as the speech act theory. Compare also Linell (2001: 116) who sees the 'written language bias' in linguistic semantics and pragmatics as "an excessive reliance on individual intentions in the explanation of utterances", i.e., an overemphasis of "individual acts at the expense of social interaction".

[37] Cf. Marnette's (2001) overview of the scope of the theory (2001: 244). Compare also Maingueneau (1999: 181-182) who talks about theories of enunciation, rather than a single model.

The issues of intention and perception, most importantly, allow detaching reported speech from the anterior/original utterance whether or not such a 'represented' entity exists. Recognising the creativity of participants in discourse, such an approach points to a certain autonomy of the phenomenon of reported speech as a polyfunctional device through which participants may intentionally negotiate their roles and meanings in discourse. Still, what has to be borne in mind is the fact that even the radical 'creative' approaches to reported speech, particularly those in keeping with Tannen (1986; 1989) and the notion of *constructed dialogue*, do not deny that in many cases speakers indeed refer to some 'authentic' speech event. The issue that remains to be resolved is the relationship between reported speech and this authentic event. Although the majority of researchers reject the verbatimness hypothesis, stemming from the written language bias in linguistics (cf. e.g., Linell 2001: 114-117). – the hypothesis which stands no chance of verification against the empirical evidence – the issue of faithfulness[38] is a more delicate one. Thus, in the present discussion it is accepted, after Short – Semino – Wynne (2002) that "the removal of the faithfulness criterion from discourse presentation theory ignores the fact that faithfulness is the central factor in a number of contexts" (2002: 349). Naturally, these contexts[39] are specific; therefore the relevance of the faithfulness criterion is utterly context-dependent[40]. For instance, Moore (2003) in a study of Early Modern English slander depositions presents evidence for the irrelevance of the faithfulness criterion for court scribes of the time. Rather than concentrate on the wording, even in direct speech records, a scribe was more focused on the contents.

For the reasons outlined above the definition of reported speech in terms of the anterior/original speech event cannot be accepted uncritically. Rather, in order

---

[38] Compare the notion of *fidelity* in Hill and Irvine (1993a: 15) defined as "the accurate representation of form and content of the quoted speech" and the context-dependent view of "responsibility for "fidelity" in representation of reported speech". Cf. also Besnier (1993) in the same volume on the understanding of faithfulness in Nukulaelae community in which children "are expected to convey complex verbal messages, repeated exactly as uttered by the sender" (1993: 165). These findings confirm Coulmas' tentative remark that "the notion of verbatim rendition, that is, identity of form, seems to be culturally variable" (1986: 1). Cf. also Shuman (1993) on the notion of accuracy in relation to authority. The author claims "while people challenge one another on the accuracy of their reports, the issue at stake is not accuracy but the appropriation of authority" (1993: 135).

[39] One of the contexts where the faithfulness criterion indeed applies is journalistic discourse (e.g., Waugh 1995). However, Sleurs – Jacobs – Waes (2003), in their discussion of what they refer to as *pseudo-quotation*, show that in press releases, an active construction process takes place, the result of which is often nothing else but invented direct quotation.

[40] There are studies of specific, institutional contexts in which the literal character of quotation (Antaki and Leudar 2001, concerning the quoting of official records during in the British Parliament) or the view of quotation as "a mirror image" of the speech event it purports to represent (Matoesian 2000: 897, on the functions of electronic records of prior witness's statements in court) are exemplified and sustained.

not to completely dismiss this relatively common view, its hedged version is sustained for the purpose of this study. As has been aptly put by Hickmann (1993), this standpoint, after all, holds true for a range of reported speech instances: "Some utterances reporting speech are inherently metalinguistic in the sense that they *refer explicitly* to speech events" (Hickmann 1993: 64). In order not to ignore the functional potential of reported speech, it has to be borne in mind, after Collins (2001), that it performs "a *metapragmatic* function of language" (2001:1), aptly defined[41] by Overstreet and Yule (2002) as allowing "language-users to anticipate, comment on, and influence the interpretation of the pragmatic impact of what they say or write" (2002: 785).

2.3.2.4 The source

The idea of the source of reported speech is very closely linked to the problem of the anterior speech event. Actually, in definitions of the phenomenon which rely on the source of the report, the existence of an anterior speech event is implied. The misunderstandings[42] concerning the source have not, however, been as frequent as the problem addressed above and they were largely concerned with the non-inclusion of self-quotation[43]. For instance, Massamba (1986) in a study of reported speech in Swahili explicitly disregards self-quotation in his discussion (though not ignoring the possibility of self-quotation, cf. 1986: 119f) when defining reported speech "as a message conveying utterance for which the reporter claims no authorship" (1986: 99). Similarly, Bolden (2004) talks about "speech attributed to another person and/or to another context (i.e., *reported speech* and especially *direct reported speech*)" (Bolden 2004: 1071, italics original) when analysing the boundaries of reported speech in conversational Russian. This omission is even more striking given that the author does refer to instances of self-quotation (e.g., Bolden 2004: 1098). Another exclusion of self-quotation in a reported speech definition is found in Koven (2001), whose focus is the "quoted performances of **self** and other" (2001: 513, emphasis MW) and who sees "[a]n instance of quoted speech ... as a clause of a story presented from the perspective of a character, reenacting the purported thoughts, speech, and other deeds of narrated characters" (2001: 526-27). Similarly, Maynard (1996), investigating self-quotation in Japanese, states "quoting someone's words, involves, by definition, the voice of another" (1996: 210). Both authors (i.e.,

---

[41] On metapragmatics, cf. Verschueren (1995).
[42] However, "a fundamental ambiguity about the relationship between the speaker and the source of reported speech" (Hill and Irvine 1993a: 12) has to be accepted, particularly in linguistic anthropology.
[43] As far as the studies of self-quotation are concerned, the phenomenon has received more interest lately (e.g., Golato 2000, Koven 2001).

Koven 2001 and Maynard 1996), though focusing on self-quotation, omit it in their definitions.

Although the idea behind the source has emerged as a transparent one, one has to be cautious enough to remember that the source of a speech event remains open to intentional manipulation by the speaker. Antaki and Leudar (2001) demonstrate instances of a "mystery source" (2001: 480), where speakers purposefully dramatise the identity of people whom they wish to quote. In doing that, the quoting speakers in this specific contextualisation (sessions of the British Parliament) are able to reveal true positions of the quoted sources, incorporate personal evaluations of these positions as well as strengthen their own (political) position. The 'mystery source', however, is a functional aspect of reported speech rather than 'a third kind,' next to 'self' and 'other'.

2.3.2.4.1 Evidentiality

The source of information a speaker is relying on at the moment of speaking is connected to a linguistically complex and typologically diversified issue of evidentiality (cf. sections 4.3.1.4 and 4.3.1.5.8). English for instance does not require the evidential status of utterances to be marked (Hill and Irvine 1993: 18), neither does it possess a grammaticalised system of evidentiality, but such systems are not uncommon in the languages of the world (cf. Palmer 2001: 35-52, cf. also Aikhenvald and Dixon 2003 for a recent typological overview of this issue). Dendale and Tasmowsky (2001) provide a neat semantic classification of evidential marking cross-linguistically:

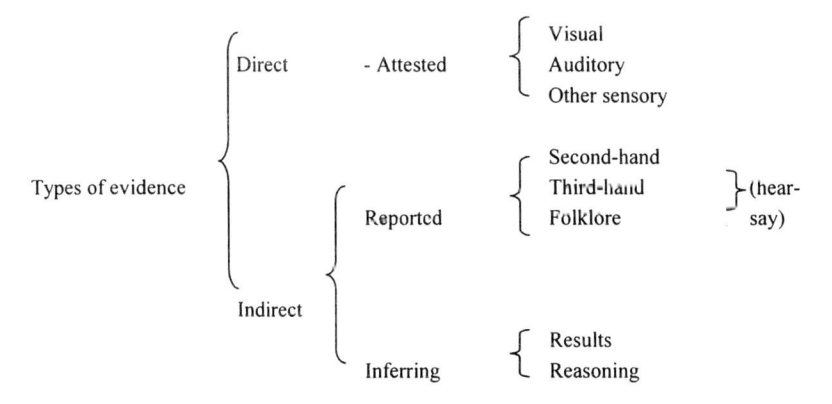

```
                        ┌ Visual
         ┌ Direct  - Attested  ┤ Auditory
         │                     └ Other sensory
         │
Types of │          ┌           ┌ Second-hand
evidence │          │ Reported  ┤ Third-hand   ┐ (hear-
         │          │           └ Folklore     ┘ say)
         │ Indirect ┤
         │          │           ┌ Results
         └          └ Inferring ┘ Reasoning
```

Figure 1: The semantic domain of evidentiality (based on Willet 1988; after Dendale and Tasmowsky 2001: 343)

Though English does not have a grammaticalised evidential system, it uses evidential strategies (cf. Aikhenvald 2003) which are mostly encoded in verb semantics and the use of modal verbs. Lacking such a system, however, English is much more difficult to analyse with respect to reported speech, as it lacks grammatical devices disambiguating problematic or unattributed instances of the phenomenon i.e., when the speaker chooses not to specify the source of information. Most importantly, from the pragmatic point of view, evidentiality systems and strategies equip the speaker with means to mark their own degree of commitment to the proposition i.e., they are ways to assess the reliability of the utterance, to include an element of personal evaluation or attitude. In this way evidentiality is connected to modality (cf. section 4.3.1.5) through which the pragmatics of reported speech is most clearly manifested.

2.3.2.4.2 Implications of 'source' for the definition of reported speech

On the basis of this modest selection of examples, one could venture to claim that the non-inclusion of self-quotation in a definition of reported speech does not necessarily have a serious theoretical bearing nor does it pose a major problem, since it would be inconceivable to imply that researchers do not allow the possibility of self-quotation. Rather, in order for the formulation to remain succinct, self-quotation may as well be implied rather than referred to explicitly. Yet, it is by all means possible to provide a balanced formulation whose brevity does not exclude self-quotation and, even more importantly, which does not introduce the anterior/original speech event condition. Such a definition is found in a syntactic study of Old and Middle Hungarian where reported speech includes "recollections of chunks of earlier texts as well as current utterances of (other) speakers even if those utterances are not real, or are not presented as such (e.g., if they occur in someone's thoughts, if they are performative, if their form is conditional, negated, or refers to the future)" (Dömötör 2001: 338).

2.3.2.5 Text, utterance, thought – the medium problem

Dömötör's definition (2001) quoted above may provide a starting point for the next step in the discussion, as it uses two keywords which are particularly sensitive to misinterpretations in the context of reported speech studies. These words are *text* and *utterance*. The latter has already been quoted above, particularly in connection with Volosinov's definition, but also with reference to other authors. Although in Dömötör's formulation the two words may be seen as standing in opposition – the former meaning instances of written and the latter of spoken language – they do not normally carry these implied meanings, at least not within the field of reported speech studies. The fact that *text* and *utterance* may imply a written vs. spoken distinction leads to another problematic dimension of reported speech, namely the medium in which the original utterance has been produced (provided there has ever been an anterior/original speech event), the medium in which it is reported as well as the possibility of thought reporting or reporting on linguistic events that have never even taken place. The last option is particularly difficult to capture because of its medium-free nature i.e., the fact that speech events may be wordless.

As far as the studies of contemporary languages are concerned, the medium problem is hardly ever recognised as a potential issue demanding a consistent treatment and there are few researchers who recognise medium distinctions or apply them to the categorisation of reported speech instances. The exceptions here are Baynham and Slembrouck (1999), Short – Semino – Wynne (2002), who are actually indebted to the aforementioned study, and Matoesian (2000).

When designing a model for the analysis of reported speech in institutional settings, Baynham and Slembrouck (1999) emphasise the contextual and situational dependency of the phenomenon and its functional dimensions which can be inferred on the basis of this dependency. The particular significance assigned to the context leads the authors to some detailed considerations upon the medium problem (Baynham and Slembrouck 1999: 447-8). Starting with the contexts in which written speech events are reported in the written medium, they claim that outside academic writing[44], for instance in the printed media, "the actual formulation of a cited utterance is not only affected by routine habits of notetaking (e.g., shorthand) but also by various types of editorial interference (e.g., 'correcting' the grammar)" (Baynham and Slembrouck 1999: 447). As the authors go on to claim, things become even more complicated if there is a shift in medium from speech to writing where all that can be afforded is a "simulation of spokenness" (Baynham and Slembrouck 1999: 447). Similarly, Short – Semino – Wynne (2002) notice: "many features of original utterances are lost in *any* report ... especially if the anterior discourse is in one medium and the posterior discourse in another" (Short – Semino – Wynne 2002: 330, italics original). This statement concerns not only representations of speech in written contexts but also representations of writing in spoken contexts. In other words, medium transfer demands special attention to what the authors refer to as the "cross-medium 'equivalence'" (Short – Semino – Wynne 2002: 331).

This approach, exceptionally sensitive to the issues of medium, is continued in McIntyre et al. (2004) in that the speech/writing/thought distinctions are carefully applied to the categorisation of speech presentation proposed. Problematic as the issue of medium may be, the emphasis placed on resolving it has led the authors to a categorisation consisting of 42 different categories, 21 for the written and 21 for the spoken data corpus. Had it not been for the strict

---

[44] Cf. Jakobs (2003), a study on the topic of what she refers to as *reproductive writing*.

medium distinctions (writing, speech, thought), the number of categories could be reduced to 7 for each set of data. It is indeed questionable whether such an intricate categorisation, although it does recognise the often-neglected lack of equivalence of the different media, may at all contribute any illuminating facts about reported discourse. For example, Short – Semino – Wynne (2002: 342) have found that direct writing and thought presentation in the overall written corpus they studied each account for less than 1% of all tags. On the basis of this evidence, it is proposed here that the threefold medium distinction need not be sustained in the present work, in the first place not to obscure the clarity of categorisation and in the second place because its explanatory potential has proved disappointing. The twofold distinction, on the other hand, keeping apart speech (comprising of reports of both spoken and written language) and thought has proved fruitful, as has been predicted earlier by Leech and Short (1981), in that it corresponds to the distinction between direct and indirect reported speech of which the former is the norm for speech and the latter the norm for thought presentation. According to Halliday (1985), speech and thought presentation have specific syntactic correlates: "Thus parataxis is naturally associated with verbal projections and hypotaxis with mental ones" (Halliday 1985: 248). Indeed, as far as spoken language is concerned, there are studies which have been able to corroborate that direct speech can indeed be seen as the norm for speech, like, for instance, Vincent and Perrin (1999). More recently this has even been taken for granted as in e.g., Dimmendaal (2001: 145) who claims that "directly reported speech is the norm" for the languages that he analyses. Therefore, the definition to be formulated for the purpose of the present discussion incorporates the twofold rather than the threefold medium distinction.

In his study of "a hyperform of direct speech" (Matoesian 2000: 881), the author shows how reported speech played through an audiotape is a tool of manipulation of the relationship between the reporting context i.e., the situation of courtroom and the original speech event. The electronic medium in this truth-seeking context has an ontological priority over other resources, like, for instance, reading the tape-script out loud by the defence attorney (Matoesian 2000: 897). Thus, in the contexts of social power "the production medium or communicative modality which transmits reported speech is ontologically ranked and ideologically loaded" (Matoesian 2000: 896). Drawing on the conclusions of this study, next to the twofold medium distinction established above, the additional implications of medium selection in the institutional contexts rendering asymmetrical power relations are incorporated in the present work.

2.3.2.6 The context

The significance of context in linguistics is profound and so is the complexity of the notion, whose scope can be well grasped on the basis of a volume edited by

Duranti and Goodwin (1992)[45]. *Rethinking*, as the title announces, the notion of context, the collection is an answer to "a trend toward a more interactive and dialogically conceived notions of contextually situated talk" (Goodwin and Duranti 1992: 1). Though the contributions discuss various aspects of the issue, the phenomenon of context continually frustrates the attempts at a single definition and one has to finally agree with the authors of the introduction that "such a definition may not be possible" (Goodwin and Duranti 1992: 2)[46].

The issue of context has so far not received a more extensive treatment in the present discussion but has appeared as a recurrent theme. This section is devoted to the presentation of the understanding of context emerging specifically in the literature on reported speech in order to define and stress the importance of this aspect for the present work. It is noteworthy to underline that courtroom records analysed here may provide no more than written attestations of specific institutionally set interactions. Therefore, adopting the figure and ground opposition[47] reflected on by Goodwin and Duranti (1992: 9-10) as an analogy to the relationship between focal event and context, one has to bear in mind that "writing ... is one of the main procedures through which the **ground** within which language emerges is systematically erased, made invisible, and excluded from analysis" (Goodwin and Duranti 1992: 32f, original emphasis). Thus, if through writing down speech the context of interaction is lost[48], the constant recovery of the context is the central task to be carried out in this study in order for the analysis of data (with limitations that it entails) to remain a feasible task. It has to be borne in mind, however, as Carroll et al. (2003) maintain, that in the case of historical material "the actual context of use and its effect on the particular texts can at best only be guessed at" (2003: 3).

Though recognising the importance of context, however defined, individual branches of linguistics usually fail to make explicit what methodological procedures are to be applied and what elements are to be analysed on the way to the discovery of context (Schiffrin 1987: 12). In order not to perpetrate a similar omission, the notion of context, in accord with the aims of the

---

[45] For some interesting approaches to context cf. e.g., Lindstrom (1992: 102 103) on the notion of context based on Michel Foucault's *orders of discourse*, Bauman (1992: 128) on the active process of contextualisation, Schegloff (1992: 195 on "distal" and "proximate contexts", Cicourel (1992: 294-296) on the broad and narrow view of context and Cicourel (1992: 303-307) on expanding the ethnographic context.

[46] Compare Van Dijk (2004: 348-369) on a mental dynamic theory of context and its application to the setting of a parliamentary debate. The author states: "Despite this earlier work, we still lack a more or less explicit theory of context. Indeed, until today, there is not a single monograph on context" (Van Dijk 2004: 348). Cf. also Van Dijk (2004: 348) for references to the research on context within social psychology.

[47] On figure and ground in linguistic systems cf. also Hanks (1992: 61-62) in the same volume.

[48] Compare Carroll et al. (2003: 3) on contextualisation of early written texts.

present study, needs to be specified on the basis of its treatment within reported speech studies.

As in the case of many themes concerning reported speech studies, Volosinov (1929 [1973]) is again the pioneer of a critical approach to syntactic accounts of the phenomenon which disregard the notion of context. In his view, "reported speech and the reporting context are but the terms of a dynamic interrelationship" (Volosinov 1929 [1973]: 119), which implies a possibility of mutual influence i.e., the speaker reporting speech may be involved in the creation of context (the revealing side to this approach) and, more obviously, the context of reporting may in turn affect the speaker and his reported speech (cf. Golato 2002: 49). The former possibility is also recognised by Buttny (1998) who sees context "as existing independently of the text and as (re)created in and through the text" (1998: 46), the text being implicitly understood as the creation of language users. Buttny (1998) defines context in its relation to text: "[i]f text is the microlevel of social interaction, context includes macrolevel dimensions in which to situate the text, such as historical background, the participants' power or economic position" (1998: 46). This approach is in line with the traditional sociolinguistic view of context as the communicative environment including a range of components (cf. Lindstrom 1992: 103-4), such as participants, setting, ends, keys, channels, forms of speech, norms of interaction and interpretation, and genres (Hymes 1967 [1972]: 58-65).

More recently, this traditional approach was extended by Baynham and Slembrouck (1999) to work specifically as an analytic tool for the study of reported speech within institutional discourse. This view advocates a "discourse-analytic perspective with a clear functionalist orientation" (Baynham and Slembrouck 1999: 442). Except for the focus on the text properties in context, as the authors continue, it also takes into account "user-related processes of discourse production and consumption" (Baynham and Slembrouck 1999: 442). Finally, Baynham and Slembrouck (1999) formulate the focus of reported speech studies within institutional context as falling on "the purposes of speech representation in the reporting context: what is the communicative work that is being achieved in terms of an overall generic purpose?" (Baynham and Slembrouck 1999: 454). This approach has been exercised in a range of studies and has indeed been able to produce illuminating results concerning aspects of reported speech such as, for instance, in the study by Short – Semino – Wynne (2002), which successfully deals with the hitherto unsolved issue of faithfulness and the anterior utterance hypothesis in reported speech.

The function-oriented approach outlined above is followed in the present work since it is well suited to its purposes and to the data it seeks to analyse, as well as – according to its proponents – as an interactive model of context, it may "enable use [sic] to capture more effectively and equitably the interaction between language and other forms of social action"[49] (Baynham and Slembrouck 1999: 445-6). It is, moreover, favoured over standpoints proposing rather restricted understandings, such as that of Maynard's *semiotic context* (1996: 224) or a Relevance-bound notion of context as advocated, for instance, by Uchida (1997), The two views on context (Maynard 1996, Uchida 1997) could be criticised after Van der Wurff (2002: 121) as global approaches ignoring generic factors or those determined by text-type.

To conclude this discussion of context, it is asserted that the pragmatic angle of this study calls for a broad conception of this term. According to Recanati (2002), one of the crucial factors in a pragmatic interpretation (understood by the author as concerned more with human action than with language) of an utterance is the fact that there is absolutely no limit to the contextual information which may be relevant to the results of this interpretation (Recanati 2002: 106). General as it may be, this notion of context informs and underlies the present study.

2.3.2 Studies outside historical pragmatics – implications for a definition

In the discussion above, the following problematic issues occurring in definitions and approaches to reported speech were identified: the anterior speech event, the source, the medium and the context. These issues were resolved in accord with the purpose of the present work. It was done in the following ways: the anterior/original speech event condition was rejected but the possibility of the existence of such event was sustained; as for the source, its variations (other versus self) were accepted as obvious and implicit; as far as the medium is concerned, a twofold (speech and writing vs. thought reports) medium distinction was accepted. Throughout the discussion, the phenomenon of reported speech emerged as pragmatic in nature, which was presented on the basis of some shortcomings of exclusively syntactic or, for instance, prosody-oriented approaches. In particular, the issues of boundaries and marking were discussed as not being sufficiently elucidated by these approaches. It was underlined that intention, mediation and perception must also be incorporated into a comprehensive account of reported speech, as these factors have crucial bearing on the functional potential of the phenomenon. Finally, the notion of context was raised in the discussion as one of the dominant factors in the analysis of reported speech and, faced with historical written material, one of the vital foci of attention.

---

[49] Quotation in accord with the original printed version of the paper.

2.4 Categorisation

The *canonical* or *prototypical* categories – as *direct* and *indirect speech* are often referred to – have for a long time been viewed as representing a clear-cut dichotomy (e.g., Jespersen 1924, Coulmas[50] 1986, Janssen and Van der Wurff 1996). In the traditional view, the categorisation of reported speech was thus restricted to three categories, of which the canonical ones posed no classification problems, while the additional mixed type (cf. footnote 3) was probably less straightforward but equally easy to distinguish. Thus, Jespersen (1924) enumerates a category which "gives, or purports to give, the exact words of the speaker (or writer): *direct speech* (oratio recta)", and another in which "one adapts the words according to the circumstances in which they are quoted: *indirect speech* (oratio obliqua)" (1924: 290). Furthermore, Jespersen distinguishes two sub-types of the former kind providing the third category, *represented speech* (1924: 291), which corresponds to what is, among other terms, referred to as *free indirect speech*. A recent comprehensive grammar of the English language, almost eight decades distant from Jespersen (1924), defines the canonical categories of reported speech in the following way: "**Direct reported speech** purports to give the actual wording of the original, whereas **indirect reported speech** gives only its content" (Huddleston and Pullum 2002: 1023, emphasis original). To this, *free indirect speech* is added as a 'third kind'. Not only do other authors rely on Jespersen (1924) particularly in their definition of direct speech, but they also commit the error of sticking to the empirically dubious direct versus indirect speech opposition[51].

The cross-linguistic evidence in favour of maintaining a clear-cut dichotomy of direct and indirect speech is not conclusive. Thus, Coulmas (1986a) gives examples of Ancient Greek, Old French, Mambila and Nootka as languages lacking clearly marked boundaries between direct and indirect speech[52] (Coulmas 1986a: 146). Similarly, Ebert (1986), a contributor to Coulmas' volume (1986), points to the fact that "[t]he idea that languages make a clear distinction between direct and indirect speech is for the most part a grammatical fiction" (Ebert 1986: 156) and supports her conclusion with empirical findings not only with regard to exotic languages like Chamling, Nepali or other African tongues, but also English and German. Not only is the distinction between direct and indirect speech not universal but it is frequently not as clear-cut at all, as has been shown by Lucy (1993): "[b]etween these two poles may lie a range of blended alternatives" (1993b: 95). The notion of a dichotomy of direct and indirect speech is dismissed by Roeck (1994), an analysis within the framework of functional grammar. Using

---

[50] Compare a less rigid view on the dichotomy as expressed in Coulmas (1986a).
[51] Compare Thompson (1996: 504) on further examples of grammatical approaches.
[52] Cf. Coulmas (1986a) for references.

data from as many as 40 languages, the author summarises evidence for the existence of over ten types of reported speech classified on the basis of the presence or absence of (1) deictic shifts, (2) pragmatic function assignment, (3) expressive or emotional components, (4) quotative markers, (5) conjunctions (Roeck 1994: 343). The results of the analysis reveal a cross-linguistic continuum of types of reported speech.

The discussion of categories of reported speech to be applied in this work will commence with the two assumptions referred to above: first of all, that direct and indirect speech do not form a clear-cut dichotomy and secondly, that even if they can be seen as extremes, in between them one has to accept the existence of a range of intermediate categories, the boundaries of which are frequently fuzzy. These cross-linguistically verifiable assumptions are applied in the present discussion to the categorisation of reported speech types within a single language in a synchronic stage.

2.4.1 Categorisation criteria

Although the classification of reported speech instances has always been central to the discussion of the phenomenon, the efforts to provide a universal categorisation[53] comprising clear-cut units of description have not been particularly successful. Moreover, it seems futile to seek absolute categories even at the cost of a lucid description. A range of studies have actually provided categorisations designed for their individual aim or the text-types under scrutiny. To give a couple of illustrations, Waugh (1995) who discusses reported speech in journalistic discourse provides her own continuum of reported speech categories to account for the specificity of the material at hand, thus demonstrating how individual text-types may determine the categorisation of speech presentation. Moreover, the author shows that in journalistic discourse the "separation between direct and indirect speech is categorical" (Waugh 1995: 163) and she sees each category as representing two separate continua, differentiated by orthography. Another continuum of reported speech, ranging from the most to the least demonstrative forms, is proposed in Schiffrin's (2002: 325) discussion of Holocaust stories. Specific discourse types, such as, for instance, political campaigns reports may also require some specific categories, such as an *embedded metapragmatic construction* proposed by Wortham and Locher (1999). Therefore, rather than a search for a universal categorisation, an overview of comprehensive proposals is presented below in order to determine a set of categories to be applied in the further discussion and to account for the choices made.

---

[53] Compare a range of accounts of philosophical approaches to quotation and the categorisation in Cappelen and Lepore (1997).

2.4.1.1 Perspective/point of view

It is generally agreed that the criterion of distinction between *direct* and *indirect speech* is the perspective of the reporter, i.e., the current speaker (e.g., Coulmas 1986a, Roeck 1994). In direct speech the perspective of the original speaker is maintained whereas indirect speech involves a shift in the direction of the reporter. The shift in question primarily concerns deictic elements which get adapted to a new deictic centre. Naturally, grammatical manifestations of these adjustments are unquestionable for some languages. Still, accepting the perspective/point of view criterion implies abiding by the original utterance hypothesis, hence it cannot be taken for granted, considering the complex of issues around the anterior speech event.

2.4.1.2 Other anterior utterance biased criteria

Accepting the fact that "the distinction between direct and indirect speech is more complicated than a mere dichotomy" (Coulmas 1986a: 143), Coulmas provides the following set of scalar parameters with respect to which instances of reported speech may vary: faithfulness to form and content of the original utterance, deictic homogeneity and syntactic integration. When it comes to the faithfulness[54] criterion, the author does not even attempt to provide ways of verifying its degrees and moreover, this parameter is another indication of the uncritical acceptance of the original utterance hypothesis. Neither does the author elaborate on the deictic homogeneity criterion instead giving a couple of isolated remarks on cross-linguistic variability of deixis as a preparation for a more in-depth treatment of the final parameter: syntactic/grammatical integration. Therefore, tense, mood, word order and complement formation together with deictic switches are the indicators of the degree to which the reported and reporting clause are "harmonised and integrated within one another" (Coulmas 1986a: 148). Coulmas' proposal includes at one pole a structure in which the reported part is minimal e.g., a noun phrase fully integrated into the reporting clause, and at another the total syntactic separation of the two clauses as occurring in direct speech. In between these two, as the author continues, there is a "transition zone of indirect speech forms of varying degrees of integration" (Coulmas 1986a: 150). Although no specific categories are named and the configurations of parameters are not defined, this classification proposal is an interesting one as it at least slightly departs from the anterior speech event hypothesis. Still, no empirical verification of Coulmas' proposal has been offered so far and his modest cross-linguistic presentation of

---

[54] Cf. Short – Semino – Wynne (2002) for a discussion of the faithfulness criterion and its application to the studies of reported speech.

the degrees of integration of reported and reporting clauses on the basis of German, English, Latin and Japanese cannot be accepted as conclusive.

Spoken data from a French corpus forms the basis for the analysis and a categorisation of reported speech in a paper by Vincent and Dubois (1996). Assuming that reported speech is more than reproduction of others' speech, the authors rely on the contextual information (time of quoted speech or tense, speaker, addressee and the content of quoted speech) to isolate "five categories of 'acts' that are carried out through reported speech" (Vincent and Dubois 1996: 361). These are placed on a continuum ranging from the +quote through reproduction, pseudo-reproduction, actualization, invention, assertion to the − quote pole. The combinations of components underlying the categorisation are given in Table 4:

Uses of reported speech	Reproduction	Pseudo-repro.	Actualization	Invention	Assertion
Indicators of reproduction					
past event	+	+	+/−	−	−
definite speaker	+	+	+/−	+	+**
definite addressee*	+	−	+/−	+	+/−
definite context	+	−	+/−	+/−	−
narrative act	+	+/−	+/−	−	−

*other than the reflexive pronoun
**The speaker can only be *I (je)*

Table 4: Indicators of the reproduction of words for the five uses of reported speech (after Vincent and Dubois 1996: 367)

The problem posed by this categorisation, as in the case of Coulmas (1986), is its reliance on the original utterance. Despite the authors' claim that they are focusing on contextual parameters, their proposal is not able to go beyond the anterior speech event thus only superficially attending to the context of the ongoing speech event. Moreover, configurations of parameters overlap for different categories, though it is not the fuzzy boundaries between them that are problematic. Rather, there is a great degree of arbitrariness to the proposed categories and finally, they do not coincide with any externally induced factors, such as i.e., pragmatic or situational needs. Vincent and Dubois (1996), though giving an apparently novel proposal, remain restrained within the limits imposed by the original utterance hypothesis.

2.4.1.2.1 Dimensions of reporter's choice

A functional perspective on reported speech viewed as "signalled voices in the text" (Thompson 1996: 501) results in a categorisation on the basis of four dimensions of reporter's choice: the voice, the message, the signal and the attitude

(Thompson 1996: 507). Proposing a functional approach is a way of overcoming the lack of consistent formal features on the basis of which distinct reported speech categories could be identified. Thus Thompson (1996) proposes the following inventory of options:

Dimensions of choice	Cline of options	
voice	self	
	specified other(s)	
	unspecified other(s)	
	community	
	unspecifiable other(s)	
message	quote	
	echo	
	paraphrase	
	summary	
	omission	
signal	separate	
		positive
		neutral
	fused	negative
attitude	relevant	
		positive
		neutral
	not relevant	negative

Table 5: Functional options for language reports (after Thompson 1996: 524)

Throughout the discussion of the main dimensions of reporter's choice that he proposes, Thompson notices a range of structural features of reports, which are also variable parameters. These parameters are summarised in Table 6:

Signal	Message
reporting clause	quote
reporting adjunct	reported clause:
reporting noun	main clause
reporting adjective	*that* - clause
reporting verb	*wh* – clause
[no separate signal]	*to* – infinitive clause
	-*ing* clause
	prepositional phrase
	nominal group
	[no separate message]

Table 6: Structural options for language reports (after Thompson 1996: 524)

Naturally, as the author emphasises, neither of the classifications may provide a complete picture, since both are essentially selective. Still, complementing a functional categorisation with a structural one is definitely a step towards an integrated categorisation of reported speech. Thompson's study, however, only to a limited degree applies the categorisation to natural language and, not unlike the proposals discussed above, its empirical potential remains unverified. One further problem posed by Thompson's proposal is that it does not incorporate the distinction between speech and thought reports, viewing it as more adequate in literary material. On the other hand, a further advantage of this categorisation in comparison with the ones dominated by the anterior utterance hypothesis is its comprehensive account of the sources of reports, in which an unspecifiable source i.e., the lack of both a clearly identifiable original speaker or speech event, is accepted as a possibility. Still, the 'message' dimension, is tightly connected to the original function or content of a presumed anterior utterance. Thus, at some points Thompson (1996) abides by the anterior utterance hypothesis, whereas in others he is able to avoid it. Some minor criticism might also be raised with respect to a range of detailed categories which are hardly to be matched with any real discourse functions and which render Thompson's (1996) categorisation too thorough, while still not exhaustive.

2.4.1.2.2 Singleness of deictic centre

A further categorisation proposal contributed lately by Vandelanotte (e.g., 2003; 2004a; 2004b) is an extension of the traditional categorisation of reported speech into three canonical types. What the author claims, following examinations of deictic shifts connected *with free indirect speech*, is the existence of a fourth category, commonly mistaken with *free indirect speech* (FIST[55]) in the literature: *distancing indirect speech and thought*, DIST. Thus, Vandelanotte distinguishes between sentences like: *He would be late, John said* (FIST) and *John will be late, he said* (DIST) on the basis of the deictic singleness of the latter (Vandelanotte 2004a: 500). Unlike the other three categories, for the new DIST proposed by the author, the speaker does not represent a truly separate consciousness even though the structures applied are those of reported speech (Vandelanotte 2004b: 547). For instance, the first person pronouns used are always co-referential with the current speaker and so are other grammatical resources (Vandelanotte 2004b: 550, 552). The only indication of reported speech is the presence of the clause (like *he said*), referred to by the author as 'distancing'. Within the new category, Vandelanotte furthermore distinguishes *representational* and *scopal* DIST on the grounds of "pragmatically distinct contextualisations" (2004b: 557). The former sub-type is concerned with voices of others since its semantic load originates in another

---

[55] On the terminology used by Vandelanotte, cf. section 2.2.2.1.

discourse whereas the latter relies on modality, illocutionary effects and evidentiality as components of the speaker's experience representing in fact the speaker's intersubjective suggestions (Vandelanotte 2004b: 573). The contextualisations the author provides for scopal (interpersonal) DIST are: conversational uses of *I think*, *I guess*; the illocutionary *I claim* in the academic discourse (cf. Baynham 1999) and evidential use for news reports. On the other hand, the referential DIST is manifested through "the echoing of a character's (or even an I-persona's) speech or thoughts, the intermingling of obliquely rendered interviewee's speech in journalistic discourse, and 'echoed' argumentation in academic discourse" (Vandelanotte 2004: 578). Furthermore, from the referential to scopal DIST, an increase in subjectification can be noticed.

Vandelanotte (2003, 2004a, 2004b) presents an interesting proposal within the framework of semiotic grammar. The explanatory potential of this categorisation, however, has not been corroborated by a comprehensive analysis of naturally occurring speech, instead a range of invented and literary examples have been used. Furthermore, the author does not differentiate between speech and thought presentation. Therefore, novel as it is, the model proposed by Vandelanotte (2003; 2004a; 2004b) is not empirically reliable enough to be applied in the present work.

2.4.1.3 Narrator/reporter control

A first elaborate categorisation of reported speech was proposed by Leech and Short (1981), whose criterion is the degree of narrator or reporter control. The authors approach reported speech as a continuum of categories ranging from those controlled by the narrator or reporter: *narrative report of speech acts* (NRSA), *indirect speech* (IS), to *free indirect speech* (FIS) where this control diminishes to *direct speech* (DS) and *free indirect speech* (FIS) which are largely independent of authorial/narratorial discourse:

NRSA   IS   FIS   DS   FDS

Figure 2: Reported speech categories; based on Short – Semino – Culpeper (1996: 115)

A very similar inventory of categories can be proposed for thought representation: narrative report of thought acts (NRTA), indirect thought (IT), free indirect thought (FIT), direct thought (DT), free direct thought (FDT).

This categorisation has been verified against empirical data in a range of contributions[56]. Short – Semino – Culpeper (1996) apply Leech and Short's

---

[56] Cf. Short – Semino – Culpeper (1996: 111) for further references to studies applying this categorisation to both literary and non-literary material. Cf. also references in this discussion and Van der Wurff (2002: 123) for further references.

(1981) model to a corpus of contemporary prose fiction and newspaper reports. From the point of view of the present work, Short – Semino – Culpeper (1996) provide a highly instructive study since, as far as categorisation is concerned – they aim at investigating the differences between literary and non-literary texts. Moreover, recognising pragmatic and contextual factors, the authors approach *speech and thought presentation* (as they refer to reported speech) from a textual/discoursal perspective. The former aspect is particularly crucial for the non-literary institutional data to be analysed here and so is the latter – a perspective in accord with the general view taken in the present study.

The findings of Short – Semino – Culpeper's (1996) paper concerning the differences between literary and non-literary texts are as follows: despite the fact that "[t]he myriad ways in which speech and thought can be represented in texts cuts across the literary/non-literary divide" (1996: 114), the corpus under investigation requires an additional category for prose fiction, while such a need does not occur in newspaper material. This category is *internal narration* comprising reports of cognitive activities and emotional states of characters (Short – Semino – Culpeper 1996: 124-126). The other major refinement proposed to Leech and Short's (1981) *speech and thought presentation* model when faced with authentic data is an additional category *narrator's report of voice*, the minimal report where an occurrence of a speech event is mentioned without any further detail (Short – Semino – Culpeper 1996: 124). The second new category is applicable both to the prose fiction and newspaper material under consideration.

Wynne – Short – Semino's (1998) study is an extension of the same project. First of all, the material under research is enriched with biographical and autobiographical texts; secondly, the categorisation proposed involves further elaboration of Leech and Short's (1981) model; and thirdly, instead of *speech and thought presentation*, the authors talk about *speech, thought and writing presentation*, thus viewing writing as a separate mode. In terms of categorisation, Wynne – Short – Semino (1998) provide instances of *Narration of Internal States* (corresponding to Short – Semino – Culpeper 1996 *internal narration*) also in newspaper reports (Wynne – Short – Semino 1998: 242). Therefore, modes of reporting in literary and non-literary texts are shown to yield an identical inventory of categories. Furthermore, the study provides an even more intricate elaboration of Leech and Short's (1981) *narrative report of speech act*, the *narrator's*[57] *representation of speech act with topic* (Wynne – Short – Semino 1998: 244) within which two further subcategories are discerned: quotation and hypothetical speech. The new categorisation is, however, not tested against the data and no statistical results are presented in the paper.

---

[57] Note the difference with the Leech and Short model: *narrative* reports (of speech *acts* or thought *acts*) (1981: 323) are substituted for with *narrator's* reports (of speech *act* or thought *act*) in the elaborations of the model by the Lancaster scholars.

The categorisation provided by Wynne – Short – Semino (1998) is tested in another study, a continuation of the earlier projects, Short – Semino – Wynne (2002). Here, the extended medium differentiation is adopted so that six separate categories are used for *speech, thought and writing presentation*, on the basis of the Lancaster written corpus. Since the aim of the reviewed study is a thorough discussion of faithfulness in reported speech, the authors concentrate on the statistics of direct rather than indirect modes of *speech, thought and writing presentation*. The categorisation model under discussion is extended even further in McIntyre et al. (2004), a review of a new corpus project, the *Lancaster Speech, Writing and Thought Presentation Spoken Corpus*. Not only do the authors provide a new naming convention for the spoken data under investigation, but they also multiply types within the proposed categories (2004: 63-67):

Discourse Presentation Categories

Written Corpus		Spoken Corpus	
Category	Definition	Category	Definition
NV	Narrator's Representation of Voice	RV	Representation of Voice
NI	Narrator's Representation of Internal States	RI	Representation of Internal State
NW	Narrator's Representation of Writing	RN	Representation of Writing
NRSA	Narrator's Representation of Speech Act	RSA	Representation of Speech Act
NRTA	Narrator's Representation of Thought Act	RTA	Representation of Thought Act
NRWA	Narrator's Representation of Writing Act	RWA	Representation of Writing Act
NRSAp	Narrator's Representation of Speech Act with Topic	RSAp	Representation of Speech Act with Topic
NRTAp	Narrator's Representation of Thought Act with Topic	RTAp	Representation of Thought Act with Topic
NRWAp	Narrator's Representation of Writing Act with Topic	RWAp	Representation of Writing Act with Topic
IS	Indirect Speech	IS	Indirect Speech
IT	Indirect Thought	IT	Indirect Thought
IW	Indirect Writing	IW	Indirect Writing
FIS	Free Indirect Speech	FIS	Free Indirect Speech
FIT	Free Indirect Thought	FIT	Free Indirect Thought
FIW	Free Indirect Writing	FIW	Free Indirect Writing
DS	Direct Speech	DS	Direct Speech
DT	Direct Thought	DT	Direct Thought
DW	Direct Writing	DW	Direct Writing
FDS	Free Direct Speech	FDS	Free Direct Speech
FDT	Free Direct Thought	FDT	Free Direct Thought
FDW	Free Direct Writing	FDW	Free Direct Writing

Table 7: Categories in the SW&TP Written corpus and their equivalents in the Spoken Corpus (after McIntyre et al. 2004: 57)

The abundance of categories in the extension of the model initially comprising ten modes (Leech and Short 1981) does not yet exhaust the meticulousness of the authors' proposal. Thus McIntyre et al. (2004) further introduce a set of categories for what is left outside discourse presentation, adding nine new types:

Written Corpus		Spoken Corpus	
Category	Definition	Category	Definition
N	Narration	A	Anything other than SW&TP (narrative and non-narrative)
		RU	Report of Language Use
NRS	Narrator's Report of Speech	RS	Report of Speech
NRT	Narrator's Report of Thought	RT	Report of Thought
NRW	Narrator's Report of Writing	RW	Report of Writing

Table 8: Categories outside the discourse presentation clines (after McIntyre et al. 2004: 57)

To sum up, the categorisation evolving out of a clear and concise model based on the criterion of narrator/reporter control (Leech and Short 1981) proposed by McIntyre et al. (2004) comprises the total of 51 categories. Thorough as it is, such an elaborate categorisation model does not contribute too much explanatory potential to the field of reported speech studies. As has been mentioned above (section 2.3.2.5), the threefold medium distinction applied to naturally occurring speech does not lead to illuminating conclusions, while unnecessarily hindering descriptive clarity. Furthermore, though possibly justified by the aims of corpus compilers who are responsible for detailed tagging, the classification of discourse outside reported speech reaches beyond the scope of studies into the phenomenon. Finally, even the authors themselves do not apply the model in its most sophisticated shape and decide to abide by the six categories for each medium in their presentation of statistical results (McIntyre et al. 2004: 67-68).

In its fully expanded form, the Leech and Short model (1981) is applied by Semino and Short (2004) in a work which sums up the efforts to provide a comprehensive analysis of speech, thought and writing presentation in a corpus (cf. Semino and Short 2004: 49). As in the case of McIntyre et al. (2004), it is not easy to resist the impression that many categories are superfluous, despite detailed descriptions of their functioning, exemplifications and justifications for their application.

This overview of the evolution[58] of Leech and Short's *speech and thought presentation* model (1981) over the last decade intended to provide some directions of development, particularly within the corpus studies of reported speech. The latest refinements of the original model cannot, however, be seen as

---

[58] Compare also Marnette (2001) for a combined framework of speech and thought presentation in which Leech and Short's (1981) model serves to explain and enrich the French models, i.e., by Oswald Ducrot and Dominique Maingueneau and vice versa (Marnette 2001: 251-8).

significant for the present study. First of all, the task of carrying out such detailed a categorisation is beyond the abilities of a single researcher. Secondly, the pragmatic angle of this study is not likely to benefit from a detailed quantitative approach, as the pragmatic strategies are not likely to differ between single instances but rather presumed to emerge in patterns encompassing more general categories. A much more transparent five-category model for *speech and thought presentation* is, for instance, applied by Collins (2001) in a comprehensive historical pragmatic study of reported speech in Old Russian. The categorisation adopted facilitates accounting for the patterns emerging from specific contextualisations and, moreover, it is treated as a flexible model to which some additional categories may be added when need arises. Similarly, Van der Wurff (2002) relies on six categories for reported speech (following Short – Semino – Culpeper (1996) minor refinement of the original model) in the presentation of various modes of reporting in Bengali newspapers. Another application of the model in question, which is particularly relevant for the present work, is found in Culpeper and Kytö (1999b). The material under investigation in this study are historical court records and witness depositions. Moreover, the authors point out that the Leech and Short (1981) model has the advantage having empirical backing (Culpeper and Kytö 1999b: 179). Thus, the original model or the one enriched with one additional category proves sufficient not only in the cross-linguistic but also historical and pragmatic perspectives.

2.4.2 Implications of categorisation proposals for the present study

Among the categorisations selected for the presentation above, the Leech and Short model (1981) emerges as the most reasonable choice for the purposes of this study. First of all, the model has already had numerous applications, both to the literary material for which it was initially designed as well as to other kinds of data. In all cases, the categorisation paved the way toward illuminating conclusions and its application has been particularly fruitful in discourse-based research. Furthermore, the Leech and Short model (1981) is able to account for the empirically and structurally observable difference between speech and thought presentation. Finally, the model proposes a concise set of categories that may be matched with clear pragmatic implications.

2.5 Implications from historical dialogue analysis

The sub-field of historical pragmatics, which is most informative as far as the present study is concerned, is historical dialogue analysis. All speech reports "are embedded structural units" (Roeck 1994: 332), while in the case of the data under discussion, lengthy stretches of dialogue are found to contain reported speech instances on a range of different levels of embedding. Dialogues as structural units are in general much more easily identifiable than instances of reported speech and, furthermore, any dialogue could be seen as direct speech in the first level of embedding in discourse. Despite the claim that "using the form of dialogue and reporting the speech of another speaker are two very different things" (Coulmas 1986a: 141), there has been a long tradition of viewing reported speech as constructed dialogue (Tannen 1986; 1989). Thus if instances of reported speech are embedded within a dialogue, it is assumed here that a higher organisational unit in discourse has to be accounted for next to the analysis of individual examples. Analyses on the level of dialogue are informed by a range of theoretical perspectives (e.g., Fritz and Hundsnurscher 1994, Jucker – Fritz – Lebsanft 1999). Some of the viewpoints applied are presumably going to lead to an illumination of some interactional aspects, thus working as explanatory devices in the search for the context of reported speech. Special attention is given to the levels of embedding as they typically occur within courtroom discourse. To illustrate the complexity of this institutional interaction, a model[59] by Culpeper and Kytö is presented:

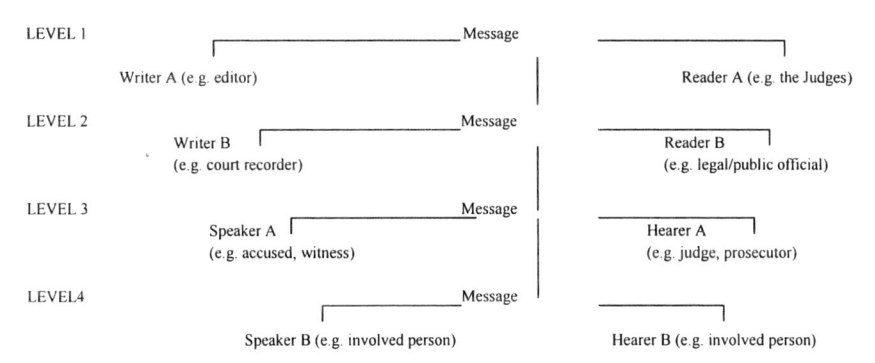

LEVEL 1	Writer A (e.g. editor)	Message	Reader A (e.g. the Judges)
LEVEL 2	Writer B (e.g. court recorder)	Message	Reader B (e.g. legal/public official)
LEVEL 3	Speaker A (e.g. accused, witness)	Message	Hearer A (e.g. judge, prosecutor)
LEVEL 4	Speaker B (e.g. involved person)	Message	Hearer B (e.g. involved person)

Figure 3: **Embedded discourse levels in the Lancaster Witches (after Culpeper and Kytö 1999b: 175)**

The courtroom interaction levels discerned by the authors are adopted as guiding lines in the present study. Naturally, modifications and adaptations required by the data are not avoided.

2.6 Dominant theoretical approaches in the studies of reported speech

Research into reported speech applies a wider range of theoretical concepts and relies on crucial philosophical underpinnings. It has to be observed that the majority of studies referred to in the present discussion share a great range of theoretical and philosophical foundations despite the versatility of the area. Thus,

---

[59] A similar, though less transparent model is advocated by Koch (1999: 411).

with no exaggeration one could state that research into reported speech is permeated with the ideas concerning language introduced by Mikhail Bakhtin[60] and Valentin Volosinov. Another source recurrent in a range of studies, with a definitely more pervasive influence on the anthropology-oriented than on purely linguistic research, is Erving Goffman[61].

2.6.1 The Bakhtinian legacy

As some researchers point out (Maynard 1996: 209, Thompson 1996: 505, Bredel 2003: 147), the fundamental assumption of the Bakhtinian view of language entails a rejection of the Saussurian abstract system as its origin. Thus, language functions in the social sphere of linguistic activity and cannot be seen as a homogenous construct, as it comprises a range of varieties specific to different social groups. This *internal stratification* of language is known as *heteroglossia*[62], the natural state of language (cf. Wortham and Lorcher 1999: 112), essentially accommodating all kinds of social *voices*. At the same time, Bakhtin's approach stems from the critique of monologic approaches which focus on the meaning inferred without recourse to the external context and, in particular, speakers' relations with others or, to be more precise, their dialogues with other *voices*. It is the dialogic relationship of the social *voices* from which the language truly originates. Bakhtin's understanding of *dialogicity*[63] does not only reflect the ubiquity of dialogue in everyday interaction but it first of all emphasises the fact that speech is invariably permeated with more and less overtly attributed or attributable words of others. Thus, in every single piece of talk there are numerous voices (*polyphony*[64], *multivoicedness*[65], *polyvocality*[66]), cultural, social and

---

[60] According to Pateman (1989) "Morris's 1946 work in behaviourist semiotics, *Signs, Language and Behavior* contains what to my knowledge is the first English-language reference to the Russian original of Volosinov's *Marxism and the Philosophy of Language*. I imagine that it could have been Roman Jakobson who supplied Morris with the reference."

[61] Goffman could actually be seen as a leading figure in anthropological linguistics in general, not only in the anthropological studies of reported speech (cf. Duranti and Goodwin 1992, Lucy 1993).

[62] This idea is referred to in: Aczel (1998), Besnier (1993: 162), Collins (2001: 1), Günthner (1999: 686), Maybin (1999: 459), Parmentier (1993: 261), Thompson (1996: 505), Waugh (1995: 168f), Wortham and Locher (1999: 112).

[63] On *dialogicity* and the notion of *dialogic* cf. Aczel (1998), Baynham and Slembrouck (1999: 450), Caton (1993: 332), Maynard (1996: 209), Vandelanotte (2004: 554), Wortham and Locher (1999: 110). Some remark on the affinity of the Bakhtinian notion of dialogue and that of Martin Buber (Friedman 2004).

[64] On polyphony, cf. Golato (2000: 47), Günthner (1999: 685), Marnette (2001: 245); on *polyphony* and *multivoicedness*, cf. Aczel (1998), Besnier (1993: 177), Golato (2002: 59), Hickmann (1993: 66), Maynard (1996: 209), Vandelanotte (2004: 571), Waugh (1995: 151). Compare also Bredel (2003) who provides an analysis of polyphony in everyday speech and introduces a differentiation of the concept into 'intrapolyphonic constructions' as self-

linguistic repetitions present, forming a never-ending, insoluble mixture of influences. The attention given by Bakhtin and Volosinov to the phenomenon of reported speech (in particular Volosinov 1929 [1973]) stems from the fact that this, rather than any other linguistic entity, is the prototypical site for the orchestra of multiple voices in language and that, as Maynard (1996) aptly put it, quotation "offers unique instances where the many 'voices' of discourse converge" (1996: 210). The frequent references in reported speech studies to these concepts are easily explainable in this light despite the fact that initially the theory has been much closer to stylistics and literary studies than to linguistic analysis. From the perspective of reported speech studies, *heteroglossia* is a particularly vital concept, as it implies the need to attend to the context of any utterance, since no utterance can be interpreted solely on the basis of its form and content. Indeed, one cannot deny the growing and deepening interest of researchers for the context[67] of reported speech, which accompanied the relatively recent shift in the area from what Baynham and Slembrouck (1999: 444) refer to as "narrative bias" to the study of language in interaction.

2.6.1.1 From voicing and speech interference to the hearer

The concept of *voicing*[68] in reported speech or, in other words, the social positioning of the reporting speaker or the evaluation and speech plans as parts of any quotation, corresponds to what Hill and Irvine (1993) refer to as *leakage* of the speaker's stance on the report or ways of expressing subjectivity toward it (Koven 2004: 480). This phenomenon corresponds to Volosinov's *speech interference*[69] (1929 [1973]: 137) where in literary discourse the

---

quotations of a range of selves (a way of dealing with inner conflicts or internalising social conflicts), 'interpolyphonic constructions' as other quotation (a way of dealing with external conflicts or externalising social conflicts), and 'hybrid constructions' involving the blending of utterances or speakers (2003: 165). The first two kinds of polyphony may be gender-related, as the author hypothesises.

[65] Cf. Golato (2000: 47) and Golato (2002: 59) on this concept.
[66] Cf. Baynham (1996: 68).
[67] Despite the fact that the importance of context in reported speech studies stems from the Bakhtinian thought, one cannot deny the fact that in his own work (published as Volosinov 1929 [1973]), Bakhtin "departs markedly from the context-sensitive methods that he uses elsewhere in his work" (Collins 2001: xv). In the face of Collins' critique of Bakhtin in this respect, the notion of context remains a highly theoretical and empirically misinterpreted concept in his work. Thus, the fact that Bakhtin is the source of the emphasis placed on the notion of context, and that it holds true not only in the area of reported speech studies, is indeed paradoxical.
[68] Cf. also Silverstein (1993: 35, 50) and Koven (2001: 515) on the concept of *voicing*.
[69] Cf. Bolden (2004:1072f) and Günthner (1999: 705) on this idea.

author's/narrator's point of view infiltrates[70] every word, particularly the speech of characters. *Speech interference*, in turn creates nothing else but *double-voiced*[71] discourse (Bakhtin 1981) in which the reporting and original speaker are in a "dynamic dialogue" (Koven 2004: 516). A fitting development of Volosinov's "dynamic interrelationship" of the two (1929 [1973]: 119), the space for this dialogue is what Matoesian (2000) refers to as an "intertextual gap" (2000: 883, 911) between the reporting and reported events. This gap[72], according to Matoesian (2000), may be maximised in indirect and minimised in direct speech as the former reduces, while the latter increases the closeness of the reported and reporting events. This relationship is, however, not the only one present in reported speech. After all, Volosinov (1929 [1973]: 85) himself emphasises the importance of the addressee who essentially enters into an interaction with the reporting speaker (e.g., Marnette 2001: 259, Vandelanotte 2004: 554). This emphasis on the hearer as a legitimate participant in linguistic interaction could, among other influences[73], be traced back to Bakhtinian thinking.

2.6.2 Goffman's legacy

Erving Goffman, "the quintessential sociologist of everyday social life" (Lemert and Branaman 1997: xlv), not unlike Bakhtin, left an indelible mark on the studies of reported speech by introducing a range of concepts which came to function as autonomous entities. Definitely, because they speak the language of Goffman

---

[70] Another way through which the relationship between the reporting and reported speech may be realised is when "the intentions of the representing discourse are at odds with the intentions of the represented discourse ... to destroy the represented language" (Bakhtin 1981: 364). This is *parodic stylisation*. This concept is referred to in Günthner (1999: 693) who rather simplistically sees it as a prosodic manifestation of speakers' evaluation. A similarly inclusive interpretation of the concept can be found in Besnier (1993: 175) who sees it as a means to manipulate the perception the audience have of the reported speaker or one way in which affect is communicated in the Nukulaelae culture by means of prosody. Prosody and accent are also shown to serve the purpose of *parodic stylisation* in a conflict between the Spanish and Galician languages and as a way the underlying linguistic ideology of resistance in Galicia may be realised (Álvarez-Cáccamo 1996: 38).

[71] On *double-voiced* discourse, cf. Aczel (1998), Baynham (1999: 486, 494, 501-2), Baynham and Slembrouck (1999: 448, 451), Buttny (1998: 48-9), Caton (1993: 332), Koven (2004: 480), Wortham and Lorcher (1999). Cf. also *double-voicing* in: Hill and Irvine (1993: 6, 14), Koven (2004: 484), Wortham and Locher (1999: 110). In the context of Bakhtin's discussion, Shuman (1993: 152) links "double-directed discourse" to the issue of responsibility.

[72] Shuman (1993: 152) sees this gap as the site for manipulating the distance between two voices in terms of solidarity and conflict.

[73] Cf. e.g., the French influences as pointed out by Marnette (2001: 259) as well as the remarks on the *participant* in the other part of this discussion.

(footing, alignment, framework, participation and *production frame(work)*[74], *participant roles, animation, response cry, replaying, detachment, distancing, creative performance, key, laminator verb* and many other concepts), reported speech studies are a source of references and citations[75].

The popularity of the theory of *footing* in the area of reported speech studies is easily accounted for with recourse to the Bakhtinian definition discussed elsewhere in this work. Assuming the "embedding function of much talk", Goffman claims: "when we shift from saying something ourselves to reporting what someone else said, we are changing our footing" (Goffman 1981: 151). The change of *footing* results in the *polyphony* of the quote (Golato 2000: 47) or, as Koven (2001: 515) claims, it is typical in reported speech that the speaker's *footing* or *voicing* finds an instantiation. Indeed, in Goffman's definition (1981: 128) of *footing*, code-switching or prosodic changes are involved to mark the changes in the alignment of participants. The attention Goffman devotes to prosody in his definition of *footing* is crucial as he proposes a 'phonemic clause', a prosodic cognitive and not a syntactic segment as a relevant unit. Thus, in a prosody-oriented analysis of reported speech, like the one provided in Couper-Kuhlen (1998), the literal application of the concept of *footing* is justified. It is, moreover, important to observe that it is in the prosody-oriented studies where *footing* can be applied as a relatively well-defined concept, while its other aspects (Goffman provides five aspects in his definition, 1981: 128) remain undefined in terms of their linguistic or other correlates. Also within reported speech studies outside the prosody-oriented ones, the concept of *footing* has so far not been clearly defined as is pointed out in Sleurs – Jacobs – Waes (2003: 197) or Jacobs (2003: 96). The fact that *footing* remains largely undefined focuses attention on the lack of a clear definition in the work of Goffman itself (Ensink and Sauer

---

[74] The concept of frame and framing in discourse has received wide interest among researchers in a variety of linguistic and non-linguistic fields, of whom Goffman is just one. For an overview and references cf. Ensink and Sauer (2003: 3-4) and other contributions in this volume.

[75] References to and citations of Goffman's work can be found in the following: Álvarez-Cáccamo (1996: 40f), Bauman (1992: 126-7), Besnier (1993: 161, 164, 180f), Briggs (1993: 179), Coleman (2004: 392), Collins (2001: 5, 22, 42, 62, 70, 71, 79, 114, 168, 203, 211, 227, 305f, 308f, 311f, 318f), Couper-Kuhlen (1998:1), Golato (2000: 47; 2002: 49, 59, 60, 66, 67), Goodwin (2003: 347f), Günthner (1999: 694), Hanks (1993: 134, 154, 155 f), Hansen (2000: 284), Hill and Irvine (1993: 8, 11-17), Holt (1996: 221; 1999: 505; 2000: 443, 444, 448), Johnstone (1987: 33, 38, 47-8, 51f), Klewitz-Couper-Kuhlen (1999: 6f, 14f), Koven (2001: 514, 515; 2004: 480), Levey (2003: 312, 317), Lucy (1993x: 15), Matoesian (2000: 880, 881-4), Maybin (1999: 362), Moore (1993: 215, 226), Myers (1999a: 378; 1999b: 573, 597), Overstreet and Yule (2002: 286), Philips (1986: 154), Schiffrin (1987: 16, 17, 22-24), Schiffrin (2002: 317, 321, 322), Silverstein (1993: 35), Sleurs – Jacobs – Waes (2003: 197), Tannen (1986: 319), Vincent and Perrin (1999: 297), Winter (2002: 17), Wortham and Lorcher (1999: 110).

2003: 8). Ubiquitous as it is, then, *footing* does not provide a powerful explanatory tool in most of the analyses of reported speech though it definitely remains a useful point of reference.

Studies in which Goffman's concepts under consideration are subject to some constructive interpretation and development are rare. Naturally, in order to attach some explanatory force to *footing*, it is necessary to identify the linguistic, or at least linguistically definable, correlates of the phenomenon. Thus, for instance Hansen (2000), an exceptional approach to code-switching as a manifestation of *footing*, is able to support a syntactic assumption with elements of Goffmanian theory (cf. section 2.3.2.2.3.2). The difference in semiotic status between direct and indirect speech can be outlined by means of Goffman's decomposition of the speaker (1981: 144-146) into easily analysable elements. In his view the term 'speaker' should be treated with caution, as the person who is usually referred to is just an *animator* of the words of others, the "sounding box in use" (Goffman 1981: 144). Except for the person physically uttering speech, there can also be other selves or voices involved, an *author*, i.e., the person whose words are produced as well as a *principal*, the person taking responsibility for the beliefs being expressed. The three *speaker roles* may be assigned to one person, but in much of discourse it is not the case, and it is here that Goffman is coming closest to the Bakhtinian idea of a word being always half somebody else's, stating: "it is not true to say that we always speak our own words" (Goffman 1981: 146).

A relatively early application of *speaker roles* to reported speech, specifically to a definition of constructed dialogue (cf. Tannen 1986; 1989) in everyday storytelling, can be found in Johnstone (1987). The creative and intentional aspect of reported speech in telling stories are explicable also with recourse to the fact that in everyday situations reporters act not only as *animators* but also as *principals* of the words uttered. Authority figures, on the other hand, as Johnstone (1987: 48) claims, are merely *animators* of messages, as they speak not for themselves as individuals but as representatives of institutional voices.

For Hanks (1993), Goffman's split is the basis for a categorisation of reported speech he proposes for Yucatec Maya with *direct*, *mentioned* and *quoted* discourse. In the first of the three categories an *animator* is also *author* and *principal*; in the second, an *animator* may or may not be the *author* but they are definitely not *principal*; in the last category: "a speaker animates the utterance of another animator, who may or may not be author or principal" (Hanks 1993: 134). The distinction between categories is specifically related to the individual deictic structures available in the language and discussed and exemplified in the further discussion in Hanks (1993).

Matoesian (2000) points to a problem inherent in contextualised social applications of *speaker roles*: Goffman himself never specifies "how these may be related to forms of discursive power" (2000: 880). The *footing* of *animator* exclusively as a typical role of reporter in direct speech involves an impression of objectivity, which is also achieved by the structural separation of the reporting and reported voice. This observation Matoesian (2000) adopts from Goffman and applies it to the Bakhtinian strategic applications of reported speech. Thus, both thinkers provide a background against which Matoesian (2000) presents the case of an ultimate evaluation involved in the "hyper-form of direct speech" (Matoesian 2000: 881) as the author refers to the use of audiotaped depositions in court. Both Goffmanian and Bakhtinian thinking provide powerful explanatory tools when it comes to linguistic ideologies.

A similar conclusion can be drawn from an analysis of politicians' lies presented by Wortham and Lorcher (1999). Embedded metapragmatic constructions, a special case of reported speech, are defined in terms of Goffman's *speaker roles*, i.e., assuming that in sentences like *Bush claimed that Clinton lied*, the reporters are able to stick to the *animator* and refrain from becoming *principal* of the accusation. In the opinion of the authors, it is clearly a responsibility-shedding[76] device applied by the reporter to defend their own objectivity (Wortham and Lorcher 1999: 120). Thus, involving three speakers usually, the reporter, speaker 1 and speaker 2, embedded metapragmatic constructions have the first embedded speaker as committed to the allegation, i.e., the *principal* of the accusation.

2.7 In conclusion: the inadequacy of a definition

Having discussed a range of linguistic aspects of reported speech as well as a range of complementary notions relevant to the understanding of the phenomenon, attention was also devoted to the theoretical underpinnings of its more general features and ways in which it functions in Western thinking. Far from brief and possibly too thoroughgoing at points, the above study was not superfluous given its initial purpose which was to conclude with a comprehensive definition of the phenomenon in question. To serve the aims of the empirical analysis, reported speech is seen here as a linguistically vague construct by means of which language exercises its internal dialogicity (Bakhtin/Volosinov) in that – through the intertextual capacity of each instance of reported speech – it invariably encompasses more than one perspective. When used in discourse, reported speech embodies multiple speaker roles and identities, not infrequently conflating more than one of those within a single utterance (Goffman). In terms of discourse functions, reported speech is not only subjectively employed by

---

[76] On the question of responsibility in relation to Goffman compare Collins (2001: 71), Golato (2002: 66) and Hill and Irvine (1993).

speakers but it ultimately performs intersubjective functions. In institutional discourse, reported speech has to be seen as a major linguistic means for the exercising or assignment of authority. Viewed from the perspective of linguistic systems, reported speech overlaps in its further functions with the highly intricate and diverse – in terms of linguistic realisations – domains of evidentiality and modality. This overlap might complicate the pragmatic implications of different categories of the phenomenon. Finally, the clarity of linguistic analysis of reported speech in terms of its categories is even further blurred by the Proteus principle advocated by Sternberg (1982) with respect to the linguistic form and function of reported speech. Thus, "the many-to-many relationship between linguistic form and contextual function", as Sternberg phrases it (1982: 152), does not sound optimistic as to the explanatory potential of any categorisation and constitutes a researcher's predicament calling for a degree of caution in the categorisation procedure as well as with respect to the generalisations made on its basis.

Unfortunately, the formulation of a succinct and conclusive definition of reported speech was not a conceivable task, as has appeared above. Still, it is maintained that as faulty as it may be, the descriptive statements provided in conclusion sum up the considerations of this chapter, while at the same time pointing to the still hazy, though less and less obscure, direction of a successful pragmatic analysis of the phenomenon.

Chapter Three

A historical sketch and methodological preliminaries

3.1 Introduction: source texts

The interest of this study in legal material is not an unusual pursuit given the functional, pragmatic and contextual orientation of the thesis (cf. Levi 1990: 6). Although serious linguistic interest in legal language is not a recent phenomenon, the constantly widening scope of research in this direction definitely is (cf. e.g., Hiltunen 1990: 16, cf. Shuy 2001: 437-38). The assumption that court records offer the most appropriate historical evidence for the study of functional aspects of language (cf. 1.3.4) has determined some further selection criteria with respect to source texts applied in the early stages of research.

As regards the chronological criterion, the lack of extant material prior to the year 1550 is essentially the predicament of all studies of courtroom discourse (e.g., Culpeper and Kytö 1999b: 152). The explanation for this situation has to be sought in the complexity of the linguistic situation in the British Isles after the Norman Conquest, manifested principally in the legal domain. Throughout the Middle English period French was dominant particularly in the spoken[1], and Latin in the written legal language (Mellinkoff 1963: 99). On the other hand, the commonly accepted view (cf. Ormrod 2003: 752) that English does not feature in the legal domain, particularly from the late thirteenth century onwards, is a myth (e.g., Hiltunen 1990: 56). Thus, the reality of legal language, obscure as it is to the modern mind, must have included a mixture of three languages whose individual roles are difficult to specify. Furthermore, at least for French and English, various forms were in use, i.e., firstly, French as the language of the north of France and the southern Low Countries (Ormrod 2003: 753, called *Old French* by Mellinkoff 1963); secondly, Anglo-Norman, i.e., the language developed out of Norman French in the twelfth and thirteenth centuries in the British Isles; and thirdly, the legal variant of the latter know also as *law French* (cf. Mellinkoff 1963: 101 106 on a degree of confusion in the literature with respect to this term).

Ormrod (2003) claims that, in the second half of the fourteenth century, French was the language of oral proceedings, whereas Anglo-Norman was used for the written record. Therefore, it comes as no surprise that the renowned *Statute of Pleading*[2], commonly held to be the first and ground-breaking regulation of the

---

[1] As Nielsen states, in the written domain "French continued to play a significant role as a language of record to the middle of the fifteenth century" (2005: 17-18).
[2] Ormrod (2003) presents a comprehensive discussion of the political context of the document, undermining the conventional interpretations of its origin and implementation by the historians of language and law. Actually, the author offers three possible backgrounds of the

complex linguistic situation in the legal domain (e.g., Mellinkoff 1963: 111), enacted in 1362 by parliament to establish the place of English in oral proceedings, did not exert any influence on the written record. According to Ormrod (2003), there was actually conscious resistance on the side of the Crown as well as civic and church authorities to adopt "English as an authoritative language of record" (Ormrod 2003: 783), which was connected with the fact that the Wycliffite and Lollard activists employed English for their subversive writings. Actually, the *Statute of Pleading* itself explicitly specifies that the records and pleas are to be held in Latin, which is no different from the hitherto exercised procedure (Ormrod 2003: 757-758). Mellinkoff argues "Latin was tentatively outlawed in the seventeenth century and legislated into a subordinate position in the eighteenth" (1963: 82). In fact, the linguistic aspect continued to complicate court procedure until the year 1731, when Latin was finally ousted by an act of parliament, as well as after this date (Baker 2002: 86-87; cf. Nielsen 2005: 15-18). As for early administrative writings, the Pepperer's Guild of London was the first to submit its record in English to parliament in 1345 (Fisiak 2000: 75). However, as Radcliffe and Cross (1927 [1946]) explain, English law reports have their beginnings in the fourteenth and fifteenth centuries, so that towards the beginning of the sixteenth century in the yearbooks, normally written in Anglo-Norman[3], there appear more and more Anglicisms (1927 [1946]: 91-92). Parliament rolls, for instance, already in the fifteenth century, used a combination of Latin, French and English, while Henry V was the first English king to use English in written communication (Ormrod 2003: 777, 784). One should not disregard the role of the Chancery – the centre of mediaeval bureaucracy situated in Westminster – "in the process of raising the profile of English in the fifteenth century" (Hiltunen 1990: 57). Nevertheless, as Radcliffe and Cross (1927 [1946]) maintain, law French did not die out until the end of the seventeenth century. Thus, the appearance of English in court records comes relatively late in the history of the language. Tiersma (1999), for instance, claims that it was no sooner than the year 1704 that all courts held their law reports exclusively in English.

Nevertheless, as Archer notices (2003: 17), evidence for courtroom discourse has been preserved in numerous library archives all over the United Kingdom. Despite this fact, the present study chooses to analyse data from edited collections, firstly because of the technicalities, which complicate access and use of archival sources and secondly as a consequence of the methodological

---

document, too detailed to allow a transparent presentation here. Most importantly, the commonly accepted view of the *Statute of Pleading* as the triumph of English in the context of victories over the French in Hundred Year War, is just one of the possibilities.

[3] Tiersma (1999: 22) talks about yearbooks as reports of oral proceedings written in Anglo-French, beginning in the 1280s and continuing through 1535. His discussions of the linguistic situation in the law after the Norman Conquest (1999: 19-34) and of the resurgence of English in the seventeenth century (1999: 35-47) are highly comprehensive.

compromise justified at length in chapter one. This compromise does not, however, exempt the researcher from verifying the faithfulness of the editions against the manuscript sources or performing a large amount of technical preparatory work on the material, which is available exclusively in printed format. Utilising the printed sources, which demands scanning and painstaking text recognition procedures in order to be converted to a readable electronic format, is a result of the reluctance towards the exclusively quantitative approaches and the uncritical use of linguistic corpora. Despite clear advantages of corpus studies in general as well as for the area of reported speech specifically (e.g., Archer 2003: 22-28; Short 2003, Semino and Short 2004: 4), it should be borne in mind that statistical presentations are likely to commit the error of ignoring the contextual aspect. This is the reason why some authors (e.g., Fludernik 1993, Collins 2001) have decided to adopt more intuition-based and qualitative approaches in their studies of reported speech. The latter stance is the one to be taken in this study, although the presentation of reported speech in the courtroom discourse of the Early Modern English period will additionally be enhanced by some quantitative results.

3.1.1 The State Trials and ecclesiastical records

The edited sources of court records analysed here include the most comprehensive, multiple-volume collection of court cases in English, known as the *State Trials*, from which the two trials analysed in this study are drawn. Despite clear advantages and its vast temporal coverage (1388-1777), this source has been subject to criticism as regards its reliability (e.g., Archer 2003). On the other hand, samples drawn from it have been included in the *Helsinki Corpus* and used in sociolinguistic and pragmatic analyses of courtroom interaction (e.g., Kryk-Kastovsky 2000; 2002). The controversy around this source with respect to its suitability for historical linguistic and particularly pragmatic research stems from a range of genre-determined features, such as vividness of presentation and low formality, both running contrary to what is expected of institutional records. Indeed, the state trials in Hargrave's collection depart from the authentic courtroom procedure by at least one additional layer of the 'filter' involved in any presentation of speech in writing (cf. Schneider 2002) i.e., they constitute creatively processed and engrossing accounts of the events in the courtroom. This distance from the authentic speech event, however, may prove beneficial for a pragmatic study of reported speech. The advantage of state trials for this specific study is demonstrated through a comparison with more formal and authentic records free from an additional 'filter' layer. The institutional character of courtroom interaction and the implications of institutionally based reported speech analysis (chapter two) necessitated choosing for this purpose ecclesiastical records as a product of a different institutional setting. In terms of Schneider's relationship between speech event and written record (2002: 72-73), church records may be viewed as 'recorded' i.e., written down simultaneously to the speech event, while state trials as 'recalled' i.e., written down subsequent to the speech event from notes and memory. Therefore, the former are characterised by a greater degree of proximity to the authentic speech event but less space for interpretation and processing than the latter.

The two kinds of data, one from the fourth edition of the *State Trials* (Hargrave 1776-1781) and the other from the records of ecclesiastical courts in the diocese of Chester (Furnivall 1897), are evidence for what can without much exaggeration be referred to as two distinct legal systems. While the former carried out the trial procedure on the basis of the common law, the latter was based on the civilian procedure. This is reflected in the trial records as "the great difference between the trials using the civilian procedure characteristic of the ecclesiastical courts and trials in the English common law was that the former were written and the latter oral" (Helmholtz 2003: 104). Moreover, according to Mellinkoff (1963), "[t]he law of the Church, with a more ancient and intimate contact with the rudiments of literacy, had always placed greater emphasis on writing than did the courts of common law" (1963: 116). However, the separation between the two systems might, after all, not have been as clear-cut, because, as is claimed by Mullholand (2003): "the oral submissions of the parties in the courts of the Church ... were vitally important" (Mullholand 2003: 10). Nevertheless, it remains an undeniable fact that "[i]n the common law courts, written pleadings[4] made a small beginning in the fifteenth century but did not become common until the sixteenth" (Mellinkoff 1963: 116). According to Tiersma (1999: 36), the printing revolution and the introduction of the printing press to England in the 1470's was a factor enhancing the impact of writing, also in the legal domain (cf. Ross 1998). After the year 1600 all kinds of legal writings were printed in considerable quantities, making reports of cases among other legal text-types widely available.

The nature of the linguistic differences between the common law and church records is not unambiguous despite the "staggering orality" (Mullholand 2003: 10) of the former trial procedure. Although in the ecclesiastical courts the procedure was based on handing in written documents, speech or dialogue – mostly formal in nature – accompanied the trial (Helmholtz 2003: 105). The dialogue in church courts, however, as Helmholtz (2003) claims in the discussion

---

[4] In the late Middle Ages there has been a major change in the procedure of the English common law from oral to written pleading (e.g. Radcliffe and Cross 1927 [1946]: 91, Mellinkoff 1963: 116, Harding 1966 [1973]: 140). According to Harding (1973) with respect to the origin of this change, "[p]aper pleading was not ... an invention of the conciliar courts, nor an adoption by them of civilian methods, but something that developed naturally in all English courts in the later Middle Ages: merely a writing-down of the complexities which had grown up in oral pleadings" (Harding 1973: 109).

of the period from the mid-fifteenth century to the 1640s, was in Latin[5]. There was still one other point in the ecclesiastical procedure where orality might come into play, namely the preliminary witness examination. This was carried out outside the court by means of *interrogatories* – lists of questions prepared in advance so that witnesses' examination and deposition could follow the interrogatory "item by item" (Harding 1973: 142). According to Harding (1966 [1973]), who discusses the civilian procedure used in the conciliar courts (e.g., the courts of Chancery, Admiralty and Star Chamber), interrogatories were generally in English and, moreover, as the formal side of pleadings was less rigid, they provided better evidence both for the circumstances of the case and the language of witnesses than plea-rolls in the courts of common law (Harding 1966 [1973]: 108).

The procedural distinction between the common law and church courts sketched above allows introducing a dividing line between the two kinds of data in the linguistic analysis carried out in this study. Thus, the main assumption encouraged by the facts outlined above, is that the two sources offer data of different institutional character, which is essentially reflected in their linguistic make-up. Therefore, it is appropriate to carry out two separate analyses of state and ecclesiastical records in order to prepare ground for a comparison of reported speech usage in the two institutional settings.

3.2 The *State Trials* – description of the source[6]

Prior to the edition used in this study, the collection had already had a long editorial history. The first edition was published anonymously (although it has been attributed to Thomas Salmon) in 1719 in four volumes, with the fifth one following shortly. The second edition, with changes, appeared in folio with an additional sixth volume in 1730 and it is attributed to Solom Emlyn, though it has also been attributed wrongly to Francis Hargrave by the compilers of the *Helsinki Corpus* and other authors (e.g., Archer 2003). This edition was followed by two volumes in 1735 (7th and 8th) and was reprinted in 1766 with two supplementary volumes (9th and 10th). The third edition was published in a six volumes folio in 1742 but without the additional volumes that accompanied the previous one. The edition used in this study appeared in six volumes reprinted from the third edition, the next four volumes were reprinted from the supplements to the previous edition and one volume (eleventh) was added. This supplementary volume "is reserved

---

[5] Still, as Helmoltz himself observes, one can find records even in the fifteenth century containing informal remarks about the language, which was sometimes English and sometimes Latin (Helmholtz 2003: 107).

[6] The main source for this section is Lowndes (1984: 2710-11). Information provided by this source is encyclopaedic.

wholly for the additional matter ... to supply any omissions in the former part of the collection" (Hargrave 1775).

The collection comprises over 130 cases from the courts of England and Scotland, the majority concerning treason, though other crimes are also included. The proceedings of the trials took place in a range of different courts, such as e.g., Star Chamber, King's Bench and the Court of Chivalry. The prosecuted parties tended to come from higher social strata (i.e., gentry, cf. Nevalainen – Raumolin-Brunberg 2003: 36) and in many cases treason charges they faced were political manipulations. Each case is supplemented with some information on the participants and the fate of the accused. In the case of a death sentence, which indeed was passed more frequently than not, the so-called death speeches are attached with descriptions of the execution. There is great discrepancy with regard to the space devoted to individual cases, ranging from page- to book-length accounts. The collection constitutes a rich source of information on the history and politics in the British Isles, not to mention its value from the point of view of legal history.

As to the sources of trials and proceedings included in the collection, these are mentioned in most cases with detailed references. In the preface to the second edition one reads: "the following TRIALS being plain Narrations of Sayings and Facts, for the most part published by the authority of the respective Courts, or by indifferent Hands; where it happens to be otherwise, the Reader is inform'd of it in the Title and in the Head of the Trial" (Emlyn 1730: i-ii), which indeed sounds promising. Similarly, the preface to the first edition has it: "as to manuscripts, such care has been taken to avoid all mistakes" (*Preface to the first edition* 1719). Considering, however, the experience of historical corpora compilers as to the truth-value of solemn meta-statements confirming the veracity of many printed sources in this period (cf. Kytö and Walker 2003), these remarks have to be taken with a degree of caution. Very telling indeed is one of the final comments in the preface to the second edition: "several Notes are added to explain and illustrate the Text" (Emlyn 1730: xv-xvi).

3.2.1 Trial of Sir Nicholas Throckmorton

Hargrave's edition gives "Holinshed's" *Chronicles*[7] as the ultimate source of the trial (Hargrave 1776: 64). Patterson (1998) provides detailed information as to this fact. According to her, initially the trial "appears as a large insertion" (Patterson 1998: 8) in the first edition of *Chronicles* in 1577, accompanying the account of Wyatt's rebellion. The way it is inserted indicates that it is a reprint of something else; as Patterson continues: "Its presentation in the *Chronicles* typographically

---

[7] Patterson provides the following details for this publication: Raphael Holinshed, *The Chronicles of England, Scotland and Ireland*, 3 vols., London 1587 (Patterson 1998: 9).

mimics the title page of a pamphlet; and in other instances where the Chronicle's typography does the same thing, the original pamphlet has survived" (1998: 9). The uniqueness of this trial in the *Chronicles* is indubitable as "the only instance in the *Chronicles* of a major political trial in which both prosecution and defence are fully represented, so fully indeed, that we are given what appears to be a verbatim transcript of the entire proceedings" (Patterson 1998: 9).

Indeed, the inspection of the Throckmorton trial in Holinshed's *Chronicles* (vol. II: 1737-1754) leaves no doubt as to the source of Hargrave's account. Hargrave follows the *Chronicles* exactly, except for the differences in spelling and, less regularly, punctuation. As regards the graphic design of the text, Holinshed version has two columns on one page, with the speakers in dialogue marked on both sides of the margin. In the margins, there are some infrequent remarks, referring to what was happening at a certain moment. The list of jury members must have been provided by Hargrave, as it is missing from Holinshed.

Having pointed out the source of Hargrave's account, Patterson fails to compare it with the manuscript sources of the Throckmorton trial, although she is aware of their existence (Patterson 1998: 97). One of the surviving MSS[8] copies of the trial, preserved as Stowe 280 in the British Library allows drawing important conclusions as to the adequacy of Hargrave's account for historical linguistic research. Namely, the examination of Throckmorton trial in the MSS (Stowe 280 ff.75), Holinshed and Hargrave demonstrates that all the differences (spelling and punctuation aside) between Hargrave's account and the MSS result from the modifications (insertions, omissions, word order changes) made by Holinshed. This observation validates the statement that, despite the date of publication at the end of the 18th century, Hargrave's account preserves the linguistic features of English preceding the date of the edition of Holinshed *Chronicles*, i.e., 1577, thus providing evidence of the 16th century English.

Exploring further the origin of the Throckmorton trial, Patterson dwells on Bellamy (1989). At this point, her observations are worth quoting at length:

"Bellamy ... assumed that the account of the trial was probably compiled by Throckmorton himself after Mary's death, though "based on notes taken at the time"...its air of completeness demands one of three possibilities: very extensive notes made by another interested party or parties, since Throckmorton could scarcely have been scribbling while he spoke; subsequent fabrication by someone with a great ear for dialogue and a lively political imagination – a political playwright, as it were; or some combination of the two. Any of these could have been followed by pamphlet publication; though the non-survival of an original suggests that it was published surreptitiously during Mary's reign ... Included in this edition is a reprint of what looks like a preface to the trial, produced by the protestant martyr John Bradford while himself in prison in the summer of 1555. Given the strength of his

---

[8] One more publicly available MSS version, which I have not consulted, is Bodleian Library, Oxford. Ms. Rawlinson C.408.

advertisement for its usefulness, his friends might have been persuaded to risk an illicit publication" (Patterson 1998: 10).

The mystery as to the details of the composition of the trial have to remain unsolved, which, however, does not affect the course of the linguistic analysis.

3.2.1.1 Throckmorton, the defendant

The trial took place on the 17th April 1554, in the Guildhall of London, for high treason. Nicholas Throckmorton (1515-1570), cousin of Catherine Parr[9], member of the Privy Chamber, the undertreasurer of the Tower at the time of the trial, (later ambassador to France 1563-4, to Scotland 1565, 1567) faced high-treason charges in connection with Wyatt's rebellion, a protestant uprising against the Spanish marriage of the Queen, Mary Tudor. Throckmorton's trial followed a horrifying revenge taken by the Queen on the collaborators in the plot. It was not only the number of people killed (over a 100 executed, mostly randomly chosen, Loades 1999: 195), but also the atrocious punishments that are bound to shock a modern mind: the convicted were sentenced to be hanged, drawn and quartered, and on the day of Wyatt's surrender (6th Feb 1554), around a hundred bodies were swinging at the gates of the City and at St. Paul's Churchyard. In this event, Throckmorton was in an extremely frail position, the gravity of charges no less than those faced by the late Wyatt:

> "Thou art before this time indited of High-Treafon, &c. that thou then and there didſt falſly and traiteroufly, &c. confpire and imagine the Death of the Queenes Majeſtie, &c. and falſly and traiteroufly didſt leuie Warr againſte the Queen within hir Realm, &c. and alſo thou waſt adherente to the Queenes Enimies within hir Realm, giuing to them Ayde and Comfort … " (Hargrave 1776-81: 63).

Even though Throckmorton's involvement in the rebellion was not direct, for he was neither involved in military actions, nor did he speak out openly in Parliament against the Spanish marriage, he definitely conspired with Wyatt to undermine the Queen's decision. Therefore, Throckmorton's acquittal is indeed worth examining in greater detail. Even more so bearing in mind that Hargrave's is the most comprehensive printed collection of Early Modern English treason trials and it contains 27 cases before the year 1600, out of which only two were concluded with acquitting sentences, extremely rare in state trials (Green 1985: 147, cf. also Green 1985: 144 on the commonly accepted view of harshness of early modern treason, murder and felony trials).

---

[9] Catherine Parr was the last wife of Henry VIII whom he married in 1543.

By way of conclusion, there is anecdotal information provided by Camden[10] (2001) concerning the life and death of Throckmorton which may be quoted in order to illustrate the perception of the character by his contemporaries:

> "Sir Nicholas Throkmorton also payed his debt to Nature, ... A man of great experience, passing sharpe wit, and singular diligence. Who busily attempting many things in Queene Maries dayes hardly saved his life by his eloquent wisdome; and under Queene Elizabeth, having with indefatigable paines discharged many Embassies with great commendations, yet could hee rise but to small wealth, and those slight dignities (though glorious in title) of Chiefe Butler of England and Chamberlaine of the Exchequer, whilest he opposed himself as an emulator against Cecyl in favour of Leicester[11]. In whose house as he fed hard at his supper on sallats [salads], he was taken (as some report) with an impostume of the lungs, as others say, with a vehement Catarr, not without suspition of poyson, and died in a good time for himselfe and his, being in great danger of life and estate by reason of his restlesse spirit" (Camden 2001).

Implicit in Camden's account is the belief that, although acquitted by the law, Nicholas Throckmorton was, nevertheless, sixteen years after the trial, judged, sentenced and executed by an unknown hand.

3.2.2 Trial of Thomas Howard, Duke of Norfolk

The source of the text of the trial as published in Hargrave's collection is debatable. The contents, however, agree in general with the description found in a contemporary chronicle written by Camden in Latin (2001), though evidence provided by this source has to be treated with caution as the book is biased towards Elizabeth and the protestant faith. Regrettably, there exists no account similar to that of Patterson (1998) with respect to Throckmorton's trial, on the basis of which the textual transmission of the trial in question could be determined.

As for the sources of Hargrave's account, there are two potential originals: the roll of the trial preserved in the *Public Record Office* (from the Court of High Steward and Peers, *Public Record Office* 2005) and one of the manuscripts in the *British Library*. The latter is accepted, though not substantiated, by Kytö and Walker (2003), who recognise as the original version the trial included in the

---

[10] William Camden (1551-1623) published some of his annals for the first time in 1615.
[11] Earl of Leicester since 1564, Robert Dudley, a favourite of Queen Elizabeth, since 1562 also member of the Privy Council, an enemy to Cecil opposing his international policy, collaborated with the proponents of the marriage between Mary and Norfolk (Loades 1999: 225).

manuscript Sloane 1427[12]. The straightforward choice of this manuscript appears even more arbitrary if one takes into consideration the fact that there exists another 'candidate' manuscript in the British Library (Sloane 2172[13]), containing a fragment of the trial which at some points overlaps with the other manuscript. Both manuscripts are dated to the 17th century.

In any case, Kytö and Walker (2003) compare a piece of the trial as it occurs in *State Trials* with the allegedly original version, pointing out numerous inadequacies of the former (2003: 237-239). Indeed, as my own examination of Sloane 1227 has shown, there are numerous instances of spelling modernisation (e.g., *accompt* as *account*, *besides* as *beside*, the most striking modifications concern personal names), and definite inaccuracies, such as ignoring the unintelligible points or the application of some spelling conventions (e.g., abbreviations, such as *Q^s* for *Queen's*) in Hargrave's text. Spelling modifications in the edition are regular with regard to adverbial endings which are regularly *-y* and not the MSS *-ie*, or the use of *i* for the MSS *y*. Quite obviously, the MSS numerous instances of final silent *-e* were omitted in Hargrave's edition; so was the frequent doubling of the final and medial *p* or *t*. The MSS spelling is, not surprisingly, very inconsistent. The editor's way around this inconsistency was to apply their own interpretive punctuation. The use of commas is much less frequent than in the MSS.

The above-mentioned modifications do not, however, constitute unusual editorial practices and the absence of these would be much more surprising than is their presence. Nevertheless, there are more serious differences between the edited and the manuscript version, such as an insertion of a clause or a word. Naturally, editorial practices of this sort definitely distort the data and render it unsuitable for phonological or morphological investigations. As far as the focus of this study is concerned, however, the linguistic aspects of reported speech are less seriously affected by the practices mentioned above. Even though the added clause in the edited version (*and some here of my Lords have likewise heard it*, Kytö and Walker 2003: 237) is an instance of reported speech, one cannot ascertain when exactly it was added, and one can definitely not exclude the possibility that such a statement could have been uttered in the course of proceedings.

Also, which the authors (Kytö and Walker 2003) fail to mention, I have noticed that the major differences occur in the beginning of the account and in its descriptive part, but not within dialogues. Moreover, the differences are limited to some grammatical and stylistic amendments aiming at greater clarity of the text.

---

[12] The manuscript, according to the *British Library Catalogue* contains "The trial of Thomas Howard, Duke of Norfolk, before the Lords at Westminster for high Treason, 26 Jan. 1571. ff. 32-81" (*British Library Online Catalogue* 2005).

[13] The manuscript contains: "Fragment of the trial of Thomas Howard, Duke of Norfolk, before the Lords at Westminster for High Treason, 14 Eliz. Jan. 1571. ff. 59-66" (*British Library Online Catalogue* 2005).

One major insertion which must have been provided by the editors is the English version of the arraignment which in the MSS is in Latin. On the whole, although the discussion by Kytö and Walker (2003) provides evidence undermining the value of Hargrave's collection for linguistic research, this evidence presented by both manuscripts, as my own examination has shown, is not conclusive for the phenomenon which is analysed in this thesis.

3.2.2.1 Norfolk, the defendant

The involvement of the House of Norfolk, including that of Thomas Howard, the 4th duke of Norfolk, in the political life of England – controversial and dramatic as it was – is a vast topic belonging to the field of history rather than that of linguistics. Therefore, the following sections will only give a brief outline of the background of Norfolk's imprisonment for high-treason charges in order to explain how, a faithful servant of Elizabeth I – and her cousin by Ann Boleyn (Rowse 1976: 251 II) – involved in Scotland against the French in 1559-60, Duke found himself in the Tower, where he spent (with brief intervals) two and a half years before he was executed on June 2nd 1572.

Towards the end of the 1560s, the Duke of Norfolk engaged in two events aimed at the dethroning the English Queen: the Northern Rebellion and Ridolfi Plot. The latter event, referred to as the Hispano-papal plot (Black 1959: 148), was designed to reinstate Mary Stuart to the throne of England and, with her assistance, to introduce the Catholic religion to Protestant England. The crucial part of the plot was the marriage of Norfolk and the Scottish Queen (Loades 1999: 225). Despite Norfolk's misgivings concerning the Italian conspirer, Roberto Ridolfi (Black 1959: 149), the Duke became involved in the matter of marriage, against an open veto on the side of Elizabeth (Black 1959: 137), making himself guilty of high-treason by intending marriage with the sovereign's relative. Norfolk's participation in the plot was discovered by William Cecil (Lord Burghley, Lord High Treasurer of England), the most influential Elizabethan advisor, and the whole "muddle-headed and half hearted treason" (Loades 1999: 238) became a tool in the hands of the latter and in the hands of the Privy Council. Camden (2001) suggests that Cecil, with his favour towards the House of Suffolk in the matter of succession, was himself a target of a conspiracy devised by a group of nobles (including Nicholas Throckmorton and, of course, the Duke of Norfolk) in the year 1569. This explains Cecil's vital interest in the most decisive actions against the wrongdoers. Ultimately, the removal of Norfolk by means of trial and execution, very much encouraged by Cecil, put an end to the crisis caused by Mary's arrival in England four years back though the matter of Marian inheritance still remained unresolved (Loades 1999: 238).

The trial of the Duke of Norfolk, which took place on the 16th of January 1572[14] in the Court of High Steward and Peers, has been aptly described as "a travesty, a form of "judicial murder"" (*Richard de Vere Newsletter No 14* 1990). Evidence was tampered with; fortuitously, condemning letters and facts were discovered, while the weightiest deposition against the Duke was provided by his servant, one Barker, a man of dubious credibility. Nevertheless, some historians have the following opinion on the procedure:

> "The trial was quite regular, even according to the strict rules observed at present in these matters; except that the witnesses gave not their evidence in court, and were not confronted with the prisoner: A laudable practice, which was not at that time observed in trials for high treason" (Hume 1778 [1983]: 107).

The Duke himself kept denying many points on which the treason charges were based but, as will be shown in the linguistic analysis of his defence, his denial proved an unsuccessful strategy. Naturally, the influence of external circumstances on the fate of the accused cannot be disregarded, as this trial was one of those where "great art in persuading juries of the defendant's guilt" (Green 1985: 106) was used by the court officials under pressure from the government. As Green continues, one of the ways to secure the sentencing verdict was careful selection of jury members and discouraging them efficiently from failing to fulfil the expectations of the monarch, also by means of fines and imprisonment. Thomas Howard was sentenced to death and was executed six months after the verdict.

According to information collected in *Edward de Vere Newsletter* (1990), there exist documents (from the years 1569-1572) pointing to the above-mentioned Earl of Leicester (cf. section 3.2.1.1 and note 10) as the major instigator of Norfolk's downfall. The perception of the contemporaries was that Leicester deliberately manipulated the Duke in the matter of marriage, then withdrew at the last moment and shed the whole responsibility on Norfolk. The Duke was supposedly warned about Leicester's conspiracy by Nicholas Throckmorton but the warning came too late (Camden 2001).

---

[14] Hargrave's collection mistakenly dates the trial to the 16th of January 1571 (Vol I, p. 81-118), although the dates of letters and written depositions presented in the courtroom (e.g., Nov 1571, Hargrave, Vol I, p. 96) and the note which states that the trial took place in the 14th year of the reign of Elizabeth indicate that it was a year later, i.e., 1572. As the *British Library Catalogue* indicates (*British Library Online Catalogue* 2005), the mistaken 1571 is also found in both manuscripts (Sloane 1427 and 2172). It is possible that the wrong date comes from Howell's edition of *State Trials* (1809-28, cf. Allebone 1859-71: 904), as descriptions of both *British Library* manuscripts refer to it as the printed edition of Norfolk's trial. *Public Record Office* gives the 14th year of Elizabeth's reign as the date (KB 8/42) and is correct. As for the day of the trial e.g., Hume gives 12th of January (1778 [1983]: 107).

3.2.3 Acquittal and death sentence: towards a pragmatic explanation

The above fragmentary historical sketch of the background of the two trials was aimed at drawing a clear dividing line between them. All the historical facts apart, the major assumption throughout the linguistic analysis is that both defendants – whose prospects prior to trials were undoubtedly equally bleak – had a chance of proceeding with their own defences according to their judgments and means. These means, to a significant, if not decisive degree, were linguistic strategies, such as e.g., reported speech, and they were of no trivial bearing on the fate of the accused. It could be claimed that these means were used successfully only by Throckmorton, while Duke, the unsuccessful defendant, failed to exploit this linguistic potential for the purpose of saving his life. Thus, thrust in the same institutional role in the trial, the two speakers proceeded in two different directions. This fact becomes even more evident if trial is defined in the following way:

> "There is, in the concept of 'trial', a strong undercurrent of the idea of a contest. The trial is necessitated by the existence of a dispute – one that is resolved by the application of the law to the facts as authoritatively found and terminated by one side or the other securing the verdict of the court" (Jaconelli 2003: 24).

The assumption as to the existence of linguistic correlates for the two defences, one resulting in the acquittal and the other in a death sentence, will be verified in the sections devoted to the pragmatic analysis of reported speech in the speech of the defendants.

3.3 Furnivall (1897) – description of the source

The collection of over a hundred samples from the "Depositions in Trials in the Bishop's Court from Nov. 1561 to March 1565-6" (Furnivall 1897: xiv) was discovered by Frederick Furnivall in the Chester Diocesan Registry in 1893. This experienced editor found the collection extremely interesting on the grounds of the sensational topic – child marriages and divorces – to which it pertained. The accounts of cases range from half a page to several pages, though longer ones are rare. The source is less controversial in terms of its usefulness for linguistic research because of the editor's standards and explicit information as to the selection and editing procedure. Also notation conventions, such as e.g., the use of italics in the case of expanded quotations or indistinct graphemes and the use of square brackets for editor's additions are explicitly clarified (Furnivall 1987: lxvi-lxvii). The edition marks chunks of reported speech with double quotation marks separating them clearly from the editor's comments, which is very useful for this study. Another argument in favour of the linguistic reliability of the collection is the fact that even the most methodical among the corpus compilers working on the *Corpus of English Dialogues* find Furnivall (1897) reliable enough to draw samples from it (cf. Kytö and Walker 2003).

The divorce cases collected in the volume are pleadings of the representatives of the local middle-class "from ...mansion-owning squires to the little alehouse-keepers, farmers and cobblers, the maids and the men" (Furnivall 1897: lxxxviii) representing speakers of a social milieu distinct from the one depicted in the *State Trials*. As can be seen from the sample provided below (Figure 4), individual depositions contain names and age of the interested parties and the approximate date (month and year) in the title. Very often, a Latin description follows the title, comprising relevant information as to the allegations and sometimes also the exact date of the deposition. Latin intros also delimit depositions of different witnesses included in one sample. Unlike the *State Trials*, ecclesiastical depositions do not contain dialogue other than embedded in the speech of witnesses but no graphic cues are used to mark it. As has been mentioned above (section 3.1.1), the depositions were most probably collected as the so-called *interrogatories*.

```
6  I. Child-Marriages.  § 1. Divorces.  4. Jn. Bridge v. Eliz. Bridge.
her, but wold have Lovid her yf she wold have bene content : of the
which premises, all the parishe talkis, & can be witnes in hit /
     4. John Bridge v. Elizabeth Bridge (born Ramsbotham).
                He 11 or 12 at the marriage, she ? 13-14.
         (Beginning lost.  Depositions taken on Dec. 1561.)
[1Elizabeth Bridge, born Ramsbotham, answers the Bill or Petition of
her Husband John Bridge, & says that after their child-marriage he never
```

Figure 4: A sample from Furnivall (1897)

In this study, selected samples are used as 'control' data serving the aim of comparison with the *State Trials*, both in terms of adequacy for pragmatic analysis and as evidence of two different legal procedures reflected in the linguistic make-up of the data. For this purpose a sample of 10,000 words is deemed sufficient.

3.4 Recent studies into historical courtroom discourse

As speech-based[15] genres (section 1.3.3), court records have recently become the focus of historical pragmatics (section 1.3.1). Growing interest in the surviving

---

[15] In his analysis of Anglo-Saxon legal language, Hiltunen (1990: 45-46) also notices some speech-based features (e.g., referential use of pronouns, topicalisations and comment-like clauses, abrupt turns etc.). In this case, the survival of these in the written medium is due to the previous oral transmission and the fact that in this period the law was written down for the first time. In this way legal Anglo-Saxon does not show variation as to the occurrence of speech-based features in different text-types in the way the Early Modern English period does.

trial proceedings and witness depositions as material for investigations into the history of the English language is parallel to the recent advances in corpus studies, facilitating access to uncommon sources and saving the pains of philological (or paleographical) work. Particularly, the *Corpus of English Dialogues* project, a mutual enterprise of Jonathan Culpeper (Lancaster University) and Merja Kytö (Uppsala), in preparation since 1996 (cf. e.g., Culpeper and Kytö 1999a; Kytö and Walker 2003), has encouraged research efforts by means of providing handy material for an in-depth exploration of this hitherto relatively obscure area. Similarly, the *Salem Witchcraft Trials* project, an international enterprise of teams from European and Northern American universities aiming to provide a new edition of the Salem transcripts has inspired some recent contributions (cf. e.g., Hiltunen 2004; Grund – Kytö - Rissanen 2004). The main foci of the studies into courtroom discourse are presented in Table 9. Additionally, information of source texts is included to illustrate the attitudes to the 'bad-data problem' and at the same time to demonstrate that the use of edited material (as in this study) is not uncommon. The findings of studies into the courtroom discourse are used as reference points in the linguistic analysis presented in the following chapters.

PAPER	SPECIFIC RECORD	SOURCE MATERIAL	FOCUS
Hope (1994)	Durham Court Records	Printed 19th C. edition *Surtees Society*	2nd person pronouns
Wright (1995)	Court Minute Books of the Royal Hospitals of Bridewell and Bedlam	manuscript	syntax of witness narratives
Kryk-Kastovsky (1998)	Late 17th C. trial proceedings	The *Helsinki Corpus*, compiled from an 18th C. edition (Hargrave)	pragmatic particles
Culpeper and Kytö (1999a)	Trial proceedings, witness depositions 1590- 1720	*Corpus of English Dialogues*, bibliographical details lacking	Hedges
Culpeper and Kytö (1999b)	Lancaster witches depositions, end of 16th C.	Early 17th C. printed version in a 20th C. imprint	levels of embedding, modes of speech reporting
Koch (1999)	Lio Mazoi Court records	20th C. editions	parameters of linguistic immediacy
Ramge (1999)	Record of 1309 proceedings, Wetzlar	20th C. edition	procedures in the compilation of an official legal text of on-the-record drafts
Culpeper and Kytö (2000a)	Trial proceedings, witness depositions 1600- 1720	*Corpus of English Dialogues*, bibliographical details lacking	conversational diagnostics

Culpeper and Kytö (2000b)	Trial proceedings 1560-1640; 1680-1760	*Corpus of English Dialogues*, bibliographical details lacking	conversational routines
Culpeper and Kytö (2000c)	Witness depositions, parliamentary debates	18th C (Hargrave), 19th C. editions	discoursal aspects
Culpeper and Semino (2000)	Depositions of witchcraft 1593-1664	16th C edition, two 17th C. printed edition, three 20th C. editions of 17th C. material	speech act analysis
Kryk-Kastovsky (2000)	Late 17th C. trial proceedings	*Helsinki Corpus*, compiled from an 18th C. edition (Hargrave)	discourse markers, examination strategies
Collins (2001)	Russian trial transcripts 1400-1505	manuscripts and editions	reported speech strategies
Archer (2002)	Salem witchcraft papers	20th C. edition	examination strategies
Dotty and Hiltunen (2002)	Salem witchcraft papers	20th C. edition	examination strategies
Archer (2003)	Trial proceedings	*Corpus of English Dialogues*	questioning strategies
Moore (2003)	Slander depositions 1475-1700, England and Scotland	20th C. editions	Direct speech reporting strategies
Hiltunen (2004)	Salem witchcraft examinations	20th C. edition	speech representation, witness strategies
Kahlas-Tarkka and Rissanen (forthcoming)	Salem witchcraft examinations	manuscript	examination strategies

Table 9: A selection of recent studies into trials and depositions as speech-based genres

3.5 Some methodological preliminaries

Some methodological issues have been referred to in the introductory part of this chapter, while the general theoretical and methodological directions of this study were characterised in greater detail on several occasions in the previous chapters. At this point, it is necessary to focus on some technicalities of linguistic analysis in order to clarify the analytic procedure performed for the purpose of the thesis. Conventionally, the following sections will touch upon the size of the samples analysed, the identification of the basic unit for investigation and the annotation of the data.

The processed version remains faithful to the original punctuation, including the preservation of the original italics for proper nouns and capitals for the majority of common nouns. The issue of punctuation and graphic representation is sometimes a useful tool in the analysis of reported speech e.g., the turns in the dialogue are graphically delimited and assigned to individual speakers but quotation marks are not used as reported speech signals. Single quotation marks occur only when a letter or earlier deposition is presented in the courtroom. Although neither of the surface text features can be viewed uncritically as a reliable clue to its interpretation, it should be mentioned that, particularly in the case of reported speech embedded in dialogue, there are isolated cases when e.g., the use of italics disambiguates the reported speech category which otherwise could not be identified as either direct and indirect (cf. example (1) below). Therefore, all surface text features are retained.

(1) Chrift faid, *Bleſſed are they that hunger and thirſte for Righteouſneſſe*[16].

3.5.1 Size and representativeness of the samples

The accounts of the two trials in Hargrave's collection contain nearly 60,000 words (Throckmorton trial, henceforth <TH>, 16,352; Norfolk trial, henceforth <N> 42,857). This sample is considered sufficient to gain insight into the pragmatics of reported speech in the courtroom of Early Modern England, mostly because of ample dialogue and several narratives of witnesses, in which the phenomenon is well represented (cf. Table 10). In <TH> the relative frequency of occurrence of reported speech tokens is slightly higher than in <N>, with a distinctiveness ratio[17] (henceforth DR; cf. Kenny 1982: 67-69) at 1,17. Naturally, the overall size of the samples is by no means comparable to the quantities of data collected in corpora of present-day English (cf. Semino and Short 2004: 24-26 for an overview) or other historical collections. It is, however, important to emphasise the synchronic, rather than diachronic, perspective of this study. Focusing on a single stage of language development, the sample in question may indeed be considered representative. Obviously, pragmatically-oriented diachronic studies of language usually incorporate greater amounts of data. For instance, taking a closer look at the corpus used in one specific study, which purports to be a comprehensive diachronic monograph of the role of the question in the Early Modern English courtroom (Archer 2003), i.e., the *Sociopragmatic Corpus* (the total of the court trial section is 121,189 words, Archer 2003: 149), which is a part of a larger *Corpus of English Dialogues*, one discovers that the word counts for synchronic 40-year periods approximate 40,000 (cf. Archer and Culpeper 2003: 43). In the face of the above figures, the size of the sample investigated in this study is well suited for a synchronic analysis on condition that the linguistic phenomenon under investigation is well-represented.

---

[16] In the *State Trials*, a grapheme easily confused with < f >, i.e., < ſ >, the so-called long <s>, is used for <s> in all positions in the word except for capitals.

[17] Distinctiveness ratio, a simple statistic invented by A. Ellegård enables the researcher "to compare proportions characteristic of one text with proportions characteristic of another" (Kenny 1982: 69).

90 Chapter Three

Naturally, there are studies into reported speech, such as e.g., Semino and Short (2004), which analyse extant material. As the authors emphasise, however, the completion of the investigation of 250,000 words, had only been achieved because a team of experts were involved in the work on the data since 1994 (Semino and Short 2004: 41f). Such collective enterprises, impressive in scope, are not infrequently undertaken in the course of corpus projects, and can, regrettably, not be matched by the efforts of a single researcher.

	<TH>	<N>
TOTAL INSTANCES	1133	2523
NORMALISED FIGURE PER 10,000 WORDS	692,88	588,70
DISTINCTIVENESS RATIO		1,17

Table 10: Reported speech instances in the data

3.5.2 Between the turn and the report – basic description units

As outlined above, reported speech operates on the level of discourse rather than syntax and as such, its instances are not easy to single out for the purpose of analysis. As is commonly known, speech reports are neither equivalent to syntactic units (sentences) nor to the units of discourse (e.g., turns in conversation). Moreover, the complexity of some reports and the diversity of occurring categories pose further problems when attempting to define *report*. Consequently, singling out these units inevitably involves a degree of subjectivity[18] and necessitates handling some cases individually. A preliminary strategy is to view reports as uninterrupted presentations of points of view different from the perspective of the author or current speaker: in other words, those introducing 'voices' that stand out from the authorial discourse. Frequently, however, reports of speech bring in more than one voice or comprise more than one category within an uninterrupted presentation, rendering this approach unacceptable:

(2) DS [1] [*Throckmorton.* ... DS [2] [Chrift faid, [NRSA PASS [3] [*Bleſſed are they*] that *hunger and thirſte for Righteouſneſſe.*]]
(3) DS [*Shrewſbury.* Come you hither to checke us, *Throckmorton?*]

Instances like (2) call for splitting the text into parts: [1], [2] and [3] as constituting separate reports. This would, however, neglect the issue of embedding: [1] is an instance of direct speech embedded in the authorial discourse, [2] is embedded in [1] as an instance of direct speech within a

---

[18] The lack of graphic cues for speech reports in pre-modern texts is an additional difficulty. Here, editorial punctuation is not accepted uncritically.

character's turn, and finally [3] as a NRSA, is embedded in [2], i.e., it is a part of a direct quotation from the words of Christ. Still, [1], [2] and [3] are different categories, which, in formal analysis, makes it possible to view them as individual reports. Thus, a report can be defined as a single, formally detachable instance of a category of reported speech. On this view, (2) comprises three different reports, while (3) is an instance of a single report. This viewpoint serves the needs of the categorisation procedure, simplifies the formal description of reported speech and is essential for a statistical picture of the phenomenon, which is complementary to the qualitative discussion. In order to incorporate the phenomenon of embedding (cf. section 2.3.2.2.3.2), the definition of a report is combined with the notion of a turn in dialogue, slightly adapted for the present purpose. A turn is defined here as an uninterrupted statement of a character or an interrupted presentation of a point of view or voice in narration. Thus both (2) and (3) above are single turns. Turns are not split into separate reports, but the latter are categorised and formally analysed as integral parts of the former.

3.5.3 Annotation of the data

The first step taken in the analysis of reported speech is labelling its instances with proper category labels. The categorisation model to be followed here has been sketched out in the previous sections but it has to be borne in mind that emendations and departures from Leech and Short (1981) are possible, given the specific problems posed by the material under investigation. Therefore, the next chapter contains an empirical discussion of the suitability of the selected model for the investigation of two treason trials and numerous illustrations of categorisation decisions. The basic categorisation is, moreover, informed by the findings of other models reviewed in the previous chapter (section 2.4 and subsections). Particularly some structural aspects enumerated by Thompson (1996) and Collins (2001), like, for instance, selected syntactic and morphological features, the position of tag against the report, tagging strategies, supplementary tagging and levels of embedding (Collins 2001: 4) are taken into account. As becomes clear in the course of the discussion, the completion of the categorisation is not an aim in itself; it is the categorisation procedure and a range of considerations pertaining to it that prove revealing in terms of the pragmatic nature of reported speech.

Apart from the abbreviations for the basic reported speech and thought categories introduced above (section 2.4.1.3), labels encoding additional information will be used in the annotation of the samples (cf. Abbreviations). All the information encoded by the additional labels may have clear pragmatics correlates in the analysis of reported speech strategies; therefore they were included despite their detailed nature.

3.6 Concluding remarks

The sections above were devoted to three areas constituting essential preliminaries to the linguistic analysis of reported speech. Firstly, the discussion clarified some historical issues determining source text selection. Secondly, the source texts were presented with a view to their suitability for linguistic research. For the *State Trials* outlining the historical background of the treason trials investigated in this study was deemed both useful and necessary. Thirdly, some technicalities and introductory methodological information were presented in order to justify some decisions and to facilitate the reading of the examples quoted in the following empirical discussion. On the whole, these sections prepared the ground for the analysis to follow.

Chapter Four

Reported speech as a marker of stance – pragmatic aspects of categorisation

> "Trial discourse rest on a theory of intertextuality decontextualising speech from one speech event and recontextualising it in a new one, to constitute its evidentiary and epistemological field"
>
> (Matoesian 2000: 879).

As has been shown in chapter two (section 2.4.1.3), Leech and Short's model (1981) provides a sound basis for a description of individual categories of reported speech. Still, accounting for some pragmatic aspects of reported speech cannot be postponed till the categorisation has been completed, since without an immediate justification and incorporation into the procedure, the pragmatic features in question are left unexplained. Such an approach leaves room for extensions and emendations of the selected model. Therefore, the linguistic analysis of reported speech in Early Modern English common law court records (second half of the 16th century) commences with an in-depth qualitative discussion of controversies accompanying categorisation decisions. The analysis aims to show that the resolution of controversies as to the scope and structure of individual categories involves a noteworthy explanatory potential with respect to the pragmatic aspects of reported speech.

4.1 Accounts of reported speech in Early Modern English

The categories of reported speech in many cases have well defined structural correlates. Unfortunately, comprehensive syntactic treatments of reported speech in Early Modern English are not available and in the discussions of the period the phenomenon is not commented on (e.g., Barber 1976 [1997], Görlach 1991, Denison 1993). Even Visser (1966), comprehensive as he is in illustrating all stages of the development of the language and who does devote some space to reported speech (§821-833), is not very useful when it comes to categorisation problems, as he only relies on the traditional three-category view of reported speech. Also, as can be inferred on the basis of the monograph devoted to the descriptive adequacy of Early Modern English grammars of the period (Dons 2004), the issues pertaining to reported speech were not discussed by the contemporary grammarians. Some occasional empirically-based remarks on reported speech in Early Modern English can be found in the studies into courtroom discourse (cf. Table 9), e.g., Culpeper and Kytö (1999b), Archer

(2003), Moore (2003). These, however, are rare and cannot provide a sound basis for a synchronic treatment of Early Modern English data.

Naturally, the accounts of reported speech in other periods of the history of English, including present-day English reported speech, cannot be transferred uncritically to the data under research. The present study in its general approach rejects the convenient position resulting form the Labovian uniformitarianism, for two reasons. First of all, the institutional factor determining a range of linguistic phenomena in the analysed texts is subject to constant change and so are the mechanisms of legal institutions. As Berger and Luckmann (1981) maintain: "Institutions always have a history, of which they are the products. It is impossible to understand an institution adequately without an understanding of the historical process in which it was produced" (1981: 72). Secondly, it may be extremely dangerous to apply modern ideas and linguistic interpretations to those stages of the language which are linguistically not strikingly different from present-day language, or which appear to be intelligible to a modern reader. The ability of modern readers to understand Early Modern English texts is only superficial and often deceptive, particularly when it comes to the lexicon. One can easily forget the need for a 'translation' of any text from a different linguistic period as well as the fact that such a 'translation' is a prerequisite for an insight into the realities of the past. Thus, lacking the support of existing investigations or ready-made solutions to the problems posed by reported speech in Early Modern English, the structural analysis determining the categorisation needs to be carried out with extreme caution.

4.1.2 Extensions and emendations of Leech and Short's model (1981)

Leech and Short model (1981) will essentially have to undergo some modifications in order to accommodate the specific nature of courtroom discourse. On the basis of Goodrich (1990) it is accepted here that legal language is a specific way of structuring communication as well as a kind of specialised rhetoric. This basic view stems from two aspects of its institutionalisation:

> "... the unity of the legal system which, in sociological terms, refers to ... the limitation of legal discourse to a restricted set of hierarchically defined speakers together with the internal shielding or valorisation of specific 'authorised' texts and the strictly delimited rhetorical settings of legal communication and contact with the non-legal world" (Goodrich 1990: 174-5).

As Goodrich goes on to claim, the areas of lexicon and syntax most clearly reflect the above dimensions of institutionalisation. The former area, including specialised vocabulary, is significant in terms of its expressive and intentional aspects and it comprises something one could refer to as "a primarily symbolic lexicon" (Goodrich 1990: 177). As far as the latter area is concerned, syntactic form itself is determined by vocabulary, with the meanings mediated by "the syntax of generalisation" (Goodrich 1990: 180). Tiersma (1999: 40) points to the conservatism, fixation on words, formality and ritualistic character of legal language as fostered by historical developments connected with the introduction of writing into the legal domain and its growing importance after the printing revolution. The specific linguistic features reflecting the above-mentioned features of legal language are: conjoined phrases and lists of words, unusual sentence structure, special uses of negation and impersonal constructions (Tiersma 1999: 61-69), as well as the use of passives and nominalisations (Tiersma 1999: 74-79). All these are naturally common in present-day legal discourse but the standardisation of legal language initiated by the invention of print, the permanence of the law fixed in written record and the use of "exact language of the statute, even if the public no longer understands it" (Tiersma 1999: 39), lead one to assume that some of these features may have a lengthy institutional history and that many modern features of legal language may be present in Early Modern English courtroom discourse. In many points the phenomenon of reported speech coincides with either lexical, syntactic or both kinds of peculiarities of legal language as described by Goodrich (1990) and Tiersma (1999), hence the institutional aspects necessarily take precedence over aspects of reported speech.

With regard to categorisation, the following discussion concentrates on those aspects which – when faced with historical legal records – turn out to be insufficiently developed in the Leech and Short model (1981). For one thing, the ritualised character of the linguistic data as reflected in the frequent use of formulas and other fixed phrases is taken into consideration. Secondly, the semantic aspect of verbs used as tagging devices in reported speech receives much more attention than it so far has enjoyed in the Leech and Short model (1981). Finally, some of the potential instances of reported speech are excluded from the analysis, mostly on syntactic grounds.

4.2 Preliminary verification of Leech and Short's (1981) categories and further aspects of reported speech analysis

The initial step towards the verification of the model for the purpose of this study is a technical emendation concerning terminology. This emendation is necessary, as the differences between the original data for which Leech and Short's categorisation (1981) was designed and the institutional data are not inconsequential. It pertains specifically to the *narrator's report of speech act* (NRSA) and *narrator's report of thought act* (NRTA) categories (cf. the confusion over *narrator's* vs. *narrative*, section 2.4.1.3). In a utilitarian text, the concept of narrator, or even author, does not function as a central explanatory notion as is the case in a fictional text. Despite the fact that definitely every text has an author, only in fiction does he/she/it receive an independent existence as a constructed consciousness. Although the concept of narrator's or author's discourse and its distance from reported speech instances is primary grounds for the categorisation in Leech and Short's model, the data analysed here may only be viewed as an instance of self-constituting discourse (cf. Maingueneau 1999) devoid of the presence of any representing consciousness. Therefore the concept of *narrator* in the institutional data is redundant, which allows substituting the NRSA and NRTA categories for RSA (*report of speech act*) and RTA (*report of thought act*) respectively.

The following examples illustrate the basic categories in the preliminary categorisation carried out on the basis of Leech and Short's model (1981):

RSA

(4) <TH>
Sendall. DA [*Nicholas Throckmorton* Knighte], hold up thy hande, RSA PASS [Thou art before this time indited of High-Treafon,]
<N>

(5) RSA PASS [Then was produc'd an Examination of the Bifhop of *Roffe*, taken at the Tower, Nov. 5. 1571...

IS

(6) <TH>
IS DO SUP [I did fay to *Winter*, RTA [that *Wyat* was defirous RSA INF [to fpeake with him]],] as RSA PAR [I underftoode].
<N>

(7) IS [The Lord Chief Juftice anfwer'd, RSA PASS [That in cafe of High-Treafon he cannot have Counfel allow'd]

FIS

(8) <TH>
Bromley. DA [*Throckmorton,*] IS [you confeffed THAT-DEL RSA [you talked with *Wiat* and others againft the comming of the *Spanyardes*, and of the taking of the *Tower* of *London*]] FIS [wherevpon *Wiat* levied a Force of Men againft the *Spanyardes* THAT-DEL; POSTPOSED he fayde]
<N>

(9) IS [He gave Advice, that fhe fhould in no wife deliver her Son, for it was againft her own Safety, IT GERUND [not knowing whether fhe delivered him into her Friends hands or no].] FIS [As for the Rebels, fhe would in no wife deliver them, for it were againft her Honour: And as for the Holds, fhe fhould not deliver any; for it were againft the Safety of her Friends in *Scotland*.]

DS

(10) <TH>
DS [*Throck-morton* aunfwered, RTA [I miflike it for diuers refpects;]
DS [Chrift faid, THAT-DEL [RSA PASS [*Bleffed are they*] *that hunger and thirfte for Righteoufneffe.*]

(11) <N>
DS [The Clerk faid, By whom RTA [wilt thou RSA Q PASS [be try'd]?]

FDS
(12) <TH>

IS [I ſaid ᴛʜᴀᴛ-ᴅᴇʟ RTA [I was glad of it;] and ꜰᴅs [as for the *Frenchmen,* ʀᴛᴀ [I care not much for them], I will ſo handle the matter, that the Queenes ſhippes ſhall bee ʀsᴀ ᴘᴀʀ [I warrante you] in ſafegard.]

RTA
(13) <TH>

ʀᴛᴀ [I meant ʀsᴀ ɪɴꜰ [not to touche your Lordſhip],]

(14) <N>

ʀᴛᴀ [he ſhould underſtand his whole Mind particularly from time to time]

IT
(15) <TH>

ʀsᴀ ᴘᴀʀ [I pray you] ɪᴛ ɪᴍᴘ ᴛʜᴀᴛ-ᴅᴇʟ [remember I am not alienate from you, but that I am your Chriſtian Brother;]

(16) <N>

Duke. ɪᴛ [That you may underſtand ʀsᴀ [that I ſpeak it not without ſome ground],]

FIT
(17) <N>

ʀsᴀ ᴘᴀss ɪɴᴠ [Then was produced his own Examination the 6th *of November,* 1571].] ʀsᴀ ᴘᴀss [and it was read], ʀsᴀ ꜰᴀᴅᴇ ɪɴ [and he confeſſed his Concealment of thoſe Speeches and Conferences before uſed about the Marriage, and ɪs [that ʀsᴀ ᴘᴀss [it had indeed been moved], ʀsᴀ ᴘᴀss [but not concluded on]]: ꜰɪᴛ [He remembreth ʀsᴀ [that the Queen charged him ſtraightly not to proceed in that Marriage];] ɪᴛ [but he remembreth not ʀsᴀ [that ſhe charged him upon his Allegiance].]

4.2.1 Thought presentation in institutional discourse

Thought presentation, as can be seen on the basis of the instances demonstrated above, does not find a full-scale reflection in the material under investigation. This is not a surprising discovery since *free* thought presentation categories in particular as well as direct thought serve the aim of presenting internal speech and are clearly narrative devices. Hence the lack of these in the institutional non-literary material is observed. The single exception here is example (17) of FIT from the trial of the Duke of Norfolk, which can be viewed as an isolated case – an exception confirming the rule. It would indeed be absurd to imagine courtroom interaction as involving witnesses and the jury expressing their thoughts on a regular basis in ways illustrated by the examples given by Leech and Short (1981: 337):

(18) Does she still love me? [FDT]
(19) Did she still love him? [FIT]

Or for the court reporter to come up in his records with examples like:

(20) He wondered, 'Does she still love me?' [DT]

After all, access to internal speech of others is not a real-life phenomenon and, therefore, cannot be expected to occur in courtroom records. This fact is actually an implicit argument for the reliability of this kind of material with respect to the ways in which it reports speech. In other words, coming across typically narrative devices or strategies in utilitarian texts would be a serious indication of their fictional rather than institutional character. On the other hand, even the lack of unambiguous instances for some thought representation categories from the data will not result in excluding the speech vs. thought distinction in the categorization of reported speech. The two thought categories (RTA and IT) are not uncommon and moreover, a general pattern may be discerned i.e., a character's report of their own reflections (example 21), which adds an additional layer of embedding to the discourse. Because of the lack of formal clues, 1st person thought reports fluctuate between direct and indirect thought, the speaker taking on a different perspective in relation to his/her own thoughts:

(21) <TH>
[I <u>doubte</u> not] THAT-DEL RSA PASS [Sir *Thomas Wyat* <u>hath</u> <u>bin</u> <u>examin'd</u> of me]

At this point, a study Maynard (1996) contributes on Japanese self-quotation, as representation of speech and thought, comes in handy. In the opinion of the author, self-quotation is direct and not indirect speech or thought. Firstly, as Maynard (1996) points out "self-quotation by directing attention to the act of saying [thinking, MW] itself, offers a place for the speaker to qualify one's speech [thought, MW] act in a variety of ways" (1996: 224). Indeed, changes in perspective, particularly in self-reports, allow some manipulative ground to the speaker so that personal attitudes, etc., are often verbalised in this way (e.g., Koven, 2001, Golato 2002). Secondly, the qualification function of verbal predicates in self-quotation may take over the propositional function totally (cf. sections in 4.3.1.3 below), rendering the occurrence of speech and thought representation questionable. Maynard (1996) solves this predicament only partially, assuming that it is exclusively the first-person present affirmative that can be interpreted as having a conventionalised rather than referential function (1996: 219). Unfortunately, the author does not provide any clues as to distinguishing between those self-quotations which are and those which are not speech act qualifiers, rather than instances of reported speech. Less ambiguous are cases of reporting thoughts of others, when, as is observed by Mushin (2001a), an indirect form must be used "that expresses some information about how the speaker came to know something that is not in their territory of information" (2001a: 1364, cf. Shinzato 2004: 878, Bolden 2004: 1112). Actually, some authors claim that there is a tendency on the side of speakers to use speech rather than thought representation when stating what others may think (Shinzato 2004: 869). Indeed, as Fairclough (2003) notices, representation of thought of others "can only be based upon speech or writing" (2003: 50). Wierzbicka (1987) makes an even more radical claim: "first person mental phrases are not only more common than third person ones: they are also more basic semantically" (1987: 115). Some of these claims with regard to thought representation found in the literature are subject to verification in the analysis of Early Modern English data.

At this point another reference to the extended Leech and Short model (1981) as presented in Semino and Short (2004) is called for. In their elaborate categorisation of thought reports, the authors propose an additional label *inferred* when presentation of thought of others takes place. Indeed, in the light of the arguments above *inferred* with respect to thought reports, is superfluous, as there is no other way of accessing the thoughts of others than through one or another kind of inference.

4.2.2 The status of reporting clauses in speech and thought presentation

There is one further point in the revised Leech and Short (1981) model which appears objectionable. As McIntyre et al. (2004: 56) and Semino and Short (2004: 29) emphasise, their categorisation includes separate tagging of reporting clauses (or reporting signals) as *narrator's reports* introducing presented speech, thought or writing despite the traditional understanding of each instance of reported speech as the whole sentence (Semino and Short 2004: 35). As the authors explain: "Strictly speaking ... the reported clause is the IS or DS string, while the reporting clause is the reporter's link between that report and the discourse in which the report is embedded" (Semino and Short 2004: 35). This serves the purpose of keeping apart speech representation subsequent to the reporting clause or signal and in this way it facilitates the word count of reported speech (*reported* clauses as opposed to *reporting* clauses).

Thus, following this separation in example (6) above only the clause following *I did fay to Winter* is seen as an instance of speech presentation, and therefore taken into consideration when it comes to statistics, while the reporting clause itself is an instance of (N)RSA[1]. In this way the whole single instance of indirect speech as in (22):

(22) IS [I did fay to Winter, RTA [that *Wyat* was defirous RSA INF [to fpeake with him]],] becomes:

(23) NRS [I did fay to Winter], IS [that RTA [*Wyat* was defirous RSA INF [to fpeake with him]],]

---

[1] As concerns the NRSA category as in Leech and Short's model (1981), labelled RSA in this study, the (N)RSA label is used with reference to the literature on the issue.

In (23) an additional embedding level is added, even though it is a redundant one – signalling the point of view of the author/narrator – which is normally taken for granted in any text. On the other hand, the reporting clause is excluded from the word count of the indirect speech report and at the same time falls outside speech presentation so as to ignore this additional embedding level. There are two consequences of such an approach and none of them is acceptable here. First of all, introducing a separate category label for each reporting clause multiplies the number of instances of speech presentation: for a single instance (in the traditional understanding) there are two categories. This undermines the capacity of reported speech to reflect the dynamic relationship between the anterior and the ongoing speech event, reflected in the reporting and reported clause respectively, as the two are clearly set apart. Secondly, the structure of many NRS's (*narrator's report of speech* as opposed to *narrator's report of speech act*, cf. example (6); repeated in (22) and (23)) is that of a main clause and not like in the prototypical example of (N)RSA (in bold below; by the way, NRS and NRSA are labels easy to confuse) given by Semino and Short (2004: 9):

> (24) He looked straight at her and **told her about his imminent return**. She was pleased.

The authors give the following structural description: "NRSA, unlike IS, prototypically has only one clause, with the 'speech report' verb often followed by a noun phrase or a prepositional phrase indicating the topic of the speech presented" (Semino and Short 2004: 10). That this description fails to match cases of reporting clauses as in (23) is absolutely clear. Furthermore, NRS's have a structure more similar to IS than to (N)RSA. Consequently, putting reporting clauses of this kind into a new separate category outside the speech presentation cline rather than viewing them as instances of IS, which they structurally are, results in blurring the indubitably functional distinctions between the categories. This would have serious impact on the interpretation of some general quantitative findings of this study, as these are essentially based on the different functions that reported speech categories perform in discourse. Finally, as the authors themselves admit, the status of NRS has not been a straightforward issue and in the initial stages of the project the NRS label corresponded to NV i.e., narrator's report of voice (Semino and Short 2004: 65f), being incorporated into one of the existing categories rather than viewed as a separate one. Undoubtedly, the issue has been a source of considerable confusion and the label is far from unambiguous.

This study does not introduce separate labels for reporting clauses also because excluding the introductory clause from the word count of reported speech equals disregarding one of the constitutive elements present in the majority of instances. Cases of free (i.e., not signalled by any element overtly introducing represented speech or thought) categories of speech and thought presentation are indeed marginal in the data analysed by various authors who follow the Leech and Short model (1981). Moreover, excluding the reporting clause (*indited*) in (N)RSA's as in example (4), *Thou art before this time indited of High-Treafon*, leaves the question as to which elements are still to be included in speech presentation, unanswered. This example shows that frequently the degree of syntactic integration of the reporting and reported clauses is too great to allow separation of the two. Despite deciding to devote a separate section to the discussion of (N)RSA's which, as Semino and Short (2004: 29) notice, "are not reporting clauses grammatically" (Semino and Short 2004: 34-38), the authors do not account for cases similar to example (4).

A pragmatic argument for the constitutive role played by the reporting clause in any instance of speech or thought representation is provided by the existence in languages of the so-called *de dicto* domain discussed by Frajzyngier (1991). As opposed to the *de re* domain, the *de dicto* domain is the domain of speech, not reality, and the distinction between the two is linguistically encoded in many languages, for instance in the marking of embedded clauses. In English there are semantic differences between sentences which include a complementiser and those which lack it (Frajzyngier 1991: 235), as in the examples below:

a. I saw that he fell down.
b. I saw him fall down.

The semantic implication of complementiser use is indirect evidence rather than direct experience because "there is little doubt that its primary function was, synchronically and diachronically, to introduce complements of the *verba dicendi*" (Frajzyngier 1991: 225). Following the course of argumentation proposed by Frajzyngier (1991), reporting clauses could be viewed as functioning similarly to complementisers i.e., as signals and constituents of *de dicto* domain in language.

As reporting clauses are not redundant in the linguistic make-up of reported speech, their structure and semantics are very often the basic criteria for the categorisation of reported speech phenomena and hence they are not excluded from the word counts. In fact, the opposite decision of McIntyre et al. (2004) and Semino and Short (2004), which is neither well justified nor difficult to challenge, is an unfortunate blight in this otherwise elegant and elaborate model.

4.3 Pragmatic aspects of the verb in reported speech

It is commonly accepted that overt use of reported speech (i.e., excluding *free* reports, which are unmarked) involves signalling this fact which is mostly realised through a *tag* by means of which "the report is indexed or attributed in the authorial context" (Collins 2001: 5). In other words, framing of the report i.e., its recontextualisation within the ongoing discourse, involves a choice of a reporting word (Fairclough 2003: 52). Of all word categories verbs serve this function most frequently. As far as other word categories are concerned, Thompson (1996) provides the following classification of tags: reporting adjunct, reporting noun, reporting adjective, no separate signal (cf. section 2.4.1.2.1). Of these the last three are applied in this study. The following table contains statistical distribution of tags in the analysed material.

	VERB	ADJECTIVE OR VERB-ADJECTIVE COMBINATION	NOUN	FREE (TOKENS)
<TH>	95,70%	3,05%	1,25%	4
<N>	92,15%	3,14%	4,71%	7

Table 11: Distribution of tags: grammatical categories

Verbs in general pose a real challenge as to categorisation owing to their complex semantics and a range of 'special' uses which is not accounted for in the Leech and Short model (1981). One additional problem pertains to the lack of a coherent classification of Early Modern English verbs on the basis of their semantic scope or pragmatic function. Naturally, such classifications exist for present-day English (e.g., Biber 1988: 242[2], cf. also Quirk et al. 1985, Biber et al. 1999) but, as the uniformitarian principle is rejected here, none of these can be utilised in full, though some insights might be gained. Therefore, the classification in the table below (Table 12) is only tentative and temporary.

The most commonly occurring verbal tag, *say*, represents the group of *verba dicendi*, comprising semantically faded verbs of speaking (Table 12[3]). As concerns related groups, phase verbs and manner-of-speaking verbs are also used, though with much lower frequencies. All these categories are relatively unambiguous predicates of reporting clauses, provided they do not occur in fixed expressions or as parenthetical or evidential expressions (cf. 4.3.1.3, 4.3.1.4 and 4.3.1.5). The *verba dicendi* tags, contrary to the commonly held assumption, do not dominate among the 15 most frequent verbal tags (1/3 in both trials) whereas the number of speech act verbs, a much more semantically and pragmatically loaded group, is not significantly different. Moreover, an instance of a mental verb (*know*), used for the representation of thought, is of 2nd (<N>) and 3rd

---

[2] Cf. reporting verbs and their classification in Caldas-Coulthard (1994: 306).
[3] The following abbreviations are used: VD – verbum dicendi, SAV – speech act verb, MenV– mental verb, ModV – verb of modality, PV – perception verb. The classification reflects the specific features of verbs, as they occur in the data, e.g., *read* is considered a VD, because its occurrence is limited to neutral reports of court procedure.

(<TH>) highest frequencies. This group is extremely problematic for reported speech analysis (cf. 4.3.1.4 and 4.3.1.5). To complicate matters even further, a verb of perception, *hear* (also in the legal meaning), has the 5th highest frequency. Quite surprising is also the common occurrence of *prove*, a copula of modality. On the whole the distribution of most frequent verbal tags determines some directions for analysis.

	<TH>	VERB TYPE	TOKENS	%	<N>	VERB TYPE	TOKENS	%
1	ſAY	VD	111	9,95	ſAY	VD	153	6,16
2	ſPEAK	VD	41	3,67	KNOW	MenV	93	3,74
3	KNOW	MenV	40	3,58	CONFEſS	SAV	85	3,42
4	PRAY	SAV	34	3,05	TELL	VD	64	2,58
5	HEAR	PV	24	2,15	HEAR	PV	62	2,50
6	CONFEſſ	SAV	18	1,61	PROVE	ModV	59	2,38
7	PROVE	ModV	18	1,61	READ	VD	53	2,13
8	TALK	VD	18	1,61	ſPEAK	VD	46	1,85
9	AUNſWER	VD	17	1,52	ANſWER	VD	43	1,73
10	REMEMBER	SAV	17	1,52	THINK	MenV	35	1,41
11	TRIE	SAV	16	1,43	DECLARE	SAV	33	1,33
12	WIL	MenV	16	1,43	PRAY	SAV	32	1,29
13	DECLARE	SAV	15	1,34	ACCUſE	SAV	25	1,01
14	READ	VD	15	1,34	MOV'D	SAV	25	1,01
15	THINK	MenV	15	1,34	CHARGE	SAV	24	0,97

Table 12: Most frequent verbal tags and percentages in <TH> and <N>

4.3.1 Reported speech as a marker of stance – a working assumption

The pragmatics of reported speech, as has been shown in the previous chapter, may surface in a range of forms resulting in a range of functions (cf. section 2.3.2.2.3.3). Most importantly, participants in discourse apply a range of reported speech strategies to negotiate their roles in communication. With respect to this, a crucial dimension of reporter's choice is attitude (Thompson 1996). It is proposed here that this aspect overlaps with a range of phenomena that can be referred to by a cover-term – *stance*[4] or *intersubjective positioning*. Following Precht (2003), *stance* is understood as "one way in which language encodes the interlocutors' relationship" (2003: 240). Biber (2004) defines *stance* as "epistemic or attitudinal comments on propositional information" (2004: 107, cf. Reilly et al. 2005 for a similar understanding).

---

[4] A wide range of phenomena is studied under this label, cf. Field (1997) on epistemic vs. affective stance; Mushin (2001b) on epistemological stance in cognitive linguistic; Kärkkäinen (2003) on epistemic stance as a pragmatic notion in spoken American English; Berman (2005) for a developmental analysis of a complex of issues referred to as discourse stance.

Studies of the phenomenon have been carried out under a range of different labels[5], all of them, according to Biber (2004), dealing with personal expression. Defined in this way, *stance* is related to modality and evidentiality. In a more narrow sense, studies in evidentiality (cf. section 2.3.2.4.1) talk about *a stance*. For instance, in the concluding chapter of a recent collection devoted to this issue cross-linguistically, Joseph claims (2003): "marking for evidentials involves the speaker's adopting a particular point of view – I hereby call this a *stance* – with regard to information sources" (2003: 308). Taking into consideration the expressive potential of a range of linguistic means which mark stance, the present study views the phenomenon not solely as an expression of speaker attitudes but, following e.g., White (2003), as possessing "dialogic functionality" (2003: 261), hence seen as an intersubjective rather than a purely subjective device. This is in accord with Martin (2003), who uses the term *appraisal*[6] for a range of interpersonal resources and points to the "social function of these resources, not simply as expressions of feeling but in terms of their ability to construct community – to align people in the ongoing negotiations of communal life" (2003: 171). The analysis of intersubjective stance allows, according to White (2003), tackling challenging issues of meaning in discourse, such as e.g., "how it is that the relations of status, power, social contact and solidarity are construed in the text" (White 2003: 260). These issues are of profound importance when analysing institutional data.

Moreover, it is claimed here that in terms of grammatical devices applied, reported speech – more often than not – is a means for the realisation of stance. This view is akin to that of Mushin (2001b) who claims, "most, if not all, languages will utilise reported speech representation, direct or otherwise, as the most explicit means of expressing the adoption of a reportive epistemological stance"[7] (Mushin 2001b: 70). The realisation of stance, in other words, is one of crucial pragmatic aspects of reported speech. Naturally, there are other linguistic means serving as markers of stance, such as e.g., adverbs and modal verbs, but the importance of phrases analysable as reported speech in this respect is undeniable. For instance, the findings of Kärkkäinen (2003) for present-day conversational American English show that 'epistemic phrases' (containing a verb potentially tagging reported speech) constitute over 60% of all markers of stance (2003: 36). Similarly, the findings presented in Biber (2004), a diachronic study of the full system of stance resources in English from 1650, show that in present-day

---

[5] The following terms occur in the literature: *evaluation, intensity, affect, evidentiality, hedging* (Biber 2004: 107, cf. also his references).

[6] Martin (2003) talks about a theory of affect comprising two basic sets of resources: engagement i.e., attributing appraisal to one source or another; and graduation, i.e. grading of the feelings themselves (cf. Martin 2003 for details).

[7] For Mushin (2001b), reportive epistemological stance is just one kind, other types being: personal experience, inferential, factual and imaginative.

English, complement clauses introduced by speech reporting verbs are most frequent stance-marking devices across registers. Although diachronically the frequency of complement clauses has been growing steadily, as Biber (2004) shows, one cannot exclude the possibility that complement clauses in the period analysed in this study were also significant, both as markers of stance and as reporting clauses. Thus, complement *that-* and *to-* clauses emerge as one of the most important ways of expressing stance (cf. remarks on the *de dicto* domain, section 4.2.2). Controlling verbs of these clauses are semantically classified in the following way:

That complement clauses
a. *That* clauses controlled by a verb (e.g., *we predict that the water is here*)
– non-factive verb
{commenting on how information is said/communicated}
add, announce, advise, answer, argue, allege, ask, assert, assure, charge, claim, confide, confess, contend, convey, convince, declare, demand, deny, emphasize, explain, express, forewarn, grant, hear, hint, hold, imply, inform, insist, maintain, mention, mutter, notify, order, persuade, petition, phone, pray, proclaim, promise, propose, protest, reassure, recommend, remark, remind, reply, report, respond, reveal, say, shout, state, stress, suggest, swear, teach, telephone, tell, urge, vow, warn, whisper, wire, write
– attitudinal verb
accept, admit, agree, anticipate, boast, complain, concede, cry, dream, ensure, expect, fancy, fear, feel, forget, foresee, guarantee, hope, mind, prefer, pretend, reflect, require, resolve, trust, wish, worry
– factive verb
acknowledge, affirm, ascertain, calculate, certify, check, conclude, confirm, decide, deem, demonstrate, determine, discover, find, know, learn, mean, note, notice, observe, prove, realize, recall, recognize, recollect, record, remember, see, show, signify, submit, testify, understand
– likelihood verb
appear, assume, believe, bet, conceive, consider, deduce, detect, doubt, estimate, figure, gather, guess, hypothesize, imagine, indicate, intend, perceive, postulate, predict, presuppose, presume, reckon, seem, sense, speculate, suppose, suspect, think, wager
*To-*clauses
a. *To-*clauses controlled by a verb (e.g., *He ordered to stay*)
– speech act verb
ask, advise, beg, beseech, call, claim, challenge, command, convince, decline, hear, invite, offer, pray, promise, prove, remind, report, request, say, show, teach, tell, urge, warn
– mental/cognition verb
assume, believe, consider, estimate, expect, be felt, find/be found, forget, hear, imagine, judge, know, learn, presume, pretend, remember, see, suppose, take, be thought, trust, understand, watch
– desire/intent/decision verb
aim, agree, bear, care, choose, consent, dare, decide, design, desire, dread, hate, hesitate, hope, intend, like, look, love, long, mean, need, plan, prefer, prepare, refuse, regret, resolve, schedule, stand, threaten, volunteer, (can't) wait, want, wish
– modality/cause/effort verb
afford, allow, appoint, arrange, assist, attempt, authorize, bother, cause, counsel, compel, defy, deserve, drive, elect, enable, encourage, endeavour, entitle, fail, forbid, force, get, help, inspire,

instruct, lead, leave, made/be made, manage, oblige, order, permit, persuade, prompt, require, raise, seek, strive, struggle, summon, tempt, try, venture
– probability/simple fact verb
appear, come, came, happen, seem, tend

Figure 8: Complete list of verbs occurring in the analysis of stance (adapted from Biber 2004: 133-135)

The above list does not exhaust the inventory of devices that can be used as markers of stance or signals of reported speech but – as will be shown below – it provides a sound basis for claiming that a considerable number of reported speech tokens in the analysed data are indeed markers of intersubjective *stance*. As a *stance*-expressing device, reported speech and its pragmatic function in general will be revealed as influencing "beliefs, attitudes, expectations and modes of interrelating" (White 2003: 259). The fact that this aspect of the phenomenon is crucial in the courtroom is not surprising and it is accepted here, following Matoesian (1999), that "when presenting their cases, attorneys and witnesses incorporate a number of interpersonal, linguistic and evidential strategies designed to persuade the fact-finder about the truthfulness of their claim" (1999: 492). This observation, although based on interaction in the present-day courtroom, is considered valid for its Early Modern English counterpart. Such a conjecture can be made on the grounds of the relatively unchanging social roles (disregarding, naturally, the changes in court organisation in the course of history, such as the introduction of the assumption of innocence or a defence lawyer) in this ancient institution i.e., the truth-seeking role of the court officials and the defending position of those standing trial.

A justification for the universality of these roles can be found in Luckmann's theory of the *communicative budget* (cf. Gloning 1999: 84-84, Knoblauch 2001: 24) which in the case of courtroom interaction has not changed substantially over the centuries. That is to say, the communicative problems in the courtroom, such as proving the defendant's guilt or providing arguments for their innocence, etc., are no different now from what they were in the Early Modern English period. The originally wide concept of *communicative budget* is seen here in a narrow sense, as the inventory of *communicative tasks* that have to be performed in a specific court case under analysis. Although the structure of *communicative acts* employed to equalise this specific *communicative budget* might have changed over the centuries, the stability of *communicative tasks* permits the assumption that reported speech strategies as markers of intersubjective *stance* may have been employed as means of equalising the courtroom's *communicative budget* in the past and that they continue to perform this function to this day. It is also possible to view the Early Modern English *communicative budget* in a much wider sense, regarding the courts of law "as instruments of social control, serving the interests of variously defined elites, while high levels of both civil and criminal litigation ... as evidence of an acutely conflict-ridden society" (Shepard 2004: 5-6).

4.3.1.1 Formulas and fixed phrases – some statistics

As has been mentioned above (section 4.1.2), legal language is formulaic. This feature surfaces also in the analysis of reported speech, as fixed expressions occur in reporting clauses or as potential instances of reported speech because they include verbs, nouns verbal nouns and adjectival phrases normally signalling speech and thought presentation. Characteristically for legal language, the so-called binomials (cf. Hiltunen 1996: 54-55) i.e., synonymous or complementary pairs of words, are frequent in both trials. Mellinkoff refers to this lexical feature as "the law's habit of doubling words" (1963: 121), though there also exist fixed phrases containing three or four complementary elements. Etymologically, binomials typically are bilingual phrases, with one element originating in Old English and the other in Latin or Old French. As the alliterative character of many of these suggests, the history of binomials goes back much further than the Norman Conquest, as these phrases have been commonly viewed as evidence of oral transmission of the law and devices of its "solemn recitation" (Hiltunen 1996: 26). As the functions of binomials are rhetorical, their constitutive elements are not viewed as separate reporting clauses even if one verb e.g., *debate*, as in the phrase DEBATED AND CONſIDER'D (<N>) typically tags reports of speech and the other, i.e., *consider*, typically reports of thought. The distinction into speech and thought presentation is based on the semantics of the first element or, alternatively, as in e.g., PREſENT AND ſAY (<N>), if one of the elements is not straightforwardly a reporting verb[8], it is bases on the less ambiguous element i.e., *say*. Except for binomials, there are also other fixed phrases characteristic for the legal discourse, as presented below (Tables 13-15).

	FIXED PHRASE	TOKENS	%	LEMMAS
BINOMIALS 47,82%	COMPAſſING AND IMAGINING(N)	2	2,90	
	COMPAſſING OR IMAGINING(N)	2	2,90	
	CONſERENCE AND ſENDING, BE	1	1,45	
	INDICTED AND ARAIGNED(1)	4	5,80	indicted and arraigned(1), indited and arraigned(2)
	ADUOW AND ſAY(1)	2	2,90	ſay and aduow(1)
	CHARGED AND ENJOYNED(1)	2	2,90	charged or called(1)
	CONſPIRE AND IMAGINE(1)	2	2,90	conſpire or talke(1)
	DEUIſE AND CONCLUDE(1)	2	2,90	deuiſe and conſpire(1)

---

[8] For the complexity not only of the semantic but also of legal interpretations of some verbal elements of binomials, cf. Barrell (1992, chapter 6).

	ALLEDGED AND PROUED	1	1,45	
	AUDITED AND ARREIGNED	1	1,45	
	DECLARED AND RECITED	1	1,45	
	EXPOUNDE AND EXPLAINE	1	1,45	
	ſAID AND LYED	1	1,45	
	FORGYUE AND FORGETTE	1	1,45	
	ſWEARE AND LYE	1	1,45	
	ILEARNE AND PROUE	1	1,45	
	IMPLIE AND ARGUE	1	1,45	
	INTIſE OR PROCURE	1	1,45	
	KNOWE AND HEARE	1	1,45	
	REMEMBRED AND LEARNED	1	1,45	
	TAKEN AND REPUTED	1	1,45	
	THINKE AND JUDGE	1	1,45	
	WARRANT AND ſIGNIFIE	1	1,45	
	WRITTEN AND CONFEſſED	1	1,45	
FORMULA 21,74%	HOW SAY YOU	15	21,74	ſaye(5), ſay(10)
VERB-ADJECTIVE COMBINATIONS 13,04%		7	10,14	proue giltie(1), proue guiltie(1),finde not guiltie(1), founde not giltie(1),founde not guiltie(2), finde guiltie(1)
		2	2,90	pleade not giltie(1),pleaded not guiltye(1)
ADJUNCTS 11,60%	AMOUNTING TO THIS EFFECT(1)(G), tending to this effect(1)(G)	2	2,90	
		2	2,90	read to this effect(1),was of this effect(1),
		4	5,80	ſaid as followeth(1), ſayde as here enſueth(1), had conference as enſueth(1), ratified as enſueth(1)
OTHER VERBAL PHRASES 5,8%	BEGIN TO READE	1	1,45	
	PLEADE	1	1,54	
	PROCLAMATION MADE	2	2,90	

Table 13: The distribution and classification of fixed phrases in <TH>

	FIXED PHRASE	TOKENS	%	LEMMAS
BINOMIALS (57,67%)				
ADJUNCTS	ſPAKE AND ſAID THUS	4	3,60	ſpake and ſaid to this effect(1), produced and read as followeth(2)
	BEGAN AND ſAID TO THIS EFFECT	2	1,80	
GERUNDS	KNOWING AND UNDERSTANDING (G)	4	3,60	
	IMAGINING AND PRACTIſING(G)	1	0,90	

NOUNS	IMAGINING AND CONfPIRING(N)	1	0,90	
	COMPAfflNG AND BRINGING TO PAfS(N)	1	0,90	
	INTENTION AND DEflGN(N)	1	0,90	
	MEfTAGE AND COMMIfflON(N)	1	0,90	
	PROMIfE AND PROTEfTATION(N)	1	0,90	
VERBAL PHRASES	PREfENT AND fAY	6	5,41	
	ADVANCE AND MAINTAIN	2	1,80	
	CLAIM AND PRETEND	2	1,80	
	PAUfED AND fAID	2	1,80	
	ADVIfED AND AGREED	1	0,90	
	AGREED AND fET DOWN	1	0,90	
	COMMANDED AND CHARGED	1	0,90	
	COMPOfED AND WRIT	1	0,90	
	CONfPIRED AND PRACTIfED	1	0,90	
	DEBATED AND CONfIDER'D	1	0,90	
	DECLARED AND ANfWERED	1	0,90	
	DENY'D AND RENOUNCED	1	0,90	
	DEPOfED OR fAID	1	0,90	
	DETEfT AND ABHOR	1	0,90	
	fAID AND AFFIRMED	1	0,90	
	fEARCH AND CONfIDER	1	0,90	
	FORBID AND PROHIBITED	1	0,90	
	fOUGHT AND ENDEAVOUR'D	1	0,90	
	HEAR AND CERTIFY	1	0,90	
	IMAGINED AND COMPAfTED	1	0,90	
	IMAGINE OR COMPAfS	1	0,90	
	INfPECTED AND READ	1	0,90	
	INfTITUTED AND ORDAIN'D	1	0,90	
	INVENTED OR DEVIS'D	1	0,90	
	KNEW AND UNDERSTOOD	1	0,90	
	OUTLAW'D AND ATTAINTED	1	0,90	
	PRETENDED CLAIM AND TITLE	1	0,90	
	PRODUC'D AND READ	2	1,80	produced and read(1)
	PUBLIfH'D AND PROCLAIM'D WAR	1	0,90	
	REPORT AND JUfTIFY	1	0,90	
	REQUIRED AND WILLED	1	0,90	
	REVOK'D OR RENOUNC'D	1	0,90	
	WHIfPER'D AND fHEW'D	1	0,90	
	WRIT AND COMPOS'D	1	0,90	
NON-FINITE PHRASE (past participle)	DISCONTENTED AND NOT fATISFY'D	1	0,90	
NP+VP	CARRIETH PROOF AND CONfENT	1	0,90	
	LAID CLAIM AND PRETENDED	1	0,90	

110 Chapter Four

	MADE OYER AND PROCLAMATION	1	0,90	
TRINOMIALS (9,01%)				
	CONſPIRED CONſENTED AND AGREED	1	0,90	
	CONſPIRED IMAGIN'D AND GONEABOUT	1	0,90	
	CONVEY'D DECLAR'D AND COMMUNICATED	1	0,90	
	DECLARE ſHEW AND AFFIRM	1	0,90	
	IMAGIN'D COMPAſS'D AND CONſPIR'D	1	0,90	
	IMAGINED DEVIſED AND CONſPIRED	1	0,90	
	IMAGIN'D DEVIS'D AND PRACTIS'D	1	0,90	
	OUTLAW'D ATTAINTED OR INDICTED	1	0,90	
GERUND	INTENDING WILLING AND DEſIRING(G)	1	0,90	
NOUN	IMAGINATION COMPAſſING AND CONſPIRACY(N)	1	0,90	
FOURNOMIALS (1,8%)				
	CONſENTED CONſULTED ADVIſED AND PROCURED	1	0,90	
	ſOUGHT IMAGIN'D COMPAſS'D AND PRACTIſED	1	0,90	
FORMULA 2,7%	ſAY	3	2,70	ſayeſt(1),ſay'ſt(1)
VERB-ADJECTIVE COMBIATIONS 9,01%	PLEADED NOT GUILTY	10	9,01	prove guilty(2), found guilty(3)
ADJUNCTS 12,61%	MADE OYER AND PROCLAIM'D THUS	5	4,50	made an oyes and proclaim'd thus(1)
	TO THIS EFFECT(N)	5	4,50	tended to the effect(1), read to the ſame effect(1), ſpake to this effect(1), tending to the effect (1)(g)
	IS AS FOLLOWETH	3	2,70	made proclamation as followeth(1), produc'd examination as followeth(1)
	AS FOLLOWETH	1	0,90	
OTHER VERBAL PHRASES 3,6%		4	3,60	produced(1), proclaim'd war(1), proclamation made(2)
NOUNS 3,6%	ITEM(N)	4	3,60	

Table 14: Distribution and classification of fixed phrases in <N>

	TOTAL FIXED PHRASES	FIGURE NORMALISED PER 10,000 WORDS	% OF TOTAL TAGS	VERB	ADJECTIVE OR VERB ADJECTIVE COMBINATION	GERUND	NOUN
<TH>	69	42,2	6,18%	**78,26%**	13,04%	2,9%	5,8%
<N>	111	25,9	4,47%	**74,75%**	9,01%	6,31%	9,92%
DR			1,63				

Table 15: A comparison of the distribution and tag categories of fixed phrases in both trials

The DR (Table 15, cf. section 3.5.1) at 1,63 shows that <TH> is more formulaic than <N>. The results as to the grammatical category of tags are similar for both trials, with a particularly insignificant difference between the frequencies of verbal reporting tags (gerundival phrases viewed separately). The distribution of the fixed phrases in the trials is clustered at the beginning and at the end coinciding with the reading of the indictment and verdict. On the whole, as can be concluded on the basis of dispersion plots, in <TH> fixed phrases are more evenly distributed than in <N>. This is due to the fact that the successful defendant occasionally employs them in his speech, also when quoting legal sources with which he is well acquainted, while in <N> the majority of legal fixed phrases are used in the reports of court procedure.

4.3.1.2 Pragmatic aspects of formulas and fixed phrases

This section is devoted to a discussion of some more fixed phrases, which – unlike the majority discussed above – are not unambiguous in speech and thought presentation. As Moon (1994: 126) observes, fixed expressions may perform a variety of textual functions, such as conveying new information and the speaker's/writer's evaluation or attitude, modalising (conveying attitude to the truth value of an utterance) and organising functions. Accompanying the choice of fixed expressions, as Moon claims (1994: 117), there is a meaningful decision on the side of a language user. As such fixed expressions have important bearing on interaction both in speech and writing. Often, fixed phrases function as introductory words, syntactically not connected to the sentence and moreover "many of these are codified or formulaic" (Grenoble 2004: 1956). Not infrequently the degree of conventionalisation of a given expression as well as its textual functions may provide grounds for excluding it from reported speech analysis, despite the presence of a verbal signal of reported speech. According to Aijmer (1996: 214-215), there is a formal test to which many fixed phrases with a modalising function could be put in order to verify their propositional content.

Unlike propositional elements, "speech-act adverbials[9] cannot be the focus of a so-called cleft construction" (Aijmer 1996: 212). Some other formal tests may be based on whether the element may be a focus of an alternative *or*-question or a negative sentence (Aijmer 1997: 4). Nevertheless, formal criteria are not always sufficient to fully justify classification decisions although they will definitely provide clues as to the distinction between true reporting clauses in direct speech and speech act adverbials. For instance, Quirk et al. (1985) propose some parallels between reporting clauses in direct speech and comment clauses[10] (i.e. hedges, parentheticals) and many other adverbials. Still, unlike speech act adverbials, propositional reporting clauses can be made into the subject complements of pseudo-cleft constructions (Quirk et al. 1985: 1022-1023). Table 16 below presents the occurrences of problematic fixed verbal phrases in the material:

VERBAL PHRASE	NUMBER OF OCCURRENCES
that is to say	9 <TH>
how say you	9 <TH>, 3 <N>
may it please you	<TH> 19, <N> 7
I pray you	32 <TH>, 11 <N>
I beseech you	<N> 18

Table 16: Problematic fixed verbal phrases in <TH> and <N>

The following sections provide an illustration of the instances of some of these expressions in the analysed texts and an interpretation from the point of view of a pragmatic analysis of reported speech.

4.3.1.2.1 *that is to say*

According to *OED* the phrase is used to:

> "introduce a more explicit or intelligible re-statement of what immediately precedes, or a limiting clause necessary to make the statement correct. Sometimes used sarcastically to introduce a statement of the real fact which a quoted statement misrepresents or euphemistically veils" (*OED say*, v[1], B, 4b).

The phrase is similar to *so to say*, identified by Quirk et al. (1985: 618) as an adverbial disjunct used as a hedge to provide a metalinguistic comment. The majority of instances are of a type quoted below:

---

[9] Speech-act adverbials are a subgroup of discourse markers which are boundaries in discourse, while the name indicates their adverbial function in the sentence (Ajimer 1996: 203).
[10] A definition by Quirk et al.: "comment clauses are parenthetical disjuncts. They may occur, initially, or medially, and thus generally have a separate tone unit" (1985: 1112).

(25) RTA [I will ſuppoſe *Vaughan* to be in as good Condition as any other Man here, FORMULA [that is to ſay], an uncon-demn'd Man.

Among the instances of the phrase there are two which indeed include quotation or reference to the authority of legal documents on which the trial relies. These references are, however, introduced by other tags and *that is to say* cannot be interpreted as serving the tagging function:

(26) RTA [Here may you ſee RSA DO SUP [this Statute doth referre all the Offences afore-ſayde, to the Statute of the xxv. of *Edward* III.]] DS [which Statute hath theſe Wordes touching and concerning the Treaſons RSA PASS [that I am indited and arraigned of;] FORMULA [that is to ſaye], RTA DO SUP [Whoſoeuer doth compaſſe or imagine the Death of the King], or leuie War againſt the King in his Realm, or being adherent to the Kings Enimies within this Realme, or elſewhere, and bee thereof probably attainted by open Deede by People of their Con-dicion, ſhall be adjudged a Traytor.]
(27) *Throckmorton.* My Caſe doth differ, RSA PAR [I graunt,] but ſpecially bicauſe I haue not ſuche a Judge: yet there is another cauſe to reſtraine theſe your ſtrange and extraordinarie Conſtructions; FORMULA [that is to ſay,] a Prouiſo in the latter ende of the Statute of *Edwarde the* Thirde, DS GERUND [hauyng theſe Wordes: Provided always, if any other Caſe of ſuppoſed Treaſon ſhall chaunce hereafter to come in Question or Trial before any Juſtice...]

According to Visser (1966: 1484), *that is to say* is a set phrase in PDE but formerly, next to *that*, other nominal and pronominal subjects could be used. Moreover, there existed a possibility of inserting adverbial adjuncts or *for to* between the infinitive and the auxiliary (1966: 1484-86). Such flexibility is not a feature of the construction in the analysed material and, moreover, its propositional value does not go beyond *that is*, rendering *say* redundant in the phrase. Rydén (1970) sees the expression as "the interpolated explanatory phrase" (1970: 18). One of many formulas occurring in the legal language, the syntactically fixed *that is to say* in the analysed court records does not fall under reported speech as it in fact does not introduce instances of speech or thought presentation. Consequently the occurrences of the verb *to say* in this phrase are excluded from the word counts of verbal reporting tags.

4.3.1.2.2 *how say you*

According to *OED*, the use of *how* in the phrase became archaic in PDE and its equivalent nowadays would be "*what?*", while formerly it was used to mean: "To what effect? With what meaning? Also, By what name?" (*OED how,* adv. (n³), A, 3). None of the examples quoted in *OED* is similar to the typical instances found in the data. The most recent example quoted in *OED* comes from Shakespere.

The phrase is still used in the legal and parliamentary discourse as well as in some other registers, though in the latter case it is clearly marked as obsolescent, sentimental or ironic. The majority of instances are of a type quoted below, where the phrase occurs as a semantically superfluous, syntactically fixed question introducer:

(28) <TH>
Sendall. $_{RSA\,Q}$ [How ſay you], $_{DA}$ [*Cutbert Vaughan,*] is this your own Confeſſion, $_{RSA\,Q}$ [and wil you abide by all that is here written?]]

In the Norfolk trial, the phrase occurs in the following shape:

(29) <N>
$_{RSA\,Q}$ [How ſay'ſt thou], $_{DA}$ [*Thomas* Duke of *Norfolk*], art thou guilty of theſe Treaſons $_{RSA\,PASS}$ [whereof thou art indicted]

Or in one case:

(30) <N>
$_{DA}$ [My Lord *De la Ware*], $_{RSA\,Q}$ [What ſay you], Is the Priſoner guilty of theſe Treaſons or not?

The distribution of the phrase suggests that it has a well-defined function in the legal procedure: except for two cases it is uttered by the attorney or jury members to emphasise the force of the following question and possibly imply hesitation on the side of the witness. This rhetorical function emphasising institutional power relations is strengthened by a direct address which follows the phrase in over half of the instances. Most occurrences cluster in the early stage of witness' examination and nearly half of all instances are utterance launchers (cf. Biber et al. 1999: 1073). The accused and a witness only use it once each in consecutive turns in a confrontational dialogue:

(31) <TH>
    a. $_{RSA\,Q}$ [How ſay you] $_{DA}$ [M. *Throckmorton,*] was there any diſpleaſure betwene you and me, to $_{RSA\,INF}$ [moue me $_{RSA\,INF}$ [to ſay aught againſt you]]?]
    b. *Throckmorton.* $_{RTA}$ [Not, that I know]: $_{RSA\,Q}$ [how ſay you $_{DA}$ [*Vaughan,*] what Acquaint-ance was there between you and me, and what Letters of Credit, or To-ken did you bring me from *Wyat* or any other to $_{RSA\,INF}$ [moue me $_{RSA\,INF}$ [to truſt you]?]

There are two cases when the phrase is not redundant, constituting a question itself:

(32) <TH>
   a. *Attourney.* Yea, ₍ₐ [Sir], but ᵣₛₐ ᵩ [how <u>fay</u> you to the taking of the Tower of *London,* which is Treafon?]
   b. *Hare.* But ᵣₛₐ ᵩ [how <u>fay</u> you to this, ₙᵣₛₐ [that *Wyat* and you <u>had Conference</u> togither fundry times at *Warner's* Houfe, and in other places?]]

In fact, it is only in the two instances above that the phrase has the illocutionary force of a question (*how fay you to*), while in the remaining cases structurally it only frames the actual question bearing no syntactic relation to it. In all cases, however, the verb *to say* does not unambiguously denote the prospective act of *saying*, though it clearly predicts a verbal reply, as the phrase could be well substituted for *what is your response to*. Given the formulaic character of the phrase, its semantic redundancy and discourse initiating function, it cannot be viewed as a reporting clause. In the speech and thought presentation cline, the phrase constitutes a separate RSA, as it invokes a statement on the side of the addressee and emphasises its subjective character even prior to its occurrence. The function of *say* in this phrase is thus closer to the function of a speech act verb, since it is an indirect way of demanding an opinion/assertion. Therefore its instances are incorporated into the inventory of tags in the analysis but will be marked as F, accounting for their occurrence within a formulaic phrase. Findings concerning this phrase can be compared to what Brown and Gilman (1989) have to say about *what can you say?* in the Shakespeare corpus. In their opinion, the phrase is interrogative only grammatically when preceding an imperative and "as a speech act it is a directive or command having the exact sense of the subsequent imperative" (Brown and Gilman 1989: 182).

4.3.1.2.3 *may it please you*

OED notes the following use of the expression in the earlier periods: "usual in deferential phrases of address or request" and "a courteous qualification to a request" (*OED please,* v. I, 3b). Brown and Gilman refer to the "magical function" (1989: 182) of the phrase and incorporate it in the list of "request verbs". Tiersma (1999: 67) includes it in the inventory of impersonal constructions with *you* substituted for *with the court* in present-day legalese used as a way of starting an argument presented to judges. Allen (1995) quotes some examples from Shakespeare where the formula is a polite device mitigating contradictions both between socially equal and asymmetrical interlocutors (Allen 1995: 289) as well as a way of expressing a wish which can be fulfilled if the experiencer allows it to happen (Allen 1995: 290-1). Indeed, in the Shakespeare corpus Busse (2002) sees the expression in terms of a polite request concerning a felicity condition on the part of the hearer (2002: 21). In the analysed data, the majority of instances involve the use of a direct address (in <TH>, for instance, direct address fails to appear twice only), strengthening the expression of deference on the side of witnesses or the attorney and the jury towards judges or other representatives of legal authority:

(33) <TH>
Throckmorton. FORMULA May it pleafe you DA [my Lords and Maifters,] RSA PASS [which be au-thorifed by the Queenes Commiffion to be Judges this day], RSA INF [to giue me leaue RSA INF [to fpeake a fewe words, which doth both concerne you and me],]

Furthermore, in the majority of instances an infinitival clause follows the formula, making it clearly a way of performing a request as in the example above. The request may also be realised by means of a *that*-clause, rendering the utterance even more formal:

(34) <TH>
Throckmorton. DA [My Lords,] fhall it FORMULA pleafe you that RSA [I fhal anfwer?]

In the trial of Throckmorton, the syntactic flexibility of the phrase is restricted to the inversion of the introductory modal verb as in (33), its occasional omission (twice) and substitution of *may* with *shall* (twice), *if* (once) or *might* (once). In 13 cases, the formula has the discourse organising function of launching a turn in dialogue. A more conspicuous deviation from the fixed pattern is observed twice, when in the place of the *you* experiencer a proper noun occurs:

(35) <TH>
fo it might FORMULA pleafe hir Excellent Majeftie RSA [to purge me in hir priuate Judgemente,] RSA [and both for-gyue and forgette my ouer rafhe Boldeneffe, that I vfed in RSA NOUN [Talke of hir Highneffe Marriage] with the Prince of *Spaine*, Matters too farre aboue my Capacitie, and I very vnable RTA INF [to confider the Gravitie therof];]

In both cases the request following the formula is addressed to the queen who is not present in the courtroom, hence she cannot be referred to directly. Furthermore, the formula may be syntactically completely independent and hence redundant as in the following example:

(36) <TH>
Stanford. And it FORMULA pleafe you, DA [my Lords], RTA [I doubt not IS INF [to proue evi-dently and manifeftly, that *Throckmorton* is worthely and rightly RSA PASS [indicted and araigned of thefe Treafons,]

Here it is clearly a polite and formulaic device to start a turn and express deference to the members of the jury.

The expression under analysis is not equally common in the trial of Norfolk where it is also more flexible syntactically. The second person experiencer, with one exception, is substituted for a proper noun, as in (35). Thus, the pattern with direct address does not occur, while the utterance launching function is not dominant as it only occurs twice. Moreover, a request is performed only twice, while the remaining instances express a wish like in the following example:

(37) <N>
to the Intent $_{FORMULA}$ it may pleafe your Majefty $_{RTA\ INF}$ [to confider of them]

There are, however, two instances similar to (36) where the phrase is syntactically not linked to what follows. The possibility of syntactic independence justifies viewing the phrase as a fixed formula, also in the trial of Norfolk, despite its relative syntactic flexibility.

Semantically the expression does not allow viewing it as an example of speech or thought presentation, despite the presence of a mental verb expressing affective attitude or – as in the case of *how say you* – as a self-sufficient instance of RSA. Therefore the phrase is excluded from reported speech analysis. As far as the verb *to please* is concerned, there is one instance which is interpretable as a report of thought, meaning 'think proper' (as in *OED please*, v. I, 3c, 1594):

(38) *Duke.* I fhall hardly come, after fo fmooth a Tale $_{RSA}$ [as Mr. Attorney of the Wards can tell]; yet one good $_{IS\ NP}$ [Proof I have to my Comfort, that they be as $_{RTA}$ [pleafe your Lordfhips $_{RTA\ INF}$ [to weigh them]].]

4.3.1.3 Verb semantics vs. discourse markers

There are numerous instances in the analysed data when verbs, which semantically may function as predicates of reporting clauses, show features of the phenomena typical of oral discourse i.e., discourse markers[11]. The not infrequent occurrence of these in the analysed data is indeed indicative of the speech-based nature of the latter. On the whole, the field of study of discourse markers is too broad to be summarised in this discussion, neither is it possible to account for the diversity of their form and function[12]. Still, it has to be emphasised that their role in discourse is crucial. Fuller (2003) points out that discourse markers are means of marking or negotiating speaker roles in discourse (cf. section 4.3.1 above), which is an important observation to be borne in mind in any institutional

---

[11] Cf. Brinton (1996: 29) for a range of names used in the literature for this concept. Notice that terms *hedge* and *parenthetic phrase* may be used as synonyms. A good overview of terms, including a taxonomy of descriptive terms and different classifications of individual items is given in Fischer (2000: 13-15).

[12] Cf. Brinton (1996) and the references. For a recent analysis of discourse markers within relevance theory, see Blakemore (2002). Other recent monographs include Andersen (2001), taking a developmental perspective within relevance theory; Onodera (2004) on Japanese discourse markers in synchronic and diachronic perspectives; Aijmer (2002) on a subset of pragmatic markers, i.e. discourse particles.

situation. As for their significance in reported speech, Sakita (2002) differentiates three ways in which speakers manipulate discourse markers in speech and thought representation:

> "(1) as modality or attitudinal indicators, in order to reconstruct reported speaker's attitudes; (2) as markers of speaker-hearer intentions and relationships, in order to reconstitute the reported speaker's intentions and their relationships; and (3) as instructions on how given utterances are to be processed" (Sakita 2002: 101).

Bearing their functional potential in mind, the focus of this study on pragmatic markers will be limited to the area in which they overlap with reported speech or, more specifically, when discourse markers occur in the form of a verbal predicate – a potential tag. Thus, a range of verbal phrases fulfil some criteria of discourse markers, i.e. firstly, the syntactic condition of independence[13] or loose connection to other clauses; secondly, optionality i.e., removal of a discourse marker does not render the sentence ungrammatical; and thirdly, the lack of propositional meaning or of the capacity to create meaning, accompanied with a clearly subjective or intersubjective function (Brinton 1996: 34). According to Jucker (2002: 213), it is the semantic level at which the status of a discourse marker may be confirmed. Unfortunately, only prototypical discourse markers, such as *well*, are semantically unambiguously empty, while the more marginal ones, as the author further maintains (Jucker 2002: 213), e.g., *you know*, have some residue of propositional meaning. Suffice it to say that in most cases, subjective decisions are made with respect to the criteria, as – clearly – each criterion involves a degree of fuzziness. Also the diachronic aspect of discourse markers will have to be taken into account in the present study because – as is commonly known – these phenomena are products of grammaticalisation or pragmaticalisation (cf. Aijmer 1997) and the degree of advancement in these processes is a crucial factor in the interpretation. For example, in present-day English *be like* is problematic in this respect as an instance of "quotative complementisers" (Brinton 1996: 62), which are not clearly verbs of saying, or which are verbs of saying but some controversy remains as to whether they are reporting clauses or not.

Discourse markers are not at all discussed in Leech and Short's model (1981), nor in the latest contribution applying the model (Semino and Short 2004), which is a serious shortcoming. Therefore, as another emendation of the model, ample attention will be devoted to clarifying some controversial matters concerning verbs as tags. The feature of discourse markers which is most difficult to accommodate within the Leech and Short model (1981), and possibly in the majority of approaches to speech and thought presentation, is the fact that quoting

---

[13] According to Aijmer "Discourse markers ... have a unique position as metalinguistic elements because they are placed in a special 'discourse marker slot' which is external to the proposition proper in the underlying syntactic phrase-marker" (1996: 207).

involves projection and hypotaxis (Halliday 1985) or, more generally, the framing of one discourse level into another (cf. section 2.5) i.e., "inserting one text into another" (Caldas-Coulthard 1994: 295). In any case, there exists a relationship between a tag and a report and the fact that this relationship is syntactically not realised in the case of discourse markers explains why reported speech categorisation models do not account for them. Finally, one more factor which adds to the complex overlap of reporting verbs with discourse markers is the issue of modality or, more specifically, its epistemic and evidential types. Most generally, following Fairclough (2003), modality[14] is seen "in terms of a relationship between speaker or writer, or 'author', and representations" (2003: 164). This definition, being one of many, is particularly well-phrased for the purpose of the present study, as it emphasises the importance of modality for reported speech which after all is nothing else but a way of verbalising speaker's, writer's or author's representations.

4.3.1.3.1 Parentheticals[15]

Discourse markers of interest for this study are parenthetical verbal expressions. Not all parenthetical expressions identified here, however, are discourse markers. As to a definition of a parenthetical, there is not much consensus in the literature (cf. Grenoble 2004 who gives an overview of approaches to this phenomenon). As Grenoble (2004) argues, this class cannot be defined structurally but functionally, as parentheticals "serve clear pragmatic functions, and are united in operating on a distinct discourse plane" (Grenoble 2004: 1954). In her discussion of parentheticals in contemporary Russian, the author abides by an all-inclusive view of the phenomenon and provides arguments for the affinity of parentheticals and reported speech as both involving changes in *footing* (cf. Goffman 1981; sections 2.6). The arguments for this view are drawn particularly from the fact that the prosodic contour[16] of statements including parentheticals is very similar to that of reported speech. Because no evidence of prosody is offered by the data investigated here, there are no grounds to uncritically include parentheticals within speech and thought presentation. Rather, the contrary view is advocated

---

[14] It is common to see modality in a more narrow sense, as e.g., in Palmer (2001: 1) as being "concerned with the status of the proposition that describes the event", i.e. narrowing the notion down to the truth-value of the proposition or the source of asserted information. Cf. also Palmer (2003) and the other contributions to the recent collection devoted to modality in present-day English (Facchinetti et al. 2003). A wider scope of interest i.e., modality in Germanic languages, is the topic of contributions to Swan and Westvik (1997).

[15] As far as the syntax of parentheticals is concerned, Fludernik (1993: 164-170) provides an overview of approaches and is not without interesting comments on their functioning in free indirect discourse.

[16] Actually, the prosodic marking of parentheticals is not unambiguously comparable to that of reported speech, as is pointed out in Blakemore (2005: 1167).

here i.e., parentheticals are not to be accepted as quotative forms. Unlike quotative forms, parentheticals are problematic and rarely straightforward for reported speech analysis, hence considerable space is devoted to providing a coherent view of parentheticals against reported speech phenomena.

As with discourse markers, parentheticals are not incorporated in the most recent developments of Leech and Short's (1981) model. For instance, Semino and Short (2004), who refer to them three times within their book-length account, reveal a comprehension of the notion which is rather different from the one central to this study. Namely, the authors give the following instances of reported speech, as including parenthetical clauses (Semino and Short 2004: 164, 192):

 a. Myers, the radio operator on duty, sounded annoyed: **every radio operator**, the tone of his voice said, **should be as expert** and efficient as he was.
 b. **The painting was proof**, he said, **that Modigliani detested him.**

In the example (a), the parenthetical status of the *the tone of his voice said* clause gives rise to the authors' uncertainty as to whether they should categorise the emboldened report as a FIS or IS. Similarly, in (b) the lack of grammatical subordination of the emboldened clause to the reporting parenthetical clause leads to portmanteau tagging, ambiguous between FIS and IS. The concluding decision with respect to similar cases is to abide by the portmanteau tagging, at the same time indicating the status of the reported clauses as intermediary between IS and FIS. It is hard to resist the impression that the problem the authors point out here is actually non-existent. In both instances, what is dealt with is the so-called intercalation of the reporting clause i.e., instead of the typical initial position it is placed sentence-medially. In fact placing reporting clauses in variable positions with respect to the reported clause does not affect the category of a given reported speech instance, although it has important consequences in discourse (cf. e.g., Collins 2001). Thus, from the point of view of the introductory discussion of parentheticals carried out above, what Semino and Short (2004) understand under the concept does not at all correspond to any of the understandings referred to in this study.

There are a range of parenthetical expressions in the data under analysis, hence for the sake of clarity the illustration of the phenomenon falls into two parts, of which the first one is devoted to those parentheticals in which a speech act verb[17] occurs, while the second to the so-called KNOW-verbs, i.e. most generally, referring to cognition. Two groups have a clear semantic affinity, as is observed by Wierzbicka (1987), and there is no denying the fact that "speech acts

---

[17] Speech act verbs and their functions have been variously defined but the following statement of Wierzbicka (1987) is accepted here: "the primary function of speech act verbs consists in **interpreting** people's speech acts, not in **performing** speech acts" (1987: 16, emphasis original).

exteriorize the speaker's mental acts and mental states" (Wierzbicka 1987: 15). The following sections provide a more comprehensive description of two speech act parentheticals, including their syntactic structure, with many points in the following description being valid also for KNOW-verbs to be discussed in due course.

4.3.1.3.2 *I pray you*

Two problems are connected with this expression: its complex historical development involving grammaticalisation to a polite marker *pray* and a range of lexical uses of the verb *to pray* which need to be distinguished from its semantically faded uses. According to *OED* the phrase is "used parenthetically to add instance or deference to a question or request" (*OED pray,* v. IV, 8a; cf. Jucker 2002: 224). Traugott and Dasher (2002: 253) add that this function also implies that the speaker/writer is paying special attention to the image needs of the addressee/respondent. As a parenthetical expression, Early Modern English *I pray you* may be viewed as falling within one set with Middle English expressions (e.g., *I gesse*) analysed by Brinton (1996) defined as:

> "containing first-person pronouns (or oblique pronouns, in the case of impersonal constructions) and verbs expressing supposition, inference, expectation or belief – what I will call KNOW-verbs – generally in the simple present tense, verbs which in other contexts require that-complementation" (Brinton 1996: 211).

The similarity between the development of epistemic parentheticals and *I pray you* has, for instance, been pointed out by Akimoto (2000: 77). Structurally, as Brinton (1996: 212) further claims, these parentheticals (first-person epistemic parentheticals, as the author refers to them) have many features of pragmatic markers, such as optionality, high frequency, fixed form, position outside the syntactic clause and little contribution to the propositional meaning. One of the functions of parentheticals indeed is the expression of emotional attitudes, as noted by *OED* (the earliest parenthetical usage noted dates from 1519). Moreover, just as in the case of the deferential uses noted in *OED*, these parentheticals are speaker-oriented and they have an interpersonal function. *I pray you* is just one of the epistemic parentheticals occurring in the analysed material and posing problems as to the status in speech and thought presentation. Not unlike some fixed phrases discussed above, first-person epistemic parentheticals are syntactically unbound and perform discoursal functions; hence their ability to introduce speech or thought reports is disputable. Furthermore, the 'truncation' of parentheticals as their syntactic incompleteness, referred to by Knowles (1980), allows drawing conclusions about their logical structure i.e., that parentheticals as one-place predicates lack a sentential complement (Knowles 1980: 397). That is to say, parentheticals do not bear any syntactic relationship whatsoever to the clause to which they are attached.

Traugott and Dasher (2002: 224) see the history of *I pray you* as the development from a performative[18] expression, through a parenthetical to a marker of politeness (adverbial). The authors see the phrase as an instance of social deictics "directly encoding within their semantic structures the conceptualized relative social standing (superiority/inferiority, (non)intimacy, ingroup versus outgroup status, etc.) of a participant" (Traugott and Dasher 2002: 225). The function of a social deictic expression *I pray you* is confirmed by the data. In the trial of Throckmorton, the defendant uses the expression (26 out of 32 occurrences) when addressing the court, the jury or the attorney as in examples (42) a, b and d. Out of the remaining 6 uses, 4 fall to the attorney who addresses his professional superiors, or the jury, whose approval he is seeking as his professional task:

(39) <TH>
    a. *Attourney.* RTA [Bycaufe you of the Jury the better may credite him], RSA PAR [I pray you DA [my Lords] let *Vaughan* RSA PASS [be fworn.]]
    b. *Attourney.* RSA PAR [I pray you DA [my Lorde Chiefe Juftice] RSA IMP [repeate the Euidence for the Queene,] RSA IMP [and giue the Jurie their Charge,]] for the Prifoner will keepe you here all day.

In a single example a jury member Cholmeley is provoked by Throckmorton to address him and phrase his question in the following way:

(40) <TH>
    Throckmorton, ... Ah, ah Maifter *Cholmely*, will this foule packing neuer be left?
    Cholmeley, Why what do I, RSA PAR Q [I pray you,] DA [M. *Throckmorton*]?

In this instance the phrase is used ironically or in a challenging way and cannot be viewed as an instance of a social deictic. This application, however, involving layered pragmatic and rhetorical functions, points to the polysemous nature of the fixed expression and its advanced semantic bleaching. In the trial of Norfolk, only half of the instances of the phrase are used by the defendant himself and are thus straightforwardly deferential, as in (43) b. There are two instances when the expression is uttered by the attorney and one by jury member, Wilbraham, both of which precede an interrogative and emphasise the forcefulness of the question, as in (43) c. Of the two remaining cases, one use occurs in the ending of a letter

---

[18] On the whole, issues of performativity and illocutionary force have been the central concerns of pragmatics since the appearance of the concept of a speech act. The interest for these in this study is, however, marginal, and no general claims are made in this respect. For interesting points, cf. e.g., Fraser (1975), Traugott and Dasher (2002).

quoted in court and is thus definitely a polite marker, and the other in a quotation of a servant's words to his master, as in the following example:

(41) <N>
This Money was delivered to one *Browne* of *Shrewfbury*, by one of the Duke's Servants, one *Hickford*; ~DS~ [who faid to *Browne, Here is* 50 *l*. ~DS~ [~RSA PAR~ [*I pray you help that it Be conveyed to Mr.* Ban-nifter's *Dwelling near* Shrewsbury].]

The findings presented above go against what has been established by Kryk-Kastovsky (1998, 2002) in the analysis of court records from 1685. Unlike in the data analysed here, the grammaticalised *pray* over a hundred years later is used mostly by the interrogators in the questioning procedure. Jucker (2002) does not find this surprising, as in his opinion "the defendants and the witnesses are not in a position to ask questions, and therefore there is no need for them to use these discourse markers" (Jucker 2002: 225). Contrary to this the use of *I pray you* in questions is rare in the material analysed here, so the above views cannot be corroborated. Different application of the expression may be due to the fact that the earlier stage of the development of the phrase i.e., that of the epistemic parenthetical, is found in the data analysed in this study; unlike as in Kryk-Kastovsky (1998, 2002), the grammaticalised *pray*.

As far as the differences between performative and parenthetical uses of the phrase throughout history are concerned, Traugott and Dasher (2002: 252-253) make several remarks that are extremely helpful here. Thus, only the clause-internal or -final position makes the phrase unambiguously parenthetical, while the initial position may also be connected with performative use, although the initial position very often introduces a directive[19] or interrogative. The parenthetical use of *I pray you* in the analysed data conforms to the pattern observed by Traugott and Dasher (2002) i.e., in the total of 43 parenthetical uses, 37 involve an imperative following or, less frequently, preceding the phrase, and the remaining 6 – an interrogative – as in the examples below:

(42) <TI>
a. *Throckmorton.* ~DA~ [My Lords,] ~RSA PAR~ [I pray you] make not too much hafte with me, neither thinke not long for your Diner ...
b. and then ~RSA PAR~ [I pray you of the Jury], ~RSA IMP~ [judge better than Maifter Sergeante doth.]
c. Firft ~RSA PAR~ [I pray you] ~RTA IMP~ [remember the fmall Familiaritie betwixt *Vaughan* and me, as ~RSA~ [he hathe auowed before you].]

---

[19] The function is that of a polite request. According to Busse (2002), *I pray you* is less polite in this function than *may it please you*, as the former expression asserts the sincerity of the speaker, while the later asks for the willingness of the listener to perform the request (2002: 280).

d. But becaufe the wordes be not fore ftrayned againſt me, RSA PAR [I praye you], DA [Maifter Atturney,] IS Q [why might not I haue tolde Maifter Arnolde, RTA [that *John Fitzwilliams* was angrie with *William Thomas*], and yet RTA [knowe no caufe of the Anger]?]]

(43) <N>
    a. RSA IMP [Note, RSA PAR [I pray you], the Advices, and fee how likely they are] but by her Highnefs's Order,
    b. RSA PAR [I pray you], let them be brought face to face to me
    c. And in what manner, RSA PAR [I pray you], RSA Q [do they difclofe it]?

PRAY	LEXICAL USE	PARENTH. USE	CLAUSE-INTERNAL POSITION	DIRECTIVE	IMPERATIVE PRECEDES PRAY	QUESTION	ADDRESS FORM
<TH>	34	2	32	23	30	4	2	17
<N>	31	20	11	9	7	2	4	-
TOTAL	65	22	43	32	37	6	5	17

Table 17: Features of *I pray you* parenthetical

As these examples illustrate, the flexibility[20] of the phrase is limited to (1) the presence of direct address (in 3 cases vocative is substituted for an 'of' genitive (42b)) and its position in relation to the phrase; (2) the position of the imperative, which may occasionally precede[21] the phrase as in (43a) (6 instances). Thus, the phrase is more fixed than the other formulas discussed above. Given its deferential functions with address forms involved frequently (17 instances), the status of the phrase as a reporting clause in speech and thought presentation is dubious not only on formal grounds (cf. remarks on 'truncation', this section). Therefore, similar to some other fixed phrases, it is interpreted as a self-standing instance of a RSA, labelled PAR (parenthetical). The tagging verb is also labelled PAR in order to distinguish this function from the performative function that speech act verbs might fulfil. This categorisation decision is extended to cover a range of verbal expressions with modalising functions – including the expressions with mental verbs – characterised by the flexibility of syntactic position and no syntactic relation to the adjacent clause.

---

[20] The findings concerning *I pray you* in the analysed data, both as to the form and function, are quite homogenous unlike e.g., in Kryk-Kastovsky (2002: 223-226), who analyses court material from 1685 and establishes a more divergent distribution and functions of the already grammaticalised *pray*.

[21] In his discussion of the phrase in late 16th century instructional texts, Fries (1998: 93-94) establishes the fixed position of *I pray you* before the imperative. This may be accidental or it may signify that the fixed syntactic position of the phrase could, in this case, be a text-type feature.

In order to substantiate categorisation decisions, further arguments are drawn from analyses of different linguistic data and environments. First of all, striking evidence for the syntactic freedom of parentheticals can be found in bilingual discourse, in cases when expressions such as *I think, I guess* are frequently code-switched between French and English (King and Nadasdi 1999). Secondly, Quirk et al. (1985) consider parentheticals as *comment clauses* and discuss some affinities the latter bear to indirect statements. Thus, the transformation of the sentence *I believe that he is stupid* into *He is, I believe, stupid* involves the reversing of the relationship of subordination i.e., the *that*-clause becomes the matrix clause, the matrix clause becomes the comment clause and, significantly, the complementiser is omitted (Quirk et al. 1985: 1113). Semantically there is a drastic change, as the authors go on to claim, "the verb in the comment clause may have only one of the meanings possible for the verb in the matrix clause ... only the hedging meaning is present in comment clauses" (Quirk et al. 1985: 1113). Finally, diachronically, as is maintained by Brinton (1996: 263), *comment clauses* derive from relative clauses with an anaphorical reference to the adjacent clause. In the opinion of the author, sentence (a) below is derived from (b), the complementiser is lost or *as* is grammaticalised in the function of a complementiser:

a. The world is flat, I believe
b. The world is flat, that/as I believe

Semantically, according to Brinton (1996), the course of development is from "an older evidential significance, by the conventionalizing of the implicature of uncertainty attached to the mode of knowing/ source of information" (1996: 263) to an epistemic meaning as in (a). Although Brinton's syntactic argument has not been conducted convincingly, the diachronic development that she proposes for parentheticals further emphasises their independence from the clause to which they are adjoined. The three arguments summarised above substantiate the status of parenthetical clauses in relation to reported speech and the categorisation decisions proposed above.

The performative function of the verb is present in its lexical uses as in the examples below:

(44) <TH>
RSA [and I pray you to help me if RTA [I miftake,]] for it is long fince I did fee them.
(45) <N>
IS [fo as I pray God, that this day it fail me not], and another time I will RSA [forgive it]

In (44) the verb is used like in *OED*, meaning: "To ask earnestly, humbly, or supplicatingly, to beseech; to make devout petition to; to ask (a person) for something as a favour or act of grace" (*OED pray,* v. I, 1). In (45) the following meaning from *OED* is realised: "esp. in religious use, to make devout and humble supplication to (God, or an object of worship)" (*OED pray,* v. I, 1). Both (44) and (45) fall under I, 1 in *OED*. Apart from those illustrated above, there are numerous instances of other lexical uses of the verb *to pray* that are not discussed here but which are included in the speech presentation inventory as different categories depending on the structural properties of the clause.

4.3.1.3.3 *I beseech you*

Although *I beseech you* has not grammaticalised into a discourse marker and hence it has not been described as going through a stage of an epistemic parenthetical like *I pray you,* the parenthetical status is proposed here for both phrases on the basis of the uses in <N>. Culpeper and Kytö (2000b) view the phrase as "a conventionalized request formula, somewhat like 'I pray you'" (2000b: 55). All the 17 instances of *I beseech you* conform to the pattern of *I pray you* discussed above, including the occurrence of the imperative form of the verb, as in the following example:

(46) <N>
If the Law do not allow me Counſel, ᴿˢᴬ [I muſt ſubmit me to your Opinions].
ᴿˢᴬ ᴾᴬᴿ [I beſeech you], ᴿᵀᴬ ᴵᴹᴾ [conſider of me]];

All the instances of the phrase occur in the speech of the defendant; hence a deferential function might be proposed. According to Brown and Gilman (1989), both expressions assert a felicity condition on the side of the speaker i.e., his sincere wish that the hearer should conform to the request (1989: 181). As the authors maintain, *I beseech you* as a marker of an indirect request is more deferential than *I pray you* in the Shakespeare corpus because the former phrase occurs 4 times as often with a honorific title than the latter (Brown and Gilman 1989: 183). Likewise, Culpeper and Kytö (2000b: 55) maintain that *I beseech you* is more formal. The affinity of this phrase to *I pray you,* except for the semantic load, can be illustrated beyond doubt with the following example (47) where the context of the expression is identical with (43) b:

(47) <N>
Duke. *Barriſter* was ſhrewdly cramp'd ᴿˢᴬ [when he told that Tale]. ᴿˢᴬ ᴾᴬᴿ [I beſeech you] let me have him brought Face to Face.

The interpretation of the phrase as an epistemic parenthetical is supported by its syntactic independence, the possibility of substituting it for *I pray you* and its occurrence exclusively in the speech of the defendant. In these cases, *I beseech you* is viewed as a RSA and labelled RSA PAR. As in the case of other fixed phrases, lexical uses of the verb *to beseech* also occur, as in:

(48) <N>
  ᴿˢᴬ [Yet one Requeſt more I beſeech of you, DA [my Peers], ᴿˢᴬ [which I with Favour may aſk,] ᴿˢᴬ [and you with Juſtice may grant]:]

This example conforms to the *OED* definition: "To supplicate, entreat, implore (a person)" (*beseech*, v. 3). One example of such a lexical use is found in <TH>. The categorisation of similar instances is carried out on the basis of structural properties, as in the case of lexical uses of *pray*.

4.3.1.3.4 Parentheticals – some statistics

The functional potential of parenthetical expressions overlapping with reported speech as well as its wide scope and the high variability included, render a more general analysis necessary. After all, apart from *pray* and *beseech*, there are a range of other verbs which, although of lower frequency, are clearly markers of stance with no less important effects on the interaction in the courtroom. Naturally, it would be superfluous to outline the analytic procedure performed with respect to each verb or to provide a detailed description of all intersubjective functions (but cf. sections 4.3.1.5.3 to 4.3.1.5.5 below). Most importantly, these verbs are subject to an analysis similar to the one of *pray* and *beseech*. It might be interesting, however, to investigate the statistical distribution of parentheticals. Particularly intriguing is the question whether the assumption of the successful vs. unsuccessful defending strategies may be corroborated by the statistical distribution of parentheticals as reported speech instances and markers of stance. That is to say, does the sheer number of occurrences of this linguistic phenomenon correlate with the defendant's success in the courtroom. The distribution of parenthetical verbs in both trials is provided in the tables below (Tables 18 and 19).

	PARENTHETICAL VERB	NUMBER OF TOKENS	%	LEMMAS
1ˢᵀ PERSON (94,93%)	I PRAY	32	40,51	I praye (7)
	METHINK	8	10,13	methinke (3), meethinke (2), methought (1)
	I ſAY	7	8,85	I ſaye (2), I ſay and aduow (1)
	I TRUſT	7	8,85	my truſt is (1)
	I AM ſURE	6	7,59	I am ſure and moſt aſſured (1), I aſſure you (1)
	I DOUBT NOT	3	3,80	I doubte not (1)
	I KNOW	3	3,80	

128   Chapter Four

	I MEANE	2	2,53	
	I VNDERſTAND	2	2,53	I underſtoode (1)
	I WARRANT	2	2,53	I warrante (1)
	I ſUPPOſE	1	1,27	
	I GRAUNT	1	1,27	
	I THINK	1	1,27	
2ND PERSON (1,27%)	YOU KNOWE	1	1,27	
3RD PERSON (3,8%)	HE THOUGHT	2	2,53	hee thought (1)
	HE TRUſTED	1	1,27	
TOTAL		79	100,00	

Table 18: Distribution of parenthetical verbs in the trial of Throckmorton

	PARENTHETICAL VERBS	NUMBER OF TOKENS	%	LEMMAS
1ST PERSON (77,61%)	I BEſEECH	18	26,48	
	I PRAY	11	16,18	
	I ſAY	6	8,83	
	I AM ſURE	4	5,88	
	I KNOW	3	4,41	
	I THINK	3	4,41	
	I HOPE	2	2,94	
	I TRUſT	2	2,94	
	I AM OF OPINION	1	1,47	
	I BELIEVE	1	1,47	
	I DOUBT NOT	1	1,47	
	I FEAR	1	1,47	
2ND PERSON (13,43%)	YOU KNOW	4	5,88	
	YOU MAY BE ſURE	1	1,47	
	YOU ſAY	2	2,94	ſay you(1)
	YOU THINK	2	2,94	
3RD PERSON (7,46%)	HE DOUBTED NOT	2	2,94	she doubted not(1)
	HE THOUGHT	1	1,47	
	HE WAS AſſUR'D	1	1,47	
	SHE TRUſTED	1	1,47	
PASSIVE (1,49%)	IT WAS THOUGHT	1	1,47	
TOTAL		68	100,00	

Table 19: Distribution of parenthetical verbs in the trial of Norfolk

The following table (Table 20) shows the statistical differences in the distribution of parenthetical verbs between the two trials:

		<TH>	<N>
ALL TOKENS	TOTAL	79	68
	NORMALISED FIGURE PER 10,000 WORDS	48,31	15,87
	DISTINCTIVENESS RATIO		3,04
DEFENDANTS' TOKENS	TOTAL	65	46
	PERCENTAGES	**82,28%**	67,65%
	NORMALISED FIGURE PER 10,000 WORDS	39,75	10,73
	DISTINCTIVENESS RATIO		3,7
OTHERS' TOKENS	TOTAL	14	22
	PERCENTAGES	17,72%	32,35%
	NORMALISED FIGURE PER 10,000 WORDS	8,65	5,13

Table 20: Comparison of parentheticals' distribution in two trials

In general, the parenthetical RSAs are more frequent in <TH> than in <N> with DR at 3,04. Particularly important is the difference between the frequency of occurrence in the speech of two defendants, amounting to over 80% of all instances in <TH> against less than 70% in <N> (c.15% fewer occurrences in the latter) with DR at 3,7. With respect to this aspect of stance i.e., the use of parenthetical RSAs, the results corroborate the assumption that the language of Nicholas Throckmorton involves more instances of stance marking by means of reported speech than the language of the Duke of Norfolk.

4.3.1.4 KNOW-verbs – a model of evidentiality

Among verbs which frequently occur as parentheticals[22] (cf. Tables 19 and 20 above), there is a group defined by Brinton (1996) (cf. section 4.3.1.3.2) as KNOW-verbs. Lexically, as the author notices, these verbs fall within the category of evidentiality[23]: "the source of knowledge being thought, belief or phantasy" (Brinton 1996: 232). According to Muslin (2001a), evidentiality is a twofold notion coding both "information about the speaker's source of information and their assessment of the validity/reliability of that information" (2001a: 1362). The following model reflects this view of evidentiality, understood as an epistemological stance, at the same time illustrating the intricacy of the issue:

---

[22] More precisely, Brinton (1996) talks about first person epistemic parentheticals.
[23] Aijmer (1997: 17) defines evidentiality as "the domain of linguistic elements expressing various attitudes to knowledge". An overview of evidentiality is provided in Dendale and Tasmowski 2001. A typological overview of strategies and systems of evidentiality is provided in the articles collected in Aikhenvald and Dixon (2003).

Actual source of information ⟶ Speaker assessment of actual source

Interactional setting ⟶ Speaker assessment of Interaction

Adoption of epistemological stance ⟶ Linguistic choices

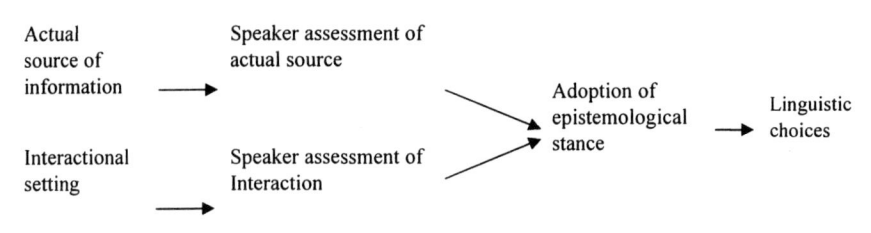

Figure 6: Model of epistemological stance adoption (adapted from Mushin 2001b: 59)

As for their function, the majority of evidentials are mental state verbs which "systematically express subjectivity" (Nuyts 2001b: 390). Fairclough (2003) sees these as markers of modality on a par with verbs of appearance i.e., *seem* and *appear* and hedges such as *sort of* (2003: 169). Mental verbs can also be viewed as "epistemic qualifiers" (modal auxiliaries, adjectives, adverbs, nouns, epistemic parentheticals) that "soften or reinforce illocutionary force" of an utterance (Aijmer 1997: 18-19). For some verbs evidential and epistemic meanings overlap[24] e.g., according to Nuyts (2001a: 113), in *think* and *believe*, which the author refers to as *mixed epistemic evidentials*. Other authors draw a clear dividing line between factive (*realise, discover, know, find out*, etc.) and non-factive verbs (*believe, think* etc.) assuming that the use of the former implies speaker's certainty as to the truth-value of the complement clause i.e., they carry such a presupposition (Kiparsky and Kiparsky 1970, Traugott 1972, Field 1997). Yet other authors explicitly exclude mental verbs and fixed expressions (e.g., *you know, I mean*) from the inventory of epistemic parentheticals (Thompson and Mulac 1991: 316). Others view the very same items as explicit discourse markers (e.g., Tree and Schrock 2002).

4.3.1.5 KNOW-verbs – epistemic modality or thought presentation

It is natural to expect that thought presentation is introduced by means of verbs signifying mental states i.e., private verbs (Quirk et al. 1985: 202-203). The subgroups identified by Quirk et al. (1985) include (1) verbs denoting intellectual states, (2) states of emotion or attitude, (3) states of perception and (4) states of bodily sensation. The last group, naturally, does not occur in the inventory of reported thought tags. In the data under analysis, the first and second groups are well represented, while perception verbs as predicates of reporting clauses are less common. Verbs denoting states of emotion or attitude (e.g., *intend, wish, want, like* etc; Quirk et al. 1985: 203) can be unambiguously classified as thought

---

[24] The relationship between the idea of epistemic modality and evidentiality has been an exceedingly complex one. For an overview of approaches, cf. Kärkkäinen (2003: 18-19).

reporting tags. Fairclough (2003) sees these as a separate category and points to their possible modalising function:

> "There is also a distinctive category of explicit evaluations with mental processes, specifically affective mental processes (e.g. 'I *like* this book', 'I *hate* this book'). Let's call them 'affective evaluations'. These are generally subjectively marked evaluations, i.e. they explicitly mark the evaluation as that of the author, and they are therefore comparable to subjectively marked modalities (e.g. '*I think* she has arrived')" (Fairclough 2003: 172).

Affective evaluations are less complicated than the 'subjectively marked modalities' expressed by the intellectual verbs from the perspective of reported speech and thought. The former actually correspond to what Field (1997) calls *affective factive* verbs or *true-factives*, while the latter are *epistemic* or *semi-factive factives* (1997: 802). *Affective factives* (e.g., *regret, resent, amuse* etc.) are clear instances of thought reporting and are categorised as such on the basis of their structural properties. As far as the intellectual states verbs or *epistemic factives* are concerned, the interpretation of their status in reported speech is more complicated.

The major problem that mental verbs pose for reported speech analysis is the difference between their 'de re' and 'de dicto' readings (Nuyts 2001a: 108) or, using less confusing terminology, the non-qualificational vs. qualificational readings (cf. Nuyts 2001a: 114). The former assume the actual thoughts or beliefs of the **reported** person, while the latter allow the **reporting** speaker to include his/her own knowledge within the reported utterance, even if the **reported** speaker does not share this knowledge. As Field (1997) points out, among mental verbs, factive verbs in particular have the potential to make language more multi-dimensional and, similar to the basic general function of reported speech, "allow speakers to create indexical ground which encodes two perspectives, or stances, at once" (Field 1997: 804-805). Thus, the interpretative problem around KNOW-verbs is to draw a line of distinction between their evidential and cognitive usages and to position these within the speech and thought presentation cline. The initial assumption made here is that thought presentation is straightforward provided that a KNOW-verb reflects a cognitive act, while other usages are analysed separately, taking into account their specific functions in discourse. This interpretation goes against Nuyts' position (2001a) which excludes the non-qualificational readings from the domain of reported speech on no substantial grounds.

The analysis commences with the verbs selected from a list of Middle English KNOW-verbs (Brinton 1996: 213) comprising first-person epistemic parentheticals which are, first of all, verified as to their survival through the Early Modern English period. Then the distribution of these in the analysed data is scrutinised. Some researchers claim that there are grounds to view first-person epistemic parentheticals (such as *I pray*) on a par with evidential parentheticals, as, first of all, both categories "do not denote an act of cognition but merely serve to mitigate or intensify the utterance to which they are attached" (Brinton 1996: 232) and, secondly, both are free syntactic forms. The latter feature does not always apply in instances performing evidential functions, which are identified also in main verbal predication, rendering evidentials a group wider than parentheticals, at least with respect to structural properties. As for the modalising or qualificational function of evidential verbs, it is not uncontroversial (cf. Turnbull and Saxton 1997: 147-148).

4.3.1.5.1 Epistemic modals and hedges

To briefly illustrate the notion of epistemic modality, the following model proposed by Palmer (2001) could be helpful:

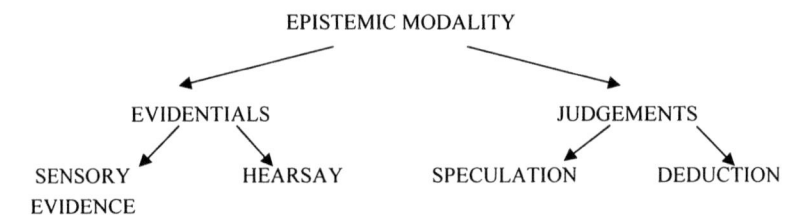

```
                        EPISTEMIC MODALITY
                       /                  \
              EVIDENTIALS                JUDGEMENTS
              /        \                 /         \
        SENSORY      HEARSAY      SPECULATION    DEDUCTION
        EVIDENCE
```

Figure 7: Palmer's model of epistemic modality (adapted from Mushin 2001b: 25)

Epistemic modal expressions perform hedging functions. This does not mean, however, that all epistemic modals are hedges. In this study a clear distinction is maintained between the two phenomena i.e., the former having a much more general functional scope than the latter. This goes against the opinions of some authors (e.g., Coates 2003) who narrow down the distinction between epistemic modals and hedges to the origin of terms i.e., the former coming from pragmatics and the latter from semantics. The main reason for keeping the two phenomena apart is the linguistic form. It is assumed here that epistemic modality overlapping with reported speech, is expressed mostly by means of parenthetical expressions which have clear-cut syntactic properties. Hedges, on the other hand, do not have to fulfil the condition of syntactic independence. Thus, the term is reserved for expressions syntactically different from parentheticals though performing some of their functions, such as e.g., intensifying or down-toning the force of the proposition (cf. section 4.3.1.5.9 below).

Pragmatic approaches to hedges include Brown and Levinson's politeness theory (1987: 145-173). Hedges in the Early Modern English courtroom are discussed by Culpeper and Kytö (1999a and 2000b) in the articles on trials, witness depositions and drama. In fact, some of fixed verbal phrases touched upon above (sections 4.3.1.1 and 4.3.1.2) overlap with hedges i.e., among the functions enumerated by Moon (1994), they perform the modalising one, signalling speaker's certainty or vagueness (cf. Biber 1988: 106), and they are used in relation to the positive face of the speaker (Culpeper and Kytö 1999a). The fact that this function is realised by verbal expressions goes against the ways in which form matches function in the opinion of Moon (1994): "With respect to function and syntactic realization, it is predictable that modalizers and organizers will be lexicalized formally as sentence adverbs or adjuncts" (Moon 1994: 126). Actually, as Grenoble (2004) points out, in the case of parentheticals which overlap with KNOW-verbs, the lack of psychological description and the clearly hearer-oriented function – providing clues as to the interpretation of the statement – allow comparing them to certain adverbs (Grenoble 2004: 1958-59). This in turn makes it possible to view some parentheticals and hedges as discourse markers whose grammatical function is adverbial, hence names such as 'speech-act adverbials' or 'illocutionary adverbials' have been coined for them in the literature (Ajimer 1996: 203). Many parentheticals (including KNOW-verbs) are fixed expressions classified by Culpeper and Kytö (2000b: 54, 58) as *modalising fragments*: downtoners/boosters (such as *I believe, I think*) and certainty markers (such as *to be sure, I am sure*). Unlike Grenoble (2004) in her contemporary material, Culpeper and Kytö (2000b) do not view the parentheticals such as *I pray you, I warrant you, I tell you, I promise you*, which occur in Early Modern English data, as hearer- but rather as speaker-oriented, hence also as evidence for a positive politeness culture (2000b: 61). It is more likely, however, that the orientation towards the speaker is related to the courtroom situation, particularly as part of survival strategies on the part of the defendant. Actually, in another paper, Culpeper and Kytö (1999a: 310f) remark that hedges like *I think, I believe* are used by witnesses in approximately 90% of instances. This point is touched upon in due course, while the hedging function of KNOW-verbs is taken into consideration next. The importance of hedges and related phenomena (i.e., hesitation phenomena, intensifiers) in the courtroom is undeniable, as has been noted by Green (1990: 273), as – among other linguistic features – these phenomena in particular are the source of inference and credibility of witnesses for the jury and the judge.

4.3.1.5.2 KNOW-verbs – a semantic classification

A semantic division of mental verbs proposed by Kiparsky and Kiparsky (1970) and followed e.g., in Traugott (1972) and Field (1997) is used in this study. Selected verbs representing the categories illustrated in the following figure are discussed in the subsequent sections in order to verify some correlations between their semantic, syntactic and modalising i.e., pragmatic aspects and the interplay of the three in reported speech. The only group that is excluded from the discussion are affective factives which are unambiguous as to their status in reported speech, introducing instances of thought presentation.

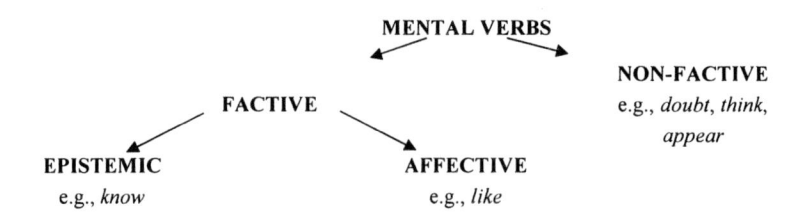

```
                    MENTAL VERBS
                  ╱             ╲
                                          NON-FACTIVE
          FACTIVE                         e.g., doubt, think,
         ╱       ╲                        appear
  EPISTEMIC    AFFECTIVE
  e.g., know   e.g., like
```

Figure 8: A semantic categorisation of mental verbs

4.3.1.5.3 *Doubt not* and *doubt*

Listed by Brinton (1996) as a first-person epistemic parenthetical in Middle English, *I doubt not* has evidently preserved this function in the analysed Early Modern English material:

(49) <TH>
for RSA PAR [I doubte not] THAT-DEL RSA PASS [Sir *Thomas Wyat* hath bin examin'd of me], RSA [and hathe fayde what he could directly or indirectly]

I doubt not with *that*-clause with *that*-deletion justifies the interpretation as being an epistemic parenthetical expressing evaluation or personal opinion. Thus, the phrase does not function as a reporting clause but as a speech act expressing assertion. Therefore, it is viewed as a self-standing RSA. The negated verb occurs also with subjects other than the first person. In such cases if a *that*-clause with *that*-deletion is embedded in other speech reports, the phrase is also viewed as a parenthetical self-standing RSA, despite the sequence of tenses typical of reported speech. This is illustrated in the examples below:

(50) <N>
IS [To this fhe reply'd, that there was no fuch Danger in the matter as RTA [I fuppos'd]; RSA PAR [for fhe trufted THAT-DEL I would find the Judges favourable, principally the Duke of *Norfolk*, who was firft in Commiffion; RSA PAR [and doubted not THAT-DEL but the Earl of *Suffex* would be ruled by him as his tender Friend]

(51) IS [and how *Sir Nicholas Throckmorton* fent me word, RSA PAR [That he doubted not] RSA THAT-DEL [the Queen would take order to my Contentation at her next Coming to a faid Houfe].]

Apart from the parenthetical function, the phrase may also signify a mental act (*OED doubt*, v. I, 1), which is the case for all propositional uses with *of* e.g.:

(52) <N>
move her Majefty ᴿᵀᴬ ᴵᴺᶠ [to alter her Favour towards me], or any ways ᴿᵀᴬ ᴵᴺᶠ [to doubt of my affured Conftancy towards her Highnefs]

The phrase under consideration may also be followed by an infinitival phrase, for which usage *OED* (*doubt*, v. I, 3) gives the following definition: "To hesitate, scruple, delay: with *inf.*". In its single occurrence this usage, because it lacks unambiguously cognitive meanings and could actually be substituted for *I certainly will*, is viewed as a hedge or, more specifically, an intensifier of the following proposition:

(53) <TH>
Stanford. And it ꜰᴏʀᴍᴜʟᴬ pleafe you, ᴅᴬ [my Lords], ʀˢᴬ ʜᴇᴅɢᴇ [I doubt not] ɪˢ ɪɴꜰ [to proue evi-dently and manifeftly, ʀˢᴬ ᴾᴬˢˢ [that *Throckmorton* is worthely and rightly indicted and araigned of thefe Treafons,]

The hedging function of mental state verbs is not surprising, according to Nuyts (2001b): "Because the mental state predicates are inherently subjective, they are frequently used as mitigating or hedging devices" (2001b: 391). On the basis of the initial analysis of the verb *to doubt* in this study, it is necessary to distinguish its parenthetical from its hedging usage, of which in the latter – as example (53) clearly shows – the verb is assumed to have lost its propositional value completely, but it is not syntactically free. Thus, usages like (53) show less semantic load than the unambiguous parentheticals and therefore could be excluded from reported speech analysis and labelled accordingly to their function. Still, in this case, the hedge may be interpreted as a promise or as another speech act (e.g., assertion or an act of evaluation, cf. Fraser 1975: 191). Thus, in order to abide by a transparent classification, the verb *to doubt* in example (53) is viewed as an instance of RSA labelled PAR.

4.3.1.5.4 *I know, you know, it is well known etc.*

There are numerous instances of the verb *to know* in the analysed data. As in the case of *I doubt not*, discussed above, a range of distinctions are made in order to incorporate its selected occurrences within the speech and thought presentation, while at the same time to exclude those instances of lexical and parenthetical uses which fall outside it. The following examples illustrate the parenthetical occurrences of the verb *to know*:

(54) <TH>
　　a. RSA PASS [*Stanley* was for thofe Words attainted,] who, RSA EV [as all the Worlde knoweth], had before that time ſerued the King very faithully and truly.
　　b. It is lawfull for you to vſe your Gifts, which RSA PAR [I know] THAT-DEL God hathe largely giuen you], as youre Learning, Arte and Eloquence, ſo as thereby you do not ſeduce the Minds of the ſimple and unlearned Jury, RTA INF [to credite Matters otherwiſe than they be]
　　c. *Throckmorton.* RSA PAR [You knowe] THAT-DEL it were indifferent RSA [that I ſhould knowe and heare the Law RSA PASS [whereby I am adjudged];]

(55) <N>
　　a. I have neither good Utter-ance, RSA EV [as the World knoweth], nor Underſtanding
　　b. RSA PAR [I know] Religion beareth a ſtroke among you]
　　c. I never RSA [made great account of you]; RSA PASS [my Lord of *Leiceſter* made us firſt ac-quainted], your Brother RSA PAR [you know] was not my Friend.

Both types of usage i.e., as in (54) and (55) (a) and the first person predicate in (54) and (55) (b), indicate correspondingly objective and subjective certainty or epistemic modality (Brinton 1996: 254). In the former, however, the evidential meaning seems to dominate, hence the label EV. *I know* in turn differs also in that it is a parenthetical clause structurally. Similarly, *You know*[25] as (54) and (55) (c), is a prototypical parenthetical. In *OED* (*know*, v. III, 11, e) it is seen as mere conversation filler, but in the analysed material its function is more interpersonal and hedging. In fact, there is no way of establishing whether this phrase historically performed any of the above-mentioned functions established for present-day English, as the written data does not provide relevant evidence. Culpeper and Kytö (1999a: 308) maintain that, as an implicit[26] modifier, *you know* was unlikely to survive the transition from the spoken to the written medium. Some authors see this item as a marker of both positive and negative politeness in present-day English (Tree and Schrock 2002). The face-saving function of expressing the shared knowledge[27] can be discerned in the analysed data, but the one of allowing the addressee more space for expressing their opinions suggested for present-day English (Tree and Schrock 2002: 730), does not occur. Actually, in this study the difference between the parenthetical and evidential functions of *you*

---

[25] For an overview of studies on this expression in present-day English and the diversity of function different authors claim for it, cf. Brinton (1996: 185-87).

[26] Authors disagree as to whether evidentials are implicit or explicit modifiers (cf. Brinton 1996: 336f, Culpeper and Kytö 1999a: 298).

[27] Fuller claims that *you know* "enhances the salience of the information it frames" (2003: 37) and includes it in the inventory of presentation markers the function of which is "that of making the information presented more acceptable and accessible for the hearer" (2003: 36).

know is put solely to the syntactic properties (compare 54 and 55 (a) with 58 (b)). The expression is evenly distributed between the defendants and the court officials and it accounts for approximately 0,5% of the total occurrences of the verb *to know*. The function of this parenthetical usage seems to be that of challenging the addressee's intentions or pointing to the fact of concealing their knowledge as in (55) (c) above and (56) below:

(56) <N>
Wilbraham. That is no matter; for the Indictment is generally of the Queen's Enemies, and _{RSA PAR} [you know] the Money went to the Lord *Harris*.

The use of this expression marks decreased distance in the above examples; thus, it could be viewed as a marker of positive politeness. Things are, however, more complicated than that: the reduced distance allows the speaker to invade the hearer's territory and appeal to the knowledge of the addressee, which the latter would rather keep to themselves. In this way, the speaker strengthens his/her own position in front of the audience when facing controversy. Interestingly enough, unlike in present-day English where the item is commonly used to introduce new information (Fuller 2003: 36), *you know* in Early Modern English is not used for this purpose. In the example from Throckmorton's case, the expression is used in an answer to the frustrated request of the defendant to have the legal basis of his accusation presented to him and to the jury. By means of this parenthetical RSA, the defendant is able to reveal the reluctance of the court officials to allow him access to the *Law Statutes* as well as their fear that reference to these could be advantageous to the defendant's position in the trial. The obstinacy of the attorney in this matter and the assumed guilt, rather than innocence of the accused, additionally enhancing this obstinacy, are not only explained by evil intentions but also by the legal rule operating at the time of the trial i.e., the assumption of guilt rather than innocence.

Types illustrated above in 54 and 55 (b) and (c), as syntactically free, are viewed as parenthetical RSAs. One other parenthetical usage occurs with negation as a means of strengthening it:

(57) <TH> _{RSA PAR} [Not, that I know]

Illustrations in 54 and 55 (a) do not conform to the structural demands on parentheticals but they may be considered as RSAs whose function is implying an assertion based on an external source of evidence, hence they are labelled evidential. There are some further isolated uses functioning in a similar way as parentheticals but failing to fulfil the condition of syntactic independence, as in the instances below. Since the major significance of such uses is supporting the argument by referring to the source of evidence, even if this source is to remain undefined, they are labelled RSA EV, in order to account for the evidential function of the verb.

(58) <N>
    a. youre Service and Paines ~NRSA EV PASS~ [is euidently knowen to all Men]
    b. ~RSA~ [The Bifhop of *Roffe* fhortly after faid to me], and ~RSA~ [intreated to have my help for ~RSA NOUN~ [compounding of the Matter], ~IS EV~ [as you know well] ~THAT-DEL RSA~ [he can fpeak fair].]

If a syntactic relation between *I know* and the following clause exists, which is not infrequent and mostly realised by means of *that*, such an instance is viewed as thought presentation:

(59) <TH>
    a. For ~DA~ [Maifter Sergeant], ~IT~ [I knowe howe by Perfwafions, Enforcements, Prefumptions, applying, implying, inferring, conjecturing, deducing of Arguments, wrefting and exceeding the Law, the Circumftances, the Depofitions and Con-feffions, ~RSA PASS~ [that unlearned Men maye bee inchanted ~RSA INF~ [to thinke and judge thofe that bee things indifferente, or at the worft but ouerfights, to be great Treafons];]
    b. ~IT POST~ [Whether ~RSA~ [you alledge *Stanleyes* cafe trulye or no, I knowe not.]]

(60) <N>
~IT~ [I know ~RSA PASS~ [that ~RSA NOUN~ [Re-nunciation of that Claim] was offer'd,] ~RSA PASS~ [and upon certain Caufes refpited].]

In the examples above (59 and 60), the meaning of the verb is "To be cognizant, conscious, or aware of (a fact); to be informed of, to have learned; to apprehend (with the mind), to understand; with dependent statement, usually introduced by that. * With various constructions" (*OED, know,* v. III, 11). This meaning is dominant with the majority of constructions with other personal pronouns (except for *you*) as well as in the progressive and preterit forms of the verb (all persons). One other common meaning of *to know* with the preposition *of* (used also with *I* and *you* subjects), is also interpreted as report of thought as in *OED* (*know*, v. IV, 18):

know of
a. In various obsolete senses: To be or become assured of, to have or obtain information about or experience of, etc. *Obs.*
b. To be cognizant of (something as existing, an event as having occurred); to become cognizant of (*obs.*).

(61) <TH> ~RTA~ [I know nothing of the Caufe].]]

Know, however, in yet another meaning may be viewed as a report of speech rather than of thought, as in the following examples:

(62) <TH> but fithence IS VP [you would know RSA [what Communication paſſed betwixt us in *Poules* Church],]
(63) <N> IS Q [that I may know RSA [to what I fhould anfwer].]

OED (*know*, v. III, 8) defines the meaning of two instances above as "To have cognizance of (something), through observation, inquiry, or information; to be aware or apprised of (= F. *savoir*, Ger. *wissen*); to become cognizant of, learn through information or inquiry, ascertain, find out (*obs.*)". In fact it is the process of obtaining information that is central in these instances and, as is well understood, this may only be accomplished through speech, hence similar instances are viewed as reports of speech.

The parenthetical, evidential as well as reported speech and thought usages of the verb *to know* have been outlined above. Still, there are a range of lexical uses which could not have been incorporated into any of the categories. These include multi-word verbs, such as e.g., *desire to know* in which no propositional meaning of the verb in question is implied and cases where to know can be interpreted as 'to be acquainted with'. Those instances of the verb *to know* were excluded from reported speech analysis.

4.3.1.5.5 *I think, methinke and think*

The history of the decline of impersonal verbs[28], including the predecessor of PDE *think*, is interesting in itself but is skipped here for the sake of space. Suffice it to say that on the basis of Visser's examples (1966: 35) one can see that the phrase is still well represented throughout the sixteenth century. Palander-Collin (1999) sees *methinks* and *I think* as speech-based expressions which are more frequent in genres representing speech in writing, such as trial proceedings and drama, than in other genres (1999: 248). In present-day English, as is commonly observed (e.g., Aijmer 1997, Kärkkäinen 2003), *I think* functions as a discourse marker and as a marker of epistemic modality. Indeed, similar usages are found in the analysed Early Modern English data, though these are not numerous (approximately 10% of all occurrences of the verb *to think*):

---

[28] The issue received substantial attention within English historical linguistics. A comprehensive overview of approaches is provided by Denison (1993: 74-99). The author also provides a semantic definition of impersonal verbs (after Fischer and Van der Leek 1983: 246):
"The term impersonal verbs refers to a class of verbs which have a common semantic core: they all express a physical or mental/cognitive experience which involves a 'goal', in this case an animate experiencer, and a 'source', i.e. something from which the experience emanates or by which the experience is effected" (Denison 1993: 62).
For the Early Modern English accounts of this issue and the statistical presentation of usage in the relevant section of the *Helsinki Corpus*, cf. Dons (2004: 116-125).

(64) <TH>
DS [I had thefe Words to *Winter*, RSA [when he enformed me of it;] RSA PAR THAT-DEL [I think] RTA [M. *Wyat* would no *Englifhman* hurt], and this Enterprife cannot be done without the hurt and laughter of both Parties;]

(65) <N>
RTA [yet I remember one Cafe in Law], RSA PAR THAT-DEL [I think] it is in the Firft Year of King *Henry* VII.]

In the trial of Throckmorton, the above-mentioned functions are performed by the impersonal *methinke*[29] whose status in Early Modern English changes into an adverbial (Rissanen 2000: 250), which occurs in around 30% of all instances of the verb in this trial:

(66) <TH>
    a. RSA PAR [me thinke it well done], THAT-DEL you put my fayde Lorde and his Traine on Lande in the Weft Country to avoyde all Daunger
    b. I haue more neede to fee the Law, and partlye as well for the Inftructions of the Jurie, as for my owne Satisfaction, which RSA PAR [mee thinke], were for the Honor of this Prefence
    c. *Stanford.* RSA PAR [Methinke] RSA PP [the Matters confeffed by others againft you,] to-gether with your owne Confeffion, will weye fhrewdlye

In the analysed data, the distribution of the phrase indeed points to its adverbial status – the phrase is syntactically unbound and occurs in both initial and medial sentence positions. The occurrences of the phrase are too few to make generalisations, however, the fact that the impersonal form occurs twice as frequently as the personal parenthetical *I think*, is worth noting. This observation goes against what has been hypothesised by Palander-Collin (1996) on the basis of the frequencies of both phrases in the Late Middle and Early Modern English sections of the *Helsinki Corpus*. Her statistics point to the domination of the personal form of *think* from the sixteenth century onwards (Palander-Collin 1996: 146). This evidence invites the conclusion that in spite of its not infrequent occurrence in speech-like environments, such as the material under consideration here, the phrase *methinks* may have an archaic[30] touch to it. This should be true,

---

[29] The morphological form without -s is only occasional and "may be due to the supposition that the verb was a form of *pencean*, which was always 'personal'" (Visser 1966: 25). The instances in the data analysed here have the phrase spelled separately with a degree of orthographic variation. Separate spelling is typical of the earlier stages (1500-1570), as can be concluded on the basis of Wischer's (2000: 363) quantitative study of the EModE part of the *Helsinki Corpus*. This is one argument for the authenticity of the data found in the *State Trials*.

[30] Visser notices that forms like *meseems, meseemed, methinks* and *methought* are still used archaically in PDE (1966: 25).

according to Busse (2002), for all surviving impersonal constructions in the course of the sixteenth century as a result of a general trend to adapt to the SVO pattern (2002: 209). This is another argument for the phrase in the Early Modern English court material becoming conventionalised "and therefore changed into a symbol, formula[31]" (Wischer 2000: 363). On another occasion, Palander-Collin (1999) in a study of private letters in Early Modern English provides statistics showing the relatively higher degree of formality of *methinks* in comparison to *I think*, as well as the fact that the former is "part of the older generation's language" (1999: 255).

As for the functions of this expression in Early Modern English, it may be a marker of evidentiality (Wischer 2000: 355). According to Palander-Collin (1999), the verb may be classified as a *doubt* verb, following Biber and Finegan (1989), as it expresses certainty or doubt. In the trial of Throckmorton, the phrase is put to a range of different uses, and apart from strengthening personal opinion, it may also perform the function of an utterance launcher, as in 66 (c). As this example also shows, the hedging and asserting functions may overlap, which becomes clear if one takes into consideration that at this point jury member Stanford answers a rather challenging question asked by the defendant concerning the basis of the charges against him: *Is here all the Euidence againſte me that you haue to bring mee within the compaſſe of the Inditement?* The evidential function of the verb is extremely important here, as the defendant has just bluntly questioned the weight of the charges presented up to that point, and the answer has to be supported with a source of authoritative knowledge, being, paradoxically, the addressee of the question himself, rather than an external source. At the same time, the accusation concerning the lack of relevant evidence, uttered by Throckmorton in the question, is too serious to be disregarded completely, hence the hedging function of the expression. In one instance the hedging function is the dominant, if not the only, function of the item and it indeed reveals the attempt of the addressee to save face. Interestingly, the conciliatory tone of the utterance is achieved through the use of the past tense:

(67) <TH>
Throckmorton. IS THAT-DEL [I confeſs RTA DO SUP [I did miſlike the Queenes Mariage with *Spain*, and alſo the comming of the *Spanyards* hither;] and then RSA PAR THAT-DEL [me thought] I had reaſon to do ſo,

In the majority of its occurrences the verb *to think* is viewed as a verbal predicate introducing reported thought, as in the following examples (68 and 69), and is categorised in accordance with its structural properties:

---

[31] Wischer sees the development of the phrase as an instance of lexicalisation, which explains the demise of the construction as lexical units "pass out of existence more easily" than the grammaticalised linguistic units, such as PDE *I think*, which were not lexicalised (2000: 365).

(68) <TH>
RTA DO SUP [Sir *Peter* dyd thinke good to practife for Armour, Muni-cions and Money]

(69) <N>
IT PASS THAT-DEL [I am led to think I may have Counfel].]

Interestingly, access to the thoughts of others is limited to the minds of the third parties, while second person thought reports do not occur with a single exception. If the verb occurs in the second person, it is in interrogative clauses or in the imperative mood. Such a distribution of the subject of the personal *think* points to a degree of uncertainty on the part of the speaker to utter somebody else's thought and having them directly confronted with the alleged author. The third party, however, may be used in this way without consequences for the speaker, which seems crucial in the courtroom setting (cf. the reference to Green (1990) at the end of section 4.3.1.5.1).

As a non-factive verb, *think* – the personal variant – does not occur in evidential functions. Therefore, the passive occurrences of the verb, which for factive verbs, such as *know*, would be straightforwardly evidential, are viewed here as parenthetical:

(70) <N>
RSA PASS PAR [It was thought] THAT-DEL there could be none more fit Inftruments to travel for Continuance of the Amity betwixt the two Realms, than we two.

This interpretation may be objected to, as – clearly – the passive construction, just like all evidentials, refers to knowledge. In this case, however, the source of knowledge remains abstract in the sense of being alleged to the minds of an unspecified group of people rather than to common knowledge, as in the case of *as the worlde knoweth, as is* known, etc. Moreover, assigning parenthetical status to *it was thought*, is justified syntactically and it leaves more scope for interpretation than defining it as an evidential RSA. At the first sight the speaker (or to be more precise, letter writer, the Earl of Murray[32], regent of Scotland) places himself and the defendant in the advantageous position of being the most *fit Inftruments* in the reported situation. Given that, the passive construction used here may be (1) hedging, as an expression of modesty, or (2) it may emphasise the

---

[32] Lord James Stuart, the Earl of Murray, was Mary Stuart's bastard brother (Black 1959: 69). Mary's chief advisor from 1561, he lost the Queen's favour in 1565 when he opposed her marriage to Lord Darnley. He was outlawed and took refuge in England (*James Stuart, Earl of Moray* 2005). Later he was pardoned and after Mary's abdication in 1567 he became regent of Scotland. A year later, leading the Confederacy of Scottish Protestants, he defeated Mary's forces in the Battle of Langside, near Glasgow, and the queen was forced to flee to England. He was assassinated by Mary's supporter, Hamilton of Bothwellhaugh.

distance and reduced responsibility of the author from the Duke's reported discourse. The latter possibility is accepted on the grounds of complex involvement in the Murray in Norfolk's case. Actually, as Hume claims (1778 [1983]: 88), Murray and Norfolk conspired together for Norfolk's marriage to Mary, the Scottish Queen, and no one else but Murray was responsible for the idea of securing in this way the succession to the English throne for the Queen's son. As Hume goes on to explain, Murray, for this purpose, offered another marriage to Norfolk i.e., that of the Duke's daughter to the young king of Scotland. Murray's proposal, however, was most probably simulated, as he was likely to have engaged in another conspiracy, this time with Elizabeth, against Mary (Hume 1778 [1983]: 92-93). At the time of the trial, Murray had already been dead, assassinated in January 1570 in revenge for a private cause. Ultimately, the letter of Murray was one piece of condemning evidence against the defendant with respect to his attempts at marrying Mary Stuart; given all the arguments above, it is the function of distancing the reporting speaker from the Duke's speech that is to be identified in the use of the passive parenthetical RSA in this case, rather than evidential references.

4.3.1.5.6 *Appear*

Biber (2004) includes complement constructions such as *seem to* or *appear that* among the markers of stance which bear some relation to the meanings of modality (2004: 109, cf. Fairclough 2003). Indeed, Visser sees verbs such as *seem, appear, prove, look* as copulas of modality (1966: 208-209, 1370-71), functioning as modifiers of meaning of the following *to-* clause and replaceable by the derivative adverbs (*seemingly* etc.). According to Traugott (1972), *seem* and *appear* assign a clear semantic value to their complements i.e., they render the proposition in the embedded clause non-factive (cf. Field 1997) i.e., their function is to express speaker's uncertainty or hesitation. Furthermore, the semantic distinction into factive and non-factive verbs has clear syntactic correlates (Kiparsky and Kipasky 1970, Traugott 1972: 59-62). The functions of the former group of verbs in present-day English have been identified by Field (1997) as encoding two perspectives or stances, i.e. that of the reporting speaker and that of the reported speaker. The Early Modern English material investigated in this study provides grounds to identify the equally important functions of non-factive verbs, the role of which is by no means limited to the expression of the speaker's uncertainty. On the contrary, evidence shows that in the courtroom data under analysis non-factive verbs may strengthen the subjective assertion on the part of the speaker by the reference to real action or a tangible information source and at the same time they may function as expressions of institutional authority. Performing this function, non-factive verbs are viewed as tagging reports of speech and are categorised on the basis of sentence structure, though there may arise the possibility of marking them in a distinctive way.

Despite relatively frequent occurrence (21 tokens in <TH> and 27 in <N>), *appear* in many cases has to be excluded from reported speech analysis, as its meaning corresponds to *OED* "to occur" (*OED appear* v. 8), as in (a) below or "To present oneself formally before an authority or tribunal; to put in an appearance. *Hence,* to present oneself as legal representative of another; to act as counsel" (*OED appear* v. 4) as in (71) and (72) (b) below, or to "be taken as, to seem (*OED appear* v. 10) as in (71c):

(71) <TH>
   a. And laſt of all, to enforce theſe matters, ʀᴛᴀ ᴘᴀss [mine owne Confeſſion is engrieued greatly againſt me], where-in there doth appeare neyther Treaſon, neyther concelement of Treaſon, neyther whiſpering of Treaſon, nor procurement of Treaſon.
   b. when the Jury did appeare
   c. but where is *Edward Wyat's* Depoſitions of any thing againſt me, now it appeareth neither his firſte nor his laſt Tale to be true?

(72) <N>
   a. ʀsᴀ ᴘᴀss [wherein is ſignified the great Abomina-tion of the *Scotiſh* Queen, appearing in her own Letters, and the Certainty of the Truth of thoſe Letters]
   b. *ſummon'd to appear this day*

As far as the epistemic uses of the verb are concerned (12 in <TH>, 17 in <N>), these are uncontroversial when the verb is preceded by *as* or followed by a relative clause with *by* (cf. section 4.3.1.3.2 above), as in (73) and (74) (a) and (b):

(73) <TH>
   a. my Words be not peruerted and abuſed to the hurt of ſom others, and eſpecially againſt the great Perſonages, ɴʀsᴀ ᴘᴀss [of whome I have bin ſundry times (ʀsᴀ ᴇᴠ [as appeareth by my Anſwers]) examined]
   b. *Stanford.* ɪs Q [Did not ᴅᴀ [you, *Throckmorton,*] tell *Winter* ʀᴛᴀ [that *Wyat* had changed his Mind for the taking of the *Tower*;]] ɪs ᴇᴠ [whereby it appeared euidently ʀᴛᴀ [that you knew of his doings]?]

(74) <N>
   a. ʀsᴀ [which I utterly refuſed], ʀsᴀ ᴇᴠ [as by my Letters from *York* to the Queen's Majeſty it may appear]
   b. ʀᴛᴀ [yet I conceive no ſmall Comfort, ʀᴛᴀ ɪɴꜰ [to think under how gracious a Queen and Sovereign Lady I live,] ʀsᴀ ᴇᴠ [which well appeareth by her moſt gracious Proceed-ing with me according to the Courſe of Law]

In view of the asserting function – authorised by a specified information source of the above examples – it is in order to classify these as instances of RSA, similar to the range of mental verbs discussed above (cf. section 4.3.1.5.4) i.e., the evidential RSAs. By the same token, uses like in example (75) are also categorised in this way, as the verb *to appear* functions as an assertion of the proposition expressed by the complement clause:

(75) <TH>
Southwell. IS EV THAT-DEL [It appeareth] you haue added good Intelligence

Parenthetical status may naturally only be assigned (but is not, when the evidential function is dominant) if the syntactic condition of independence as marked by *that*-deletion is fulfilled, while the asserting function may also occur in other syntactic structures:

(76) <TH>
Stanford. IS EV [It appeareth RSA [that you were of Counfel with *Wyat*], RSA [in as much as you fente *Winter* downe to him,] RSA [who uttered unto him diuers traitorous Deuifes.]]

(77) <N>
   a. IS EV [Thus it appeareth, that thofe the *Scotifh* Queen's Friends in *Scotland,* RTA [for whom fhe forrowed] RTA [and feared their yielding]]
   b. IS EV [Thus appeareth RSA [how he hath given Advice againft the Queen to the *Scotifh* Queen].]

Although the above instances also clearly mark assertion, with respect to reported speech there is a need to categorise them differently from the evidential parenthetical instances with *that*-deletion. Furthermore, it has to be emphasised that the above-mentioned usages occur mostly in the speech of court officials (83,33% in <TH> and 89,47% in <N>), and are connected with the specific role they play in the trial. In these contexts, the phrase with *appear* is often turn-initial and refers anaphorically to the preceding events, previously demonstrated evidence or sums up the hitherto presented facts. Although the verb occurs in the impersonal construction with *it* being a pseudo-subject, it definitely serves the purpose of substantiating the personal opinion of the speaker i.e., it has an evidential function. The subjective aim of the speaker when using the non-factive *appear* impersonally, rather than with a raised subject, is to emphasise the general validity of the expressed subjective opinion and thus to strengthen the truth-value of the proposition, at the same time exercising the authority involved in this social role. This strategy could be referred to as an impersonalised evidential strategy. Additionally, it may also be used in conducive questions:

(78) <TH>
Stanford. RSA Q [How ſay you], RSA EV [doth not heere <u>appeare</u> euident matter RSA INF [<u>to</u> <u>proue</u> you a Principal, RSA [who not onely <u>gave</u> <u>order</u> to Sir *Peter Caroe* and his Adherents, for their rebellious actes in the Weſt Countrey];]

From the point of view of speech and thought presentation, the above-mentioned uses of *appear* fulfil the function of manipulating speaker's footing as indirect evidential strategies whose role in this respect is similar to that of factive verbs (Field 1997). Still, it is the evidential and not the reporting function that is dominant, at least when *appear* is used by a court official. Therefore in these contexts, as referring to actual anterior spoken or written evidence, the above examples are categorised as reported speech, labelled additionally EV. There are also a range of structurally similar usages common in the speech of court officials, like in the following example, which cannot, however, be considered evidential:

(79) <TH>
IS [it ſhall manifeſtly <u>appeare</u> vnto you], RSA DO SUP [that *Throckmorton* <u>did</u> <u>conſpire</u> the Queenes Majeſties Death with *William Thomas,* Sir *Nicholas Arnold,* RTA GERUND [and other Traitors <u>intending</u> the fame]

The use of the modal verb *shall* renders the evidential function less unambiguous than in the instances discussed earlier; that is to say, referring to prospective[33] evidence, the phrase is only hypothetically evidential. Therefore, the verb *to appear* is read here as an unambiguous speech reporting tag, not possessing the additional function and referring to the act of presenting evidence in speech.

In the speech of Throckmorton, the successful defendant, the verb *to appear* is used distinctively from the usage of the court officials. It is the hedging aspect of the verb that is best suited to the needs of the defendant, striving to prove his innocence and question the fact-value of the accusation that he is the subject of, as in:

(80) <TH>
RSA PASS [I <u>haue</u> <u>been</u> indited,] RSA HEDGE [as it <u>appeareth</u>]

In the trial of Norfolk a witness uses *appear* as a hedge when reporting the words of a third party:

(81) <N>
IS [ſo that *Ledington* <u>ſaid</u>, THAT-DEL HEDGE [it <u>appear'd</u> to him], RTA [that the Duke <u>had</u> ſome Intention to marry with the Queen, RSA EV [as the <u>Bruite</u> <u>was</u>]]

---

[33] Actually, the prediction and future reference expressed by *shall* are dominant among epistemic functions of the modal in Early Modern English, as has been established by Nakayasu (2005: 107) in the analysis of a selection of Shakespearean plays.

Overall, however, the evidential uses of the verb *to appear* by the defendants or witnesses are marginal.

Similar to *appear*, the verb *prove* also serves evidential functions as in the following example:

(82) <N>
Serj. IS EV PASS [It is well proved that at *Hampton-Court,* RSA PASS PROGR [being examined of the Matter by the Queen's Majefty, RSA [you diffembled it]]

Moreover, the distribution of the evidential occurrences of this verb are similar to those of *appear* i.e., all instances in <TH> are found in the speech of court officials, while in <N> this applies in 85,71% of all occurrences. Syntactically, evidentiality in *prove* correlates with the passive voice (80% instances in <TH> and c. 43% in <N>).

4.3.1.5.7 *Hear* – perception verb

Expressions such as *I have heard* may have a hedging function in present-day English, as is confirmed by Quirk et al. (1985: 1114). Next to a range of verbs (e.g., *think, assume, say, seem, appear*), *hear* in similar expressions conveys the speaker's tentativeness as to the truth-value of the clause to which it is adjoined. This function allows classifying this verb as belonging to the non-factive group. According to Brinton (1996: 234), who draws conclusions on the basis of her Middle English data, perception verbs occurring in quotative forms such as *I hear, as I've heard* are primarily evidential, as they refer to the mode of knowing or ways of obtaining information. Therefore, evaluative or other modalising e.g., hedging functions are less probable here than in the case of verbs which function as first person epistemic parentheticals (*I believe*, etc). On the other hand, one cannot deny the fact that the parenthetical status may indeed involve a degree of modalising function, as in the following examples:

(83) <TH>
    a. DS [*Throckmorton* aunfwered, at his Houſe *in Kente,* not farre from *Gillingham,* RSA EV [as I heard fay,]
    b. In communication betwixt *Winter* and me, IS EV [as he declared to me that the *Spanyards* provided to bring their Prince hither, fo the *Frenchmen* prepared to interrupt his Arrival, for they began to arme to the Sea, and had already certain Shippes on the Weft Coſt,] RSA EV [(as he heard)]

(84) <N>
    a. and how to thoſe the Duke adhered, those he comforted for thoſe he procured the comfortable Letters to be ſent, RSA EV [as you have heard]

148   Chapter Four

      b. RSA NOUN [In which her complaint, RSA EV [as I have heard her Majeſty her
      ſelf RSA BARE INF [declare it],]]

(85) <TH>
    Stanford. IS EV [That it may appeare yet more euidently howe *Throckmorton,* was a
    principal Doer and Counſellor in this matter], RSA [you ſhall heare his owne Confeſſion
    of his own hand writing.]

(86) <N>
    Serj. RSA INV [Now ſhall you hear the Duke's own Confeſſion].

Primarily, two functions are discerned: with the first person pronoun, the speaker uses the verb to support the argument, while with other pronouns he/she may be using it as a distancing and responsibility-shedding device. The evidential usage of the verb in the trial of Norfolk is a tool exclusively in the hands of court officials striving to manipulate the audience in order to condemn the accused. Thus, e.g., instance (84b) is a clear reference to a higher authority in order to add strength to the argument of the sergeant. The usage illustrated in (83 and 83) is common in both trials and serves the purpose of addressing the audience, (1) in order to emphasise the weight of the evidence that has just been heard; or (2) in order to introduce and foreground the evidence to come, thus focusing the audience's attention. Both kinds of usage have the same function: they involve an assumed rather than verifiable implication as to the truth-content and the faithfulness to real life events of the evidence already given or prospective. More importantly, the alleged truth-value of the evidence constitutes the ground on which the arguments of the court officials are actually built. Interestingly, this kind of usage occurs exclusively with the 2nd person pronouns and it comprises a substantial amount of evidential instances of the verb (37,5% in <TH> and 75% in <N>). Moreover, all these instances illustrate the fact that verbs like *hear,* when they are predicates in reporting clauses, indicate the perspective of the receiver rather than the speaker (Semino and Short 2004: 81). Actually, what the speakers achieve by means of these is manipulating the perspective of the hearer, thus employing one further pragmatic function of reported speech, surfacing this time in the use of a verb of perception. It is no accident that the use of the 2nd person pronoun with *hear* correlates with speaker roles in both trials i.e., in Throckmorton, 75% of all *you* forms occurs in the turns of the court officials, while all *I* forms in the turns of the defendant; in Norfolk, even more evidently, all *you* forms occur in the turns of the court officials.

    In the trial of Throckmorton, the defendant uses the second person perspective twice with *hear,* thus turning the tables on the judges and the jury:

(87) <TH>
   a. RSA EV [and therefore you ſhall heare RSA DO SUP [what your owne Lawe doth ſay].]
   b. RTA AP Q [And why bee yee not ſo well contented RSA INF [to heare Troth for mee, as Untroth againſt me]?]

In (87a), the defendant introduces a quotation from the legal resource he has at hand in order to support his argument and, applying a strategy which is apparently an attribute of the court official and their institutional role, he is able to foreground the weight of the written authority he is relying on. In (87b), Throckmorton addresses the jury with a rhetorical question with the legal meaning of the verb (*OED hear* v., 6. *trans.* "To listen to judicially in a court of law; to give (one) a hearing; to try a person or a case") again exploiting the strategy which is not a part of his institutional role. Whereas Throckmorton, as is clear even on the basis of the two isolated instances, is able to employ strategies belonging to other institutional roles, the Duke is much less inventive in this respect. First of all, the Duke's speech does not contain any clearly evidential instances of the verb. Although the defendant frequently uses the first person with *hear*, he refers to (1) his own prior disadvantageous confession, (2) condemning depositions of other witnesses against him, or (3) written evidence presented in court equally charged against him. The Duke strives to counteract or correct all of these and therefore such usages cannot be considered evidential, as the source of knowledge is not of major importance here, neither is its authoritative justification. On the contrary, evidence is referred to with the intention of diminishing its significance. The strategy, including the not infrequent denial – as in example (88) – is unsuccessful, as it unnecessarily repeats the accusations already stated, thus strengthening rather than undermining their weight. The pattern of use of the perception verb *to hear* in Duke's speech illustrates how, instead of employing an advantageous, though apparently accidental strategy, as is done by Throckmorton, the Duke attempts to save his own skin by means of a consistent, but highly disadvantageous, pattern of use.

(88) *Duke.* I never dealt with that Money, RSA [nor heard of it]; I dealt not at that time with *Barker,* RSA [nor heard any thing of the Rebels], ſince they went into Flanders.

As far as the status of verbs of perception within reported speech is concerned, instances of these are categorised depending on the syntactic structure, as *to hear* refers to an overt act of speech or perception, usually with a traceable anterior utterance (not in the case of negation, however). Although the instances with *as* referred to above, relative clauses have shown less straightforward evidential functions than in the case of *appear*, evidential status was nevertheless proposed for them. At the same time, the hedging function was kept apart, doing justice to the patterns discerned in the data.

4.3.1.5.8 Evidentials – some statistics

Following a qualitative presentation of reported speech instances tagged by KNOW-verbs, a general overview of evidentiality as one of the major pragmatic aspects of the phenomenon can be presented. As the tables (21-25) show, evidential usages of verbs are not limited to one semantic category but are found also with speech act verbs and verbs of saying:

EVIDENTIAL VERB	TOKENS	%
APPEAR	12	25,53
HEAR	7	14,89
fAY	6	12,76
KNOW	6	12,76
PROUE	5	10,64
DECLARE	4	8,51
CONFEfIE	1	2,13
DIfPROUE	1	2,13
DIfCUfIE	1	2,13
PRETEND	1	2,13
fEE	1	2,13
TERME	1	2,13
WITNEfIE	1	2,13
TOTAL	47	100,00

Table 21: Distribution of evidential verbs in the trial of Throckmorton

SOURCE	TOKENS	%	LEMMAS
1ST PERSON	6	12,77	as I have declared (1), I have difproued (1), as I heard fay (1), as I hearde (1), I learne and proue (1), we all know (1)
2ND PERSON	10	21,28	as you haue hearde (2), you haue heard (1), you know well (1), so you faye (1), you fay (1), as you fay (1), as you fee (1), as you did pretend (1), as you termed (1)
3RD PERSON	11	23,40	which he hath confeffed (1), as [Lord] hath fayd (1), as [counfell can] declare (1), which [judges can] declare (1), as Law fhall difcuffe (1), as [worlde] knoweth (2), as the whole [realme] knoweth (1), [vaughan's confession] doeth witneffe (1), as he heard (1), as much as he heareth (1)
PASSIVES	5	10,64	it is alledged and proued (1), as is declared and recited (1), as is faid (1), it is knowen (1), fo be said (1)
NON-FACTIVES			
APPEAR	12	25,53	appeare(4), as appeareth(3), appeareth(2), appeared(1), is apparent(1)
PROUE	1	6,38	that proueth (1)
	2 PASS		it is proued (1), it is euidently proued (1)
TOTAL	47	100,00	

Table 22: Evidential verbs in <TH>: a classification

Reported speech as a marker of stance 151

EVIDENTIAL VERB	TOKENS	%
APPEAR	19	20,64
PROVE	14	15,22
HEAR	12	13,03
KNOW	10	10,87
ſAY	10	10,87
ſEE	8	8,70
CONFEſS	4	4,35
DECLARE	4	4,35
TELL	3	3,25
ALLEDGE	1	1,09
BELIEVE	1	1,09
BRUITE WAS	1	1,09
PROPOSE	1	1,09
REPORT	1	1,09
ſEEME	1	1,09
THINK	1	1,09
WITNEFS	1	1,09
TOTAL	92	100,00

Table 23: Distribution of evidential verbs in the trial of Norfolk

	TOKENS	%	LEMMAS
1ST PERSON	9	9,78	I confeſs'd (1), I have declared (1), as I have ſaid(2), as I have heard(2), as I do know(1), as I had told (1), as we believe(1)
2ND PERSON	18	19,57	as you ſay(1), you ſee(7), as you have heard (2), you have heard(4), you have heard evidence(1), you hear(2), as you well know(1)
3RD PERSON	17	18,48	as he hath confeſs'd(2), as he told(1), it ſeemeth(1), as [lords can] declare(1), [lords can] witneſs(1), [lords] heard(1), [lords] do well know(1), as [messengers can] tell(1), as the [worlde]knoweth(1), as [duke] confeſſed(1), as bruite was(1), as [barker] ſaid (2),[god] doth know(1), as they ſay(2)
PASSIVE	15	16,30	it hath been ſeen(1), as hath been alledged(1), as hath been declared(1), as hath been ſaid(1), it is ſaid(1), it is well known(4), as he was ſaid(1), it was known (1), as was reported(1), as declared(1), as propos'd(1), have it thought(1)
NON-FACTIVES			
APPEAR	19	20,64	as (it) may appear(2), appeareth(6), it appeareth(8), as appeareth(1), it hath appear'd(1), as hath well appeared(1)
PROVE	8	8,70	this (which) proveth(3), the conveying away proveth(1), it proved(1), [questions] prov'd(1),he proveth(1), [serjeante] hath prov'd(1)
	6 pass	6,53	it is well proved(2), it is ſufficiently prov'd(1), it is plainly prov'd(1), the Duke is proved (1), as hath been proved(1)
TOTAL	92	100,00	

Table 24: Evidential verbs in <N>: a classification

The table below (Table 25) shows the statistical differences in the distribution of parenthetical verbs between the two trials:

		<TH>	<N>
ALL TOKENS	TOTAL	47	92
	NORMALISED FIGURE PER 10,000 WORDS	28,74	21,47
	DISTINCTIVENESS RATIO		1,34
DEFENDANTS' TOKENS	TOTAL	15	23
	PERCENTAGES	31,91	25,00
	NORMALISED FIGURE PER 10,000 WORDS	9,17	5,37
	DISTINCTIVENESS RATIO		1,71
OTHERS' TOKENS	TOTAL	32	69
	PERCENTAGES	68,09	75,00
	NORMALISED FIGURE PER 10,000 WORDS	19,57	16,10

Table 25: Comparison of evidentials' distribution in two trials

On the whole, DR's between the two trials are not as high as in the case of parentheticals. As the table above also shows, the statistical distribution of evidentials in the speech of the defendants does not coincide with the success criterion, as DR is not strikingly high i.e., at 1,71, though it clearly points to a definitely more frequent application by Nicholas Throckmorton. Generally, the use of evidentials by the defendants is marginal, which is not surprising given the fact that it is a strategy belonging to the institutional role of court officials, as is confirmed by the statistics. Important features of evidential RSAs are: occurrence in *as* relative clauses (cf. lemmas in Tables 22 and 24), frequent correlation with the passive and *it* impersonal subject, and the use with the perfect tense.

4.3.1.5.9 Hedges – a brief summary

A range of verbs occurring in evidential functions are viewed as hedges (*seem, doubt, appear, allege, think*). Though marginal in the data under consideration (9 instances in <TH> and 4 in <N> distributed equally between the court officials and the defendants), hedges have been discussed above on several occasions (most importantly, sections 4.3.1.5.1 and 4.3.1.5.5). It is necessary, however, to briefly summarise the findings as to this phenomenon. First of all, hedges are usually intrusive clauses or they fulfil the structural demands on RSAs and are categorised accordingly. There is a single instance which does not conform to the RSA pattern, as in (81) above (section 4.3.1.5.6), which is categorised as an instance of IS on the basis of its structure. As far as the functional properties of hedges are concerned, comparing two differently categorised examples of the same verb illustrates important points:

(89) <N>
    a. RSA INV NP [Now is the queſtion, DS Q [How far the Inſtructions extended, whether to matter of High-Treafon, RSA PASS EV [as hath been alledged,] or no?]
    b. I had not the Cipher, nor ſaw any ſuch Letter RSA HEDGE [as you alledge].

(90) <TH>
    a. And FORMULA it pleaſe you, DA [my Lordes,] RSA HEDGE [foraſmuche as it ſeemeth] theſe Men of the Jurie RSA [which haue ſtraungely acquitte the Priſoner of his Trea-ſons whereof RSA PASS [hee was indited],]...

<N>
    b. IS EV THAT-DEL [it ſeemeth you have had Books and Counſel], RSA [you alledge Books, Statutes, and *Bracton*]

(91) <TH>
    a. DS NP [I had theſe Words to *Winter,* RSA [when he enformed me of it;] RSA PAR THAT-DEL [I think] RTA [M. *Wyat* would no *Engliſhman* hurt], and this Enterpriſe cannot be done without the hurt and laughter of both Parties;]
    b. DS [Then *Throckmorton* ſaid, ſithence M. Sergeante you haue red and gathered the place RSA HEDGE [as you think,] that maketh moſt againſt me,]

Examples (89) and (90) clearly show that the distinction between the evidential and hedging function of the same verbal RSA lies exclusively in pragmatic considerations i.e., in example (89a), the court official emphasises that he is relying on a specific source of knowledge, framing his implication in a conducive question. In (89b), which is drawn from the Duke's speech, the same phrase is used to distance the speaker from the accusation that he attempts to challenge. Similarly, the different categorisations of *seem* in (90) (a) and (b) can only be substantiated with reference to the context. Both instances come from the speech of the attorney and are uttered towards the end of both trials. In (90a) the attorney expresses his negligent attitude and a degree of disbelief towards the undesirable acquitting verdict of the jury, thus *seem* has been assigned a hedging, and not an evidential function. In (90b) the attorney points out the evident recourse of the accused to legal resources, which the latter had demanded in the initial stage of the trial, thus implying that he had no access to them. Thus, the evidential function of *seem* underlines the fact that the accused has just been caught lying, which naturally damages his credibility.

As example (91) illustrates – in contrast to the distinction between hedges and evidential usages – the distinction between the parenthetical and hedging function of the same tagging verb is syntactic, not pragmatic in nature. For instance, it is not unlikely that in example (91a), the speaker (i.e., Nicholas

Throckmorton) is hedging the proposition just as he is in (91b), but the distinction between PAR and HEDGE categories is based on the structural properties and the syntactic relationship between the RSA and the proposition. Also, parenthetical expressions have a wider functional scope of functions than hedges (cf. sections 4.3.1.3 above).

4.3.2 Concluding remarks

The focus on the categorisation procedure in the investigation into reported speech illustrated three general points. Firstly, it was shown that the pragmatic character of the phenomenon surface already in the course of categorisation. Secondly, both the quantitative and qualitative significance of verbs as tags of reported speech instances were demonstrated. Thirdly, the crucial pragmatic feature of reported speech – its role as a marker of stance, understood as the relationship between the reporting speaker and their representation, was proposed and corroborated.

Most importantly, the following issues were clarified in the discussion above: Leech and Short's model (1981) has been properly extended and adjusted to the data under analysis in five major ways: (1) aspects of thought presentation were revised to account for the institutional data, so was the concept of the narrator; (2) the status of reporting clauses as reported speech was reclaimed; (3) discourse markers overlapping with potential verbal tags were incorporated in the categorisation procedure; (4) parenthetical verbal structures were accounted for and received a special status within the speech and thought representation cline; (5) the intricacy of mental verbs as instances of reported speech was pointed out and resolved; (6) concepts of epistemic modality and evidentiality were incorporated in the analysis of reported speech.

Chapter Five

Pragmatic aspects of individual reported speech categories

5.1 Introduction: embedding levels

The aim of this chapter is to present further pragmatic features of reported speech categorised on the basis of Leech and Short's model (1981) extended and emended in chapter four. The following sections apply quantitative methods of description to provide a more detailed, though selective, illustration of individual categories. Taking into account the issue of embedding, whose significance has been substantiated in the previous sections (cf. 2.3, 2.5), two levels of description are discerned, i.e. the textual and interaction level. The analysis of the former takes into consideration the organisation of the text viewed from the perspective of reported speech, focusing on the distinction between dialogic speech events (direct speech) and other (non-direct[1]) modes of speech presentation. In terms of reported speech categories this distinction corresponds to the traditional dichotomy of direct and indirect speech, the former understood as dialogue on this level. On the other hand, the interaction level, comprising all of the categories discussed in the previous chapter, is much more intricate, as the number of embedding levels that it may involve is theoretically infinite. Moreover, the distribution of some categories on this level does not always correspond to well-defined contextualisations. Still, as far as the distribution of reported speech on the level of interaction is concerned, it is assumed that a detailed quantitative presentation of the individual categories serves the purpose of identifying some further pragmatic characteristics of the phenomenon. Finally, some space is devoted to a comparison of general features of reported speech in state trials and ecclesiastical records in order to corroborate the assumption as to the greater suitability of the former for a pragmatic study (cf. 3.1.1).

5.2 Pragmatic aspects of reports and dialogue – the textual level

In order to distinguish the presentations of spoken elements of courtroom procedure from dialogic interaction between witnesses and court officials, instances of the former are generally labelled as reports; cf. the examples below:

(92) <TH>
Firſte, after RSA NP PP [Proclamation made], and RSA PP [the Commiſſion read] the Lieutenant of the *Tower*, Maſter *Tho. Bridges*, brought the Priſoner to the Barre; then RSA PASS [Silence was commaunded,]

---

[1] Distinguishing non-direct from indirect modes enables a clearer presentation on the two levels.

(93) <N>
RSA PASS [Which then was read by the Clerk of the Crown.]

Additionally, the courtroom procedure may involve bringing forth external evidence, collected prior to the trial, such as witness depositions (confessions), or letters of various parties, including the defendants. These may constitute much longer speech events than in (92) and (93), and are more frequent in <N>, as in this trial the prosecution is based exclusively on preliminary evidence with no witnesses interrogated during the trial (cf. 3.2.2.1). In <TH> dialogue in the form of witness examination in the courtroom is an additional source of evidence. This explains the difference in the word count ratio of reports against dialogue between the trials, as shown in Table 26:

	<TH>	<N>
% OF REPORTS IN THE TOTAL RS WORD COUNT	12,51%	25,18%
% OF DIALOGUE IN THE TOTAL RS WORD COUNT	87,49%	74,82%
RATIO OF DIALOGUE VS. REPORTS	6,99	2,97

Table 26: Word count of reports vs. dialogue – textual level

Naturally, the presentation of verbal interaction by means of dialogue provides a faithful reflection of the actual institutional procedure. Additionally, the pragmatic aspect of direct speech i.e., its vividness and theatrical nature (Wierzbicka 1974, Tannen 1986), contributes to the "involvement creating capacity" (Collins 2001: 68, cf. Clark and Gerrig 1990) of the text-type. Furthermore, in the case of treason trials viewed as political manipulations (cf. Barrell 1992, chapter 6), this aspect of the record is of particular significance, as it utilises one other pragmatic feature of direct speech presentation i.e., it gives the addressee a deceptive impression of objectivity (cf. Matoesian 2000: 883 on the authenticity of direct speech). Rather than presenting the actual speech events in court as processed information, which is achieved through non-direct strategies, the presentation by means of dialogue is allegedly unmediated and it puts the addressee "in the position of a witness who must evaluate the represented speech event" (Collins 2001: 68). Consequently, extant use of dialogue may result in assigning the perspective of a participant to the readers and in this way give them an illusion of being able to draw their own conclusions, rather than having to depend on ready-made interpretations. Such a presentation, relying on the semblance of verbatimness (Collins 2001: 51), may succeed in securing the preconceived interpretation of the course of events in the trial record, which shows how the legal domain may become a manipulation tool in the hands of political authorities. Indeed, treason trials used to enjoy the greatest interest of contemporary authorities, as Green claims: "In a succession of well-known state trials, mainly for treason, the Tudor and Stuart monarch pressed their advantage to the fullest" (1985: 106).

Pragmatic aspects of individual reported speech categories 157

Reports of conventional verbal activities, which are numerous in the elaborate institutional procedure, occur very often in the non-direct mode, as in example (92) above. This, in the first place, serves the purpose of economy, as RSA is basically a summarising strategy (Leech and Short 1981: 324). Besides, on the textual level, the non-direct modes are particularly well suited for repetitive speech events, such as readings of depositions and letters. By means of non-direct strategies the courtroom procedure is reduced to the background in contrast to the more prominent dialogic interaction and in this way the involvement-creating effect of the record is further enhanced, also by preventing the reader from becoming overburdened and bored with unnecessary detail. Moreover, the courtroom procedure always follows strict rules and is predictable, therefore it neither requires a meticulous account, nor does it actually deserve devoting substantial space to it. Economy of presentation by means of non-direct modes makes the record readable and saves the receivers' processing effort by providing information that has already been in a way processed by someone else.

Rather surprisingly, though generally backgrounded, presentations of court procedure may involve an emphatic strategy: in <N>, inversion in the majority of cases coincides with RSA (81,81%). This usage has a well-defined discourse function i.e., applied for the summaries of court procedure it adds prominence to the reported events by virtue of marking boundaries between different discourse levels. Thus, economy – in the use of summarising RSA – is achieved whereas the use of inversion in the reporting clause serves discourse-organising functions.

Less typically, the courtroom procedure is presented as direct speech in the form of isolated turns or turns in dialogue, as in the following examples:

(94) <TH>
Sendall. ᴅᴀ [*Nicholas Throckmorton* Knighte], hold up thy hande, ʀꜱᴀ ᴘᴀꜱꜱ ꜰᴀᴅᴇ ɪɴ [Thou art before this time indited of High-Treafon,]
(95) <N>
The Serjeant again ᴅꜱ ɴᴘ [made Oyer, and proclaim'd thus: ᴅᴀ [*Lieutenant of the* Tower *of* London], *return thy* Habeas Corpus, *and bring forth thy Prifoner* Thomas *Duke of* Norfolk].]

The number, though not the function, of similar instances is close to negligible in <TH> (2.05% of all direct speech turns) but in <N> it is not trivial at 9,56%. Despite the suitability of non-direct reporting modes for the presentation of the courtroom procedure, direct speech occurs inevitably with a foregrounding function. The distribution of similar reports is not limited to, though particularly noteworthy in, the initial and final stages of the trial, serving as frames for the entire discourse. In the initial stages of <N>, single direct speech turns coincide with the role of *Sergeant at Arms*, responsible for keeping order in court and that of the *Clerk of the Crown* "responsible for the framing, reading and recording of the criminal indictments" (Harding 1966 [1973]: 180). In the final sections in <N>

158 Chapter Five

single turns overlap with the institutional part played by Lord Steward, a court functionary who assists the jury and reads the verdict. Thus, a possible motive for the application of direct speech in the beginning and at the end of the trial is the need to enhance the salience of these stages in the courtroom procedure.

Single turns are found also in other stages of the trial in <N> where they coincide with readings of pre-trial depositions or letters which, as has been noted above, are more frequent than in <TH>. In this context two patterns of occurrence may be discerned. Firstly, a single turn of a court official typically precedes the presentation of external evidence as an introduction. Secondly, single turns of the defendant typically follow such a presentation as a response to the evidence that has been brought forth. In this contextualisation, the framing function of foregrounded direct speech is discerned not unlike in the initial and final stages of the trial. Single direct speech turns tend to mark the salience of the boundaries between different discourse levels. Their functions are, however, different from the ones identified above for direct speech (cf. Sternberg's Proteus principle (1982), section 2.7) i.e., single direct speech turns are not designed to secure the perceptual salience of their own but they are auxiliary to important points of courtroom procedure usually expressed by non-direct strategies. It can then be observed that if the principle of economy as well as figure-ground relationship (cf. section 2.3.2.6) do not allow making the crucial institutional moments prominent by presenting them as direct speech, this aim is still to be achieved by means of adjacent positioning of single direct speech turns.

5.2.1 Institutional roles

The analysis of dialogue on the textual level allows discerning the degree of involvement of individual speakers in the interaction. The crucial institutional role in the trial is naturally that of the defendant. On the part of the court in the period under analysis two officials i.e., sergeant-at-law and attorney, are by definition the most active participants. Although in terms of the present-day trial in the legal systems derived from Anglo-Saxon law the former is commonly regarded as the precursor of the barrister and the latter of the solicitor, these institutional roles differ considerably between present-day and Tudor England. To be more specific, historically, sergeants-at-law were pleaders – speakers for the litigant (e.g., Baker 2002: 156) and for that reason their oath of loyalty was made to their clients and not to the court (Harding 1966 [1973]: 174). The role of attorneys, who owed allegiance to the court, was to represent litigants in court in the event of their absence. The distinction between the two, as Baker (2002) puts it, was "between quick-witted and learned courtroom lawyers and managerial, clerkly lawyers" (2002: 157). Also the sergeants, but not attorneys, received regular salaries (Harding 1966 [1973]: 175). Most importantly, neither of the two officials served as counsel to the defendant, as at that time counsel was hardly ever allowed

Pragmatic aspects of individual reported speech categories 159

(Baker 2002: 509-510). Although the office of a solicitor, as is claimed by Harding (1966 [1973]: 177), became an important part of the attorney's profession in the sixteenth century, the function of this clerk as auxiliary to the defendant cannot be observed in the data (i.e., in <N>, where a solicitor appears). In the trials under consideration the adversarial roles of present-day barristers and attorneys are not discerned either. Rather, both sergeants and attorneys act as prosecutors and are thus actively involved in the dialogic interaction, particularly with the defendant. This is corroborated by the distribution of turns among the three most significant institutional roles:

	<TH> TOKENS	%	<N> TOKENS	%
DIALOGUES	16	--	36	--
ALL TURNS	195	100%	293	100%
SINGLE TURNS	4	2,05%	28	9,56%
DEFENDANT'S TURNS	80	41,02%	124	42,32%
SERGEANTS' TURNS	27	13,85%	65	22,18%
ATTORNEYS' TURNS	19	9,74%	34	11,6%
% OF DEFENDANT'S TURNS IN DS WORD COUNT		68,78%		36,56%

Table 27: Dialogue in <TH> and <N>

5.2.1.1 Aspects of defendants' direct speech

In both trials (cf. Table 27), the statistical distribution of turns is similar. The defendants are by far the most active speakers whereas the turns of the major court officials are approximately 10% less frequent. The sheer number of dialogic turns of the defendants does not, however, straightforwardly translate to their success or failure in trial. Rather, it is the word count of defendants' turns that is much more telling in this respect: Throckmorton's direct speech turns amount to nearly 70% of the total word count of direct speech on the textual level in <TH> whereas for Norfolk this figure is lower nearly by half at over 36%. This major quantitative difference is one of the advantages of Throckmorton's strategy.

One further beneficial pattern revealed in the analysis of Throckmorton's turns is the type-to-token ratio of reported speech tags embedded in his direct turns. For one thing, this ratio is by over 8% higher than the one for all tags in <TH>; and secondly, a similar quantitative difference occurs between tags in the turns of Throckmorton and Norfolk (Table 28).

TYPE-TO-TOKEN RATIO IN TAGS	<TH>	<N>
TOTAL TAGS	48,92	38,49
DEFENDANTS' TURNS	57,30	49,62
OTHER	60,21	46,82

Table 28: Type-to-token ratio in tags

160   Chapter Five

The type-to-token ratio measured for reported speech tags reflects the range of reporting strategies applied by the speaker; in other words, if it is high it may be viewed as speaker-based whereas if it is low as a hearer-based strategy (Collins 2001: 72). Tagging reports explicitly the speaker exploits the evaluative potential of reported speech, leaving little room for interpretation on the part of the hearer and in this way controlling the reception of information. The dominant role played by the successful defendant in his trial is thus manifested in the relatively high word count of his turns as well as in the degree to which he decides to control information processing by means of tagging strategies. On the contrary, the Duke of Norfolk fails to take advantage of either strategy. Moreover, (cf. Table 29) the third most frequent verbal tag in the Duke's turns is a speech act verb, *confess*, whose meaning is in general not advantageous to the position of the accused.

<N> Word	TOKENS	%	<TH> Word	TOKENS	%
SAY	58	7,38	SAY	51	7,92
TELL	38	4,83	SPEAKE	31	4,81
CONFESS	33	4,20	KNOW	29	4,50
KNOW	33	4,20	IPRAYPAR	26	4,04
ANSWER	22	2,80	THINK	15	2,33
HEAR	22	2,80	HEARE	12	1,86
SPEAK	18	2,29	TALKE	12	1,86
IBESEECHPAR	18	2,29	TRIE	12	1,86
PROOVE	15	1,91	ANSWER	11	1,71
THINK	15	1,91	PROOVE	11	1,71

Table 29: Comparison of the most frequent tags in defendants' speech

Given that 19 out of 33 total occurrences of *confess* in the Duke's speech (57,6%) have *I* as the subject (cf. (96) below), it becomes evident that one aspect of the Duke's strategy is confirmation of the alleged misdeeds as they are gradually brought forth in the course of the trial. Thus, in response to a conducive question Norfolk fails to stand in his own defence:

(96) <N>
Serj. How ftandeth this with the Duty and Oath of a Counfellor, to $_{RSA\ NP}$ [give Advice to a foreign Prince againft the Queen's Majefty]?
Duke. $_{RSA}$ [I excufe it not], $_{RSA}$ [herein I confefs my Error]

Similarly, reacting to his own condemning letter quoted in court, in which his attempts to marry Mary Stuart are proved, the defendant eats the humble pie:

(97) <N>
Duke. ... $_{RSA}$ [Indeed I muft confefs my Folly]; it is an ill Cook that cannot lick his own Fingers

These examples (96 and 97) illustrate the cooperative strategy of defence applied by Norfolk. The analyses of courtroom discourse based on Grice's maxims of conversation and the cooperation principle (cf. e.g., Brown and Levinson 1987: 95; Levinson 1983: 100-104; Kalisz 1993: 67-81) have been carried out by Archer (2002) and Kahlas-Tarkka and Rissanen (forthcoming) on the basis of the Salem witchcraft trials. The results of the latter study show that successful strategies involve cooperation with the interrogators i.e., providing relevant information as well as the avoidance of conflict. In terms of Brown and Levinson's politeness theory (1987), the latter is an instance of negative politeness aimed at minimising threats against the negative face of the hearer. Contrary to the claims of Kahlas-Tarkka and Rissanen (forthcoming) for the Salem defendants, cooperation and avoidance of the threatening face of court officials, to which the Duke frequently resorts, do not render positive results in his case. Although aspects of unsuccessful strategies identified in the Salem records, such as denial of guilt, definitely occur in the Duke's defence, this uncooperative response is limited only to the beginning and the end of the trial. The contradiction between the general position of innocence and the specific speech events in the course of the trial in which the defendant is fully cooperative and eager to confess, is one more factor which undermines the Duke's credibility and contributes to his downfall. This is not surprising given that admission of guilt in Brown and Levinson's theory is considered an instance of direct damage of the speaker's positive face (1987: 68) and that the accused is subject to trial by jury.

Despite the evidence provided by the Salem witchcraft trials where the defendants who do not yield to threats and refuse to confess their guilt are unsuccessful, Throckmorton saves his life even though he is not at all cooperative. His talkativeness conflates the maxim of quantity, his non-informative statements – the maxim of relevance and he resorts to face threatening acts:

(98) <TH>
 a. *Throckmorton.* Noe, I did not fo; $_{RSA\ IMP}$ [proue it.]
 b. *Throckmorton.* Truly $_{RSA}$ [I did not tell him fo,] $_{RTA}$ [but I care not greatly to giue you that Weapon to play you withal:] now let us fee what you can make of it?

In denying the accusations as in (98a), the defendant fails to apply redressive strategies recommendable for this speech act i.e., he fails to seek agreement or avoid disagreement (positive strategies 5 and 6, Brown and Levinson 1987: 112-117) and in imposing his will on the hearer by means of the imperative, he fails to apply strategies of conventional indirectness suitable for requests, or hedge the illocutionary force (negative strategies 1 and 2, Brown and Levinson 1987: 132-172). Moreover, by expressing disagreement and contempt, and by openly challenging other dialogue participants, Throckmorton threatens their positive face. Not infrequently, the defendant threatens also the negative face of the court officials by requests such as:

(99) <TH>
Throckmorton. ᴅᴀ [My Lords,] ʀꜱᴀ ᴘᴀʀ [I pray you] make not too much hafte with me, neither thinke not long for your Diner, for my Cafe requireth leyfure, and you haue well dined when you haue done Juftice truly. ᴅꜱ [Chrift faid, [ʀꜱᴀ [*Bleſſed are they*] *that hunger and thirfte for Righteoufneſſe.*]
Bromley. I can forbeare my Dinner as well as you, and ʀᴛᴀ [care as little as you] peraduenture.
Shrewfbury. Come you hither to checke us, *Throckmorton?* we will not be fo ufed, no, no, I for my part haue forborne my Breakfaft, Dinner and Supper, to ferve the Queene.
Throckmorton. Yea, ᴅᴀ [my good Lord], ʀᴛᴀ [I know it right well;] ʀᴛᴀ [I meant not ʀꜱᴀ ɪɴꜰ [to touche your Lordfhip],] ʀꜱᴀ ᴘᴀꜱꜱ ᴇᴠ [for youre Service and Paines is euidently knowen to all Men]

The exchange in (99) comes from the initial stages of the interrogation and it follows the point at which the defendant has been conventionally asked how he pleads. Rather than accept the institutionally pre-planned course of the trial, Thockmorton fails to provide an answer and in this way to satisfy the positive face of court officials, making his own request instead. In the quoted exchange the negative face of the hearers is threatened again by the next – this time unmitigated – request. Thus, in his very first turns the defendant assumes an uncooperative attitude by failing to show deference to court officials and compliance with the normative rules of the institution. As Harris points out (2003), when performing a request in institutional settings the less powerful interlocutor clearly threatens the positive face of the institutionally empowered participant. Even though through apologising for the offence taken by the court officials, Throckmorton pretends to apply a redressive strategy – at the same time threatening his own positive face – as in any apology, the excessive and irrelevant information (cf. the maxim of quantity) which he adds constitutes another threat to the hearer's positive face. By going *off record* in *youre Service and Paines is euidently knowen to all Men* i.e., implying more than one unambiguous intention and avoiding commitment (Brown and Levinson 1987: 69) in this ironic statement, Throckmorton in fact threatens the positive face of the hearers once more. In general, off-record strategies are beneficial in that they allow speakers to shed responsibility and avoid accountability for the statement (Brown and Levinson 1987: 73). The reluctance on the part of the defendant to apply redressive strategies, or applying these but out of insincere causes, as in the example just discussed (98), demonstrates his rejection and withdrawal from the role of the less powerful interlocutor. Rather than accept the degree of power inherent in the institutional position of the accused, Throckmorton in the early stage of the trial claims for himself power defined as "the ability to impose one's own plans and self-evaluation" (Harris 2003: 36). Thus, violating maxims of conversation and threatening both the positive and negative face of the court officials in his direct speech on the textual level, the defendant contributes to the collapse of the well-defined institutional hierarchy and surprisingly, this strategy turns out to be beneficial in contrast to the cooperative attitude of the Duke of Norfolk who, to his own detriment, conforms to the institutional role imposed on him.

5.2.2 Possible directions of reported speech analysis – the textual level

Some quantitative data pertaining to the distribution of non-direct strategies and dialogue in the analysed trials was presented above. Not claiming to provide a conclusive overview of pragmatic aspects of reported speech surfacing on the textual level, this selective illustration of possible theoretical directions of research demonstrates the explanatory potential of pragmatic theories (Grice's maxims of conversation, Brown and Levinson's politeness theory) in this respect. Moreover, the sections above corroborate the statements as to the pragmatic nature of the analysed phenomenon (cf. section 2.3.2.2.3).

5.3 Features of reported speech on the interaction level

The analysis of reported speech categories on the level of interaction involves all instances embedded in the textual level. The non-direct textual level reports as well as dialogic and single direct speech turns may encompass a range of embedding levels e.g., letters may include reports of conversations, etc. It is, however, not so much the degree of embedding that is of major interest here but the distribution of individual reported speech categories, their correlation with other linguistic features, and the pragmatic aspects of the identified combinations. First of all, it is striking that the quantitative distribution of categories is very similar in both texts:

	RSA	IS	DS	FIS	FDS	RTA	IT	FIT	TOTAL[2]
<TH>									
TOKENS	710	138	44	1	3	188	49	--	1133
%	62,67	12,18	3,88	0,09	0,26	16,60	4,32	--	100,00
<N>									
TOKENS	1508	403	91	6	--	405	109	1	2523
%	59,77	15,97	3,61	0,24	--	16,05	4,32	0,04	100,00

Table 30: Comparison of the distribution of reported speech categories in <TH> and <N>

---

[2] The discrepancy between the overall number of all categories and the total number of tags (cf. chapter four) occurs because in the final count the untagged reports, e.g., free categories and the fade in instances, are included, thus adding to the number of instances but not tags.

Also the order of frequency of individual categories does not differ significantly between the texts. The only marginal point of disagreement concerns the occasional free categories of which FDS does not occur in <N> at all, while FIT is absent from <TH> (cf. 4.2.1). On the whole, thought reporting comprises roughly 20% of all instances whereas the rest of cases report speech (cf. 4.2.1). The strikingly high frequency in both trials of RSAs in comparison to other categories is somewhat circularly accounted for by the wide syntactic scope of this category which was additionally extended by the revisions applied to Leech and Short's model (1981) in the previous chapter. RTA and IS categories have similar frequency, with the latter being slightly higher in <N>. DS and IT are uncommon at approximately 4%.

5.3.1 Pragmatic aspects of selected grammatical features of reported speech categories

There is more variation between the trials with respect to the distribution of the grammatical features against reported speech categories, as presented below:

	<TH>							<N>					
	RSA	IS	DS	RTA	IT	TOTAL		RSA	IS	DS	RTA	IT	TOTAL	
DO SUP	57	18	1	19	3	97	8,56%	25	8	--	11	2	46	1,82%
FADE IN	5	2	--	--	--	7	0,62%	24	2	1	3	1	31	0,83%
GERUND	7	6	2	7	3	25	2,21%	46	7	4	33	16	106	4,20%
IMP	18	1	--	8	11	38	3,35%	15	4	--	12	4	35	1,39%
INF	113	9	--	11	2	135	11,91%	173	23	1	38	6	241	9,55%
INTER	2	1	2	--	--	5	0,44%	--	--	3	--	1	4	0,16%
INV	4	--	--	--	1	5	0,44%	44	7	2	2	--	55	2,18%
Q	46	15	4	5	1	71	6,27%	27	16	4	4	6	57	2,26%
PASS	131	8	1	18	1	159	14,03%	278	46	4	38	4	370	14,66%
POST	--	1	2	--	1	4	0,35%	3	--	2	1	4	10	0,39%
PP	18	--	--	3	--	21	1,85%	48	2	--	8	1	59	2,34%
PROGR	4	1	--	2	--	7	0,62%	10	3	--	1	1	15	0,59%
						574	50,66%						1029	40,78%

Table 31: Correlation between selected grammatical features and reported speech categories

As can be seen in Table 31, this variation concerns the use of the periphrastic *do*[3] in affirmative statements, which is over 4 times as frequent in <TH> than in <N>. Also questions and imperative forms of the verb in reported speech occur roughly twice as often as in <N>. A striking difference occurs in the distribution of inversion which – though marginal on the whole – is over 4 times as frequent in

---

[3] The rise of periphrastic *do* has received considerable attention in English historical linguistics, cf. e.g., Görlach (1991), Barber (1997), Stein (1990) and Nurmi (1999).

<N> as in <TH> (cf. 5.2). Less remarkably, reported speech instances tagged with a gerund are more frequent in the former trial, and so are the occurrences with the infinitives as tags.

As far as periphrastic *do* is concerned – a marker of emphatic language at present as well as in Early Modern English (Stein 1990: 50) – its frequency is particularly revealing in the speech of the defendants at 49,48% in <TH> and only 23,91% in <N>. The use of this grammatical feature by the successful defendant is a powerful rhetorical device with 41,66% of cases having *I* as referent and 33,33% with the *Statute*, *Law* or personal names of witnesses as subjects, all providing authoritative or evidential sources supporting Throckmorton's argument, as in the following examples:

(100) <TH>
   a. RSA [I will aunſwer to the Inditement], and RSA DO SUP AP [do pleade not giltie to the whole, and to euery part...]
   b. IS DO SUP [for Wiat did purge me RTA [that I knew nothing of his ſtirre].]
   c. and therefore IS [you ſhall heare RSA DO SUP [what your owne Lawe doth ſay].]

The rhetorical function of these examples (100) is similar to that of *solemn declaration* which, according to Rissanen (1985 [1998]: 208), is a feature of official document style in Early Modern English. Also, as the author claims, in his data, paradoxically, periphrastic *do* is typical of spoken or conversational language, while its major purpose is "to put forth weighty arguments and to confirm or refute them" (Rissanen 1985 [1998]: 208). On the whole, as the author concludes, this grammatical device comprises both the official style and emotive expression. Stein (1990: 31-42) devotes substantial attention to periphrastic *do* as a marker of discourse semantic prominence. Foregrounding effects achieved by this structure are largely contrastive, frequently coinciding with negation i.e., the proposition uttered is in contrast with the pre-existing knowledge (Stein 1990: 37). Given this fact, reported speech instances with periphrastic *do* may be viewed as powerful evaluating comments by means of which the speech of the defendant becomes more persuasive. The infrequent occurrence of this feature in the Duke's speech once again demonstrates that the unsuccessful defendant fails to exploit one further linguistic tool so aptly used by Nicholas Throckmorton.

One other rather marginal advantageous strategy of Throckmorton is the use of the imperative with reported speech, which in his speech constitutes 71,05% of all cases in the trial (in <N> this figure is also high, at 51,43%). In terms of politeness, imposition of one's will on others threatens their negative face, therefore the frequency of imperative in the defendant's speech is another reflection of his conflicting strategy (but cf. sections 4.3.1.3.2). It is noteworthy that Throckmorton's imperatives are clearly correlated with thought reporting of others (two third of all instances), as in the following example:

(101) <TH>
a. Firſt ᴿˢᴬ ᴾᴬᴿ [I pray you] ᴿᵀᴬ ᴵᴹᴾ [remember the ſmall Familiaritie betwixt Vaughan and...]
b. ᴿˢᴬ ᴾᴬᴿ [I praye you of my Jurie] which haue my Lyfe in Triall, ᴵᵀ ᴵᴹᴾ [note well what things at this daye bee Treaſons...]

In the majority of cases imperatives used with verbs of cognition serve the purpose of entering the territory of the hearer's thoughts and entail attempts at influencing their prospective decisions.

The distribution of gerunds in reporting clauses in <N> shows the following interesting properties. First of all, in 84,9% of cases gerunds occur in the speech of court officials or in the quoted evidence. In the former contextualisation there is a clear correlation with thought reporting (44,44%), as in example (102) below:

(102) <N>
and yet ᴿᵀᴬ ᴳᴱᴿᵁᴺᴰ [the Duke of Norfolk knowing this], practiſed to compaſs this Marriage.

According to Collins (2001: 77), not only gerundival but all participial clauses are used cross-linguistically as backgrounding devices. This stems from the fact that, in comparison to a finite verb form, participles encode fewer descriptive categories. As Collins (2001) goes on to observe, pragmatically participles and gerunds are effective in presenting non-sequenced events of secondary order i.e., those that are dependent on other events expressed in the main clause. Given that frequently instances like (102) occur as part of elaborate narrations of evidence against the accused, involving both reports of his alleged intentions and the overt acts, the correlation with thought reporting categories becomes most suitable. Also combining the accusing evidence of intent with overt practice is not accidental. Most probably it is related to the mitigation in the year 1547 (Baker 2002: 528) of the harsh Edwardian treason law, in force since 1352, which did not require an overt act to occur as an essential prerequisite for conviction. From 1547, despite the manipulative character of treason trials (cf. 5.2), which was maintained, words or intent alone could not have been taken as treasonable activities any more. Thus, in reporting thought by means of gerund – signifying an action of secondary order – court officials and witnesses who gave preliminary depositions were able to foreground the importance of overt act as a treasonable activity, at the same time not forgetting to add even more weight to the accusation by mentioning treasonable intent.

In both texts, reported speech frequently coincides with passivisation which, in the case of an unspecified agent, is an impersonalising strategy (cf. Görlach 1991: 116, Seoane Posse 2000). This reveals a tendency in the analysed text-type to strive toward informational redundancy with the agent being either anaphorically or cataphorically retrievable or not relevant at all (cf. Seoane Posse 2000: 108). Not accidentally, the passive in reported speech tags is clearly correlated with the major summarising category i.e., RSA (82,39% in <TH> and 75,13% in <N> of all passive tags).

In certain respects the overall statistical presentation of reported speech categories on the level of interaction is less likely to reveal the pragmatic aspects of the phenomenon than a similar presentation carried out on the textual level (cf. 5.2). For instance, as Table 32 demonstrates, there are no substantial differences in the distribution of reported speech categories in the speech of two defendants. This finding reveals the weak points of exclusively quantitative approaches to reported speech, as there undoubtedly exist numerous points of disagreement between the successful and the unsuccessful defendant, which were demonstrated in chapter three and in the analysis of the textual level, as well as in some correlations with grammatical features such as periphrastic *do* or the imperative on the level of interaction.

	RSA	IS	DS	FIS	FDS	RTA	IT	FIT	ALL
<TH>									
TOKENS	423	60	21	--	2	115	33	--	654
%	64,68	9,17	3,21	--	0,31	17,58	5,05	--	100,00
<N>									
TOKENS	478	127	24	1	--	126	36		792
%	60,35	16,03	3,03	0,13	--	15,91	4,55	--	100,00

Table 32: Comparison of the distribution of reported speech categories in the speech of the defendants

5.3.2 RSA – the dominant strategy and control

The overwhelming number of instances of this strategy approximating 60% in both trials (cf. Table 31) does not permit the identification of a limited number of well-defined contextualisations in which it typically occurs. Some of the functions of RSAs have been referred to above, including the most basic summarising effect. Characteristically, the syntactic features of this strategy i.e., high degree of integration between the reporting and reported constituents, render it most suitable for embedding into other categories. The fact that RSAs are in a way immersed in other reports explains why their primary function "is not to convey messages but rather to assert that the given types of illocutionary acts or perlocutionary effects occurred" (Collins 2001: 125). Similarly, Thompson (1996), who uses the term

168   Chapter Five

summary for reports corresponding to RSAs, claims that embedding determines the fact that in this category "the focus is likely to be on the speech event more than the message" (1996: 517). This opinion, as can be concluded from the data investigated in this study, is more likely to hold true for the RSAs as one of the non-direct strategies occurring on the textual level. On the level of interaction such a claim is definitely exaggerated, as the diversity of reporting tags in this category makes RSAs the most speaker-based strategy of all. Thus, the frequency of these in the institutional data is connected with the fact that speakers representing all institutional roles, motivated by vested and conflicting interests, apply in their speech the strategies which allow exercising the greatest possible control over the interpretation process.

5.3.3 Indirect speech – hierarchy of information prominence

The distribution of indirect speech on the level of interaction differs slightly between the trials with 4% more instances in <N> than in <TH> (cf. Table 31). Similarly, there are almost 7% more examples of IS embedded in the speech of the Duke than in that of Nicholas Throckmorton (cf. Table 32). The former difference stems from the fact that the basic contextualisation of this reporting mode is within 'reports of reports' or, in other words, inside longer reporting chunks comprising several layers of embedded reported speech. Also, as far as the institutional roles are concerned, this mode is roughly evenly distributed between the speech of the defendant and the rest of discourse in <TH> but in <N> 68,49% of all IS instances occur outside the Duke's speech. This quantitative difference is linked to the more frequent occurrence of external (i.e., preliminary depositions or letters) evidence in the latter trial. Typically, indirect speech instances cluster in stretches of evidence, particularly when a reporting person, usually a witness interrogated in a preliminary hearing, refers to their conversations with others, as in the following examples (103 a and b), both drawn from depositions of the Bishop of Ross, the ambassador of the Scottish Queen and the most important witness against the Duke severely tortured into confession:

(103) <N>
    a.   RSA [I talk'd with the Duke alone in a Gallery], IS [where he utter'd to me, RTA NP FADE IN [That he bore good Will to the Queen my Miftrefs]
    b.   IS [To the 9th he faith, That the Earl of *Murray* RTA AP [was in fear to have been murdered by the way, in his Return to *Scotland*...]

The use of IS is determined in (103a) by pronoun deixis i.e., the referent of first person pronouns is clearly the present speaker if indirect speech is used for the reported speakers, but it would become ambiguous if direct speech was used instead. On the higher embedding level in (103b) similar motives determine the choice of the indirect mode. The court official reading or reporting the evidence of witnesses avoids the confusion of first person pronoun referents, at the same time avoiding changes of deictic pivot and footing (cf. section 2.6.2). As Goffman claims, changes in footing normally obstruct discourse flow (1981: 150-152). Avoidance of such changes is ultimately advantageous to the hearers who do not have to adjust their perspective as though back and forth between different levels of embedding, thus being able to save extra processing effort. Also the hierarchy of information prominence is clearly constructed by means of different strategies. That is to say, on the textual level the non-direct strategy fulfils backgrounding functions and similarly on deeper embedding levels the accounts of no special prominence, which are nevertheless perceptually challenging because of their quantity, are designed so as not to attract too much of the hearer's attention by shifts in perspective. An additional argument for this pragmatic effect of the indirect reporting mode is its not infrequent correlation with complementiser deletion as a further cohesion-promoting factor (cf. *that-del* figures in Table 33):

	<TH>IS: 138		<N>IS: 403	
	TOKENS	%	TOKENS	%
THAT	41	29,71	135	33,50
THAT-DEL	20	14,49	71	17,62
PASS	8	5,80	46	11,41
INF	9	6,52	23	5,71
DO SUP	18	13,04	8	1,98
GERUND	6	4,25	7	1,74
Q	15	10,87	16	2,48
INV	--	--	7	1,74
PP	--	--	2	0,49

Table 33: Comparison of selected grammatical features of IS in <TH> and <N>

One other pattern of indirect speech in the discussed contextualisation is dyadic exchanges i.e., in the reported exchange both turns occur in the indirect mode:

(104) <N>
Being at *Titchfield*, RSA [the Queen's Majefty called him to her Gallery, IS Q GERUND [afking of him, Whether he had dealt any wife for the Marriage of the Queen of *Scots*, RSA PASS EV [as it was reported]? IS [Whereunto he anfwered, THAT-DEL RSA PAR [He thought] THAT-DEL RSA [her Majefty had heard by others].]]

Assymetrical dyadic exchanges do, however, occur in <TH>:

(105) <TH>
Throckmorton mette with *Winter* one Day in *Tower-ftreet*, and IS [told him, RSA AP [that Sir *Thomas Wyat* was defirous RSA INF [to fpeak with him,] IS Q [and *Winter* demanded where

Wyat was]: *Throckmorton* ₍ds₎ [aunſwered, at his Houſe *in Kente,* not farre from *Gillingham,* ₍RSA EV₎ [as I heard ſay,] where the Shyps lye.]

This stretch is embedded in witness deposition recorded prior to the trial. The switch into DS is completely unexpected, as after the tag *aunſwered* the sentence develops as though it was an uncomplementised indirect report. The evidential intrusive statement with first person pronoun subject disambiguates the reported speech category. The abruptness of direct speech emphasises its responsibility-shedding function and the boundary between the discourse of the witness and that of the reported defendant. Given the fact that this specific witness does not bring forth condemning evidence, the use of direct speech in this case is probably the choice of the sergeant-at-law who on this occasion is reporting the witness's deposition. It should, after all, be in line with the intention of this court official appointed and responsible in front of the royal government to distance himself from the speech of the defendant – his adversary – even if he has to physically serve as 'conduit' for Throckmorton's words. This instance is a perfect illustration of the "leakage of the quoting voice onto the quoted voice" (Besnier 1992: 176) occurring in reported speech typically when authority is exercised (cf. also Parmentier 1993). In terms of Goffman's decomposition of the speaker into different roles (cf. section 2.6), however, the court official acts not as a *principal* i.e., the person taking responsibility, but rather as an *animator* i.e., "sounding box in use" (Goffman 1981: 144), which is typical for authority figures exercising representative institutional roles (cf. Johnstone 1987: 48). In this light, assigning individual intentions to the sergeant-at-law may not be feasible anymore.

5.3.4 Direct speech – heteroglossic information

Despite the infrequent occurrence on the level of interaction (between 3,6 and 3,9% of all instances) this reporting mode shows clear patterns, as e.g., in (105) above. The most consistent correlation is with verba dicendi or other reporting verbs which do not designate speech acts or cognition. In <TH> there is a single example of a speech act verb used as a tag of direct speech, whereas in <N> approximately 7% of instances have such a tag. The use of transparent, semantically faded verbs with direct mode, underlines the aura of objectivity inherent in this mode, achieved mainly by positioning the hearer as a witness to the reported events. Also the theatrical effect of this category (cf. 5.2) and its prominence entailed in the shift of deictic pivot (cf. Bolden 2004: 1092-3 on re-anchoring in direct speech) are moderated by means of tags of relatively low semantic load. This helps to maintain cohesion and mitigate the effects of switches of perspective which are perceptually particularly challenging on deeper embedded levels.

The distribution of the direct strategy among the institutional roles differs considerably between the two trials. In <TH> 47,72% of instances occur in the speech of the defendant, while in <N> this figure is much lower at 26,37%. Bearing in mind the manipulative potential of direct strategies and their suitability for covert authoritative functions, these numbers again point to the strategic use of reported speech by the successful defendant. Additionally, Throckmorton's direct speech conversation reports may become an occasion for employing his rhetorical skills once more, this time through the manipulation of tag position, a feature which itself is extremely rare in both trials:

(106) <TH>
in times paſt I knew another Gentleman occupying this woful place. ... It chanced one of the Juſtices upon Jealouſie of the Priſoner's acquitall, for the goodneſſe of his Cauſe, $_{DS}$ [ſaid to another of his Companions a Juſtice, when the Jury did appeare, $_{RTA}$ [I like not this Jury for our purpoſe], they ſeeme to be too pitiful and too charitable $_{RSA\ INF}$ [to condemne the Priſoner].] $_{DS}$ [No, no, $_{INTER}$ ſaid the other Judge (viz. Cholmley) $_{RSA\ PAR}$ [I warrant you], $_{THAT-DEL}$ they be picked Fel-lowes for the nonce, he ſhall drink of the fame Cup his Fellowes haue done.]

In example (106), medial positioning of the tag contributes to the cohesion of the quoted dialogue, as "[t]he unobtrusiveness of intercalated tags makes them suitable for conveying heteroglossic information" (Collins 2001: 239).

5.3.5 Indirect thought

Although according to Leech and Short (1981: 344), indirect thought is the prototypical way of thought presentation (cf. section 4.2.1), its frequency in the institutional data at 4,32% of all reported speech instances in both trials does not corroborate this claim. The distribution of this category differs significantly between the defendants constituting 67,35% of all instances for Throckmorton and only 33,02% for the Duke. Given the correlation with the imperative in the speech of the successful defendant discussed above (section 5.3.1), this quantitative difference illustrates once more failure of the unsuccessful defendant to utilise advantageous strategies. In <N> (cf. above), there is a correlation with the gerundival clauses making indirect thought a useful strategy on the part of court officials. Also the use of *I* referent is distributed differently in the speech of the defendants; Throckmorton presents his own thoughts only in 30,03% of cases, which equals the number of instances of his attempts to influence the decisions of court officials by the use of the imperative, whereas the Duke expresses his own mental states in 50% of all instances. Furthermore, a half of these coincide with negation or, in other words, when talking about thoughts and affects of his own the Duke uses denial on every second occasion (cf. section 4.3.1.5.7 on disadvantages of denial). Obviously, in denying the unverifiable, the defendant does not enhance his own credibility.

5.3.6 Reports of thought acts

The second most frequent strategy, employed in approximately 16% of all cases, is reporting thought in a prototypical way. Its high frequency in the institutional discourse may be accounted for by its low immediacy and the lack of dramatic effects (Semino and Short 2004: 131), characteristic for free thought reporting categories common in fictional genres. Providing brief insights into mental states this strategy does not undermine the formality of the situation with an inappropriate extrovert taint. Unlike the RSA category, RTA does not entail summarising functions but, as with RSA, its syntactic compactness makes it suitable for embedding in other reports. Similar to the distribution of indirect thought, the speech of two the defendants differs with respect to the frequency of this category: 61,17% of all RTA reports in <TH> belong to the defendant, whereas in <N> this figure is at 31%. Self-reports, on the other hand, are the domain of the Duke, constituting 62,69% of all his RTAs; in the case of the other defendant this figure is at 36,52%. This, once more, signifies the Duke's disadvantageous recourse to his internal reality (cf. Shinzato 2004), both for evidential and affective support.

5.3.7 Free categories and slipping

Free categories are marginal in both trials on the interaction level[4]. Naturally, to be considered free, the reports have to be embedded in other reports in the first place. As untagged, instances of free categories are much more difficult to recognise as reported speech and they are particularly well-suited for minimising the intertextual gap between the reporting context and the report (cf. Matoesian 2000). Consequently, the reduced distance between the action of reporting and the reported entity achieved by means of free categories does not allow evaluative space, rendering these categories functional on the level of discourse organisation rather than as fulfilling pragmatic aims. The following example occurs towards the end of a lengthy turn of the sergeant-at-law:

(107) <N>
IS NP [He gave Advice, that fhe fhould in no wife deliver her Son, for it was againft her own Safety, IT GERUND [not knowing whether fhe delivered him into her Friends hands or no].] FIS [As for the Rebels, fhe would in no wife deliver them, for it were againft her Honour: And as for the Holds, fhe fhould not deliver any; for it were againft the Safety of her Friends in *Scotland.*]

---

[4] On the textual level all the dialogic turns are free direct speech.

Pragmatic aspects of individual reported speech categories 173

The FIS follows an indirect report of the Duke's advice to the Queen of Scotland and it reflects the hastiness with which the court official finishes his turn, thus functioning as a cohesion-promoting device. In a more interesting instance, where an FDS is found in the speech of Throckmorton, the free category is combined with the so-called slipping (fade in) i.e., a smooth transition from one reporting mode to another:

(108) <TH>
IS FADE IN [unto whom I faide, that peraduenture not onely the Queenes Shippes under his Charge might be in jeopardy, but alfo my Lorde Priuie Seale, and all his Trayne, the *Frenchmen* beeing wel prepared to meete with them; FDS [and therefore for all Euents it were good you fhould put my faid Lord in the Weft Countrey, in cafe you efpie any jeoperdie.]]

Anything but the clarity of the argument motivates the abrupt slipping into direct speech in a dialogic turn in which the defendant reports his conversation with one of the witnesses. As unintroduced, this direct speech report (108) is extremely confusing to the hearer, therefore it is unlikely that prominence, normally achievable through direct modes, is intended or marked here. On the other hand, the propositional content of the report is crucial for the witness's defence and, given the overall rhetorical aptness in Throckmorton's speech, it is unlikely that, this time, he is intentionally non-persuasive. Most probably, the abrupt fade from an indirect into a free direct category, which disregards the double perceptual challenge, forcing the hearer additionally to infer the referent of *you*, is the result of Throckmorton's rush and impatience at this very moment. Surprisingly, it is also a rare instance when a reporting strategy backfires at the successful defendant.

On the whole, slipping is infrequent at 0,62% of all reported speech instances in <TH> and 1,23% in <N>. Clearly, the dominant pattern is different from the example discussed above (i.e., 108), where the shift from one category to another involves a substantial step over the speech presentation cline. In the majority of cases, slipping occurs from RSA into IS, the former rendering summarised messages, while the latter contrastively encodes relatively more important information deserving to be presented at greater length:

(109) <N>
Alfo Mr. Wilson, RSA PP [fworn, RSA DO SUP FADE IN [did teftify the fame]; and IS [that Barker was never offer'd Torture...]

In example (109) fade in serves the purpose of presenting new facts in a less compact way than is achieved by means of the preceding RSA category.

5.4 State trials and court records – a comparison

It is necessary to devote some attention to the issue that has been raised in 3.1.1, concerning the degree of adequacy of the material drawn from the *State Trials* for historical pragmatic research. This data could be verified through a comparison with a less controversial but more formal and conventionalised source (Furnivall 1897), a collection of ecclesiastical records. In order to carry out this task, the statistical differences between the two different institutional sources with regard to the most important features of the distribution of reported speech, will be presented.

The major difference between the two sources stemming from the institutional tradition (cf. sections 3.1.1 and 3.4) is that the ecclesiastical records, comprising witness depositions, do not contain dialogue on the textual level. This is iconic of the preliminary hearing procedure, the so-called interrogatories, in which the witnesses are interrogated on the basis of a list of questions. The interaction with the court officials is thus minimal; hence the variation observed in the *State Trials* on the textual level does not apply to ecclesiastical records. All the depositions on the first level of embedding are non-direct reports.

Secondly, the gravity of the cases recorded in the ecclesiastical material is not comparable to that of the treason trials. Obviously, no life-threats are at stake when divorces of child marriages are the focus of attention. Therefore, there is little room for conflicting attitudes and rhetoric. Rather, the deponents are cooperative and comply with the maxims of conversation. There are no instances of face threatening acts or breaches of communication.

	STATE TRIALS	ECCLESIASTICAL RECORDS
TOTAL INSTANCES	3656	438
NORMALISED FIGURE PER 10,000 WORDS	617,47	467,95
DISTINCTIVENESS RATIO		1,32

Table 34: Comparison of RS count in the two sources

In terms of the frequency of occurrence the number of reported speech instances in the *State Trials* exceeds that in the ecclesiastical records with DR at 1,32. This difference is significant but not strikingly high. The differences in distribution of individual categories are much more prominent:

	RSA	IS	DS	FIS	FDS	RTA	IT	FIT	TOTAL
STATE TRIALS %	60,67	14,80	3,69	0,19	0,08	16,22	4,32	0,03	100,00
ECCLESIASTICAL RECORDS %	22,37	51,37	3,42	0,46	--	12,56	9,82	--	100,00

Table 35: Comparison of frequencies of individual RS categories in the two sources

Pragmatic aspects of individual reported speech categories 175

Table 35 presents categories on deeper embedding levels. Strikingly, the majority of reports are in indirect speech, while the number of RSAs is 15% of that in the *State Trials*. This major difference between the dominant strategies reflects the text-type distinctions between trial transcripts and church records. Also, the high frequency of indirect speech reveals a much higher degree of conventionalisation, both of the preliminary trial questioning procedure and the record.

Moreover, conventionalisation, which was largely reflected by means of fixed expressions in the *State Trials*, is once more revealed in the type-to token ratio in tags, which is significantly lower than in the *State Trials* (43,7 to 29,52), with DR between the sources at 1,5. Moreover, the distribution of ten most frequent tags points to the almost total lack of stylistic variation with respect to reported speech in the ecclesiastical records:

	ECCLESIASTICAL	%	<TH>	%	<N>	%
1	SAY	37,53	SAY	9,95	SAY	6,16
2	KNOW	8,47	SPEAK	3,67	KNOW	3,74
3	ASK	6,18	KNOW	3,58	CONFESS	3,42
4	THINK	6,18	PRAY	3,05	TELL	2,58
5	HEAR	5,26	HEAR	2,15	HEAR	2,50
6	TO (his) KNOLEDGE	3,43	CONFESS	1,61	PROVE	2,38
7	AGREE	2,52	PROVE	1,61	READ	2,13
8	FANSY	2,29	TALK	1,61	SPEAK	1,85
9	TELL	2,06	AUNSWER	1,52	ANSWER	1,73
10	CONSENT PERCEYVE REMEMBER	1,83	REMEMBER	1,52	THINK	1,41

Table 36: Comparison of most frequent tags in the two sources

The most frequent tag, the verbum dicendi *say*, is almost four times as frequent as in <TH>, where it is still higher than in <N>. The strikingly high frequency reveals the highly informative nature of the records, as the transparency of verbs of speaking is one of the signs of the relevance of reported speech instances. This consistency also demonstrates the formality of the record which does not allow speech act verbs or other evaluative tags on a regular basis. There are two markers of stance in the records: the use of hedges reflecting the attempt on the part of the witness not to sound too authoritative, being most truthful at the same time; and the use of verbs of perception for evidential purposes. These strategies are applied exclusively by the deponents with the frequency at around 5% of all tags.

On the whole this presentation of some statistics pertaining to the ecclesiastical record bluntly shows the lack of internal motivation on the side of deponents for the utilisation of the most interesting reported speech strategies. This runs contrary to the findings arrived at on the basis of the *State Trials*. For instance, the frequency of reported speech instances is not incomparable, whereas the frequency of the most frequent tags shows that the records in the *State Trials* are stylistically much more diversified, thus possibly pointing to their shortcomings as narrative bordering on fictional, but are still more interesting from the point of view of a pragmatic analysis of reported speech. As has been hypothesised above (section 3.1.1), all of the identified differences may be accounted for by the textual and institutional traditions behind both kinds of records. It may be concluded that, despite their greater authenticity, ecclesiastical records do not provide data for multifaceted research into the pragmatic aspects of reported speech.

5.5 Concluding remarks

The discussion above was based chiefly on quantitative evidence which did not render satisfactory results in all cases, though on the whole it definitely managed to fill the gap created by the qualitative orientation of the previous chapter. The pragmatic aspects identified through a selective presentation of individual categories are numerous and do not always show well-defined patterns and contextualisations. On the whole, as a result of the above sections, the pragmatic nature of reported speech was corroborated. Naturally, on many points there is much wider scope for pragmatic considerations than has been outlined. Hopefully, despite the tentativeness of many claims, some directions for research into the area have been identified and will be pursued in more detail in the future.

Finally, it is necessary to clarify an issue whose treatment might have involved a degree of inconsistency in the above discussion. Even though the methodological predicament of historical pragmatics received considerable attention in this study (chapter one), it has to be emphasised once more that the discussions of the pragmatic aspects of courtroom discourse are not claimed to be valid, without certain qualifications, for the status of reported speech in the oral procedure of the trial (cf. Collins 2001: 204). Therefore the arguments based on the hearers' perceptions are better to remain conventional linguistic generalisations with respect to their validity for real courtroom interaction in Early Modern English. On the other hand, bringing in the arguments connected with the pragmatic aspects of the trial transcript as a text-type – a more feasible task given the nature of the evidence – requires seeking much wider empirical foundations than those provided by just two instances and, preferably, carrying out quantitative corpus analyses. Taking all these factors into consideration, the occasional switches between the pragmatic aspects potentially relevant to the reader, as proposed in the analysis of the textual level and those relevant to the hearer, as proposed on the interaction level, are one consequence of a degree of conventionality involved in a historical linguistic analysis.

Conclusions

This study constitutes an attempt to contribute to the growing body of research devoted to pragmatic studies of the history of English and other languages, such as speech act analysis, studies into discourse markers and grammaticalisation, dialogue analysis and studies within politeness theory. As was demonstrated in the discussion above, multidisciplinary studies of reported speech may be successfully accommodated within this diversity of topics and perspectives – all united by pragmatic interests and the application of relevant research tools.

First of all, as was shown in chapter one, the limitations of historical data are extremely difficult to overcome, despite the focus of historical pragmatics on the 'bad-data problem'. Therefore, a comprehensive overview of the approaches to this issue was an indispensable step towards a careful selection of data for the purpose of a historical pragmatic study of reported speech. Moreover, some criticism was presented in response to the recent uncompromising approaches to primary sources which uphold the exclusiveness of the emerging research field and recommend standards impossible to meet. In chapter one an approach aimed at compromise was justified and accepted in line with the purposes of the linguistic analysis.

Chapter two contains an overview of perspectives on reported speech in the literature, particularly in the last five years, when a rapidly growing interest in the phenomenon can be discerned in the pragmatically and sociolinguistically-oriented contributions. This, together with an outline of the most widely accepted philosophical underpinnings and a presentation of categorisation proposals, provides a sound basis for the linguistic analysis of reported speech and was intended to serve as a source of pragmatic explanations and analytical tools. Moreover, building on these overviews, a definition of reported speech – the phenomenon notoriously difficult to define – was formulated.

Chapter three provided an essential historical and methodological background for research. Ample space was reserved for outlining the institutional aspects of the data in question in order to describe the context of the interaction in the courtroom. This was an answer to the calls, summarised in chapter two, for more attention to be paid to the issue of context as the most powerful explanatory tool in pragmatic research. Moreover, in this chapter a range of technicalities pertaining to converting printed material into computer-readable format were presented. Finally, the basic unit of description was defined and the annotation conventions were clarified.

Chapter four presented a range of pragmatic considerations with respect to the categorisation of reported speech instances, with particular attention devoted to the issues that have so far not been systematically incorporated into the selected model. The discussion in this chapter resulted in the emendation of the Leech and Short model (1981) so as to account for fixed expressions, discourse markers, parentheticals, hedges and evidential expressions which overlap with reported speech. The quantitative and qualitative presentations corroborated the assumption with regard to the marking of stance as the major pragmatic function of reported speech.

Chapter five was devoted to the discussion of individual reported speech categories and provided some correlations of these with grammatical features. In many cases, clear pragmatic functions of reported speech strategies were identified, once again corroborating the assumptions as to the pragmatic nature of the phenomenon. Moreover, a quantitative comparison of two kinds of data originating from different institutional sources with respect to the distribution of reported speech instances was carried out, verifying the assumption concerning the suitability of the basic data source i.e., *State Trials*, for this kind of study.

Chapters four and five were both devoted to justifying the assumption as to the correlation between linguistic strategies applied by the defendants and their success or failure in the courtroom. The following patterns were established with regard to this issue (Table 37, percentages calculated against the overall number of a given category or subcategory in each trial):

STRATEGY	<TH>	<N>	SECTION
PARENTHETICAL RSA	80%	70%	4.3.1.3.4
DS WORD COUNT – TEXTUAL LEVEL	70%	36%	5.2.1.1
TYPE-TO-TOKEN RATION OF TAGS EMBEDDED IN DS	57,3	49,62	5.2.1.1
PERIPHRASTIC *DO*	49,48%	57,60%	5.3.1
IMPERATIVE	71,05%	51,43%	5.3.1
DS	47,72%	26,37%	5.3.4
IT	67,35%	33,02%	5.3.5
RTA	61,17%	31%	5.3.6

Table 37: Strategies of RS in the speech of the defendants

The distribution of parentheticals shows that the successful defendant, Nicholas Throckmorton, uses stance-marking devices more frequently than the Duke of Norfolk. Also, as is demonstrated in section 4.3.1.5.7, with respect to evidential strategies, the former defendant applies those strategies that do not belong to his institutional role, which does not happen in the case of the Duke. Qualitative differences in the use of evidentials between the defendants are more telling than the quantitative results of their distribution, in which there is no serious discrepancy (cf. section 4.3.1.5.8). With regard to the institutional role of the defendants, the use of deferential expressions by the unsuccessful defendant (cf. section 4.3.1.3.3) signifies his acceptance of the subordinate role in the trial. The analysis of reported speech on the textual level further supports this finding: the Duke does not reach beyond his institutional role in further assuming the cooperative stance, while Nicholas Throckmorton, through his dominance in dialogue (cf. the word count of DS on the textual level), lack of cooperation, power claims, and face threatening acts, refuses to accept the institutional role of the defendant (cf. section 5.2.1.1). Moreover, the successful defendant exercises other manipulative and persuasive strategies, such as the frequent use of the periphrastic *do* and the imperative (section 5.3.1). Also DS is a powerful strategy in his speech, as it allows performing covert authoritative functions (section 5.3.4). Similarly, IT instances are used by Throckmorton with the aim of influencing the prospective decisions of the court officials as frequent correlation with the imperative shows (section 5.3.5). The unsuccessful defendant does not utilise any of these strategies to his advantage, while in the use of thought reporting strategies he is extremely introvert and seeks to support his own credibility with internal reports (sections 5.3.5 and 5.3.6). Coinciding with unjustified denial, the thought reporting strategies used by Duke do not contribute to the persuasiveness of his speech, nor do his cooperativeness and positive politeness strategies.

All the findings of the above study may be subjected to extensions and more in-depth analyses. Some directions of research into reported speech on the textual level were identified in section 5.2.2. On the level of interaction there is definitely scope for a systematic presentation of correlations between reported speech strategies and grammatical features. As in the case of analysis on the textual level, analysis on the level of interaction might be enhanced by the application of well-know pragmatic theories i.e., the theory of speech acts, politeness or relevance. A more in-depth analysis of the context of the trials, including the social background of the participants in the discourse, might provide further illuminating findings. Finally, an analysis of a larger corpus might allow drawing conclusions as to the text-types in question, thereby contributing to another sub-field of historical pragmatics, genre studies.

Even though the study is theoretically orientated, some claims were made with respect to the patterns of reported speech in Early Modern English. The contribution that this thesis hopes to make to historical linguistics lies in providing sound analytic tools for a historical pragmatic analysis of the phenomenon in the institutional setting of the courtroom. Most importantly, this study demonstrates that the difficulty inherent in a pragmatic analysis of reported speech, both with respect to historical data and the institutional setting, is not detrimental to research efforts but possesses considerable explanatory potential. Not only the description itself, but also the process of formulating it step-by-step proved revealing and fascinating in the analysis of reported speech carried out in this study.

Appendix

	Journal of Historical Pragmatics
PAPERS	5
THEORETICAL	1
LITERARY	1
NON-LITERARY	1
literary+non-lit	2
CORPUS	2
MOD.ED.	
CONT.ED.	
FACSIMILE	
FACSIMILE + mod.ed.	1
cont.ed. + mod.ed. +corpus	1

Table 1: Speech act analysis

	Historical Pragmatics (1995)	Historical Pragmatics (1998)	Journal of Historical Pragmatics	TOTAL
PAPERS	9	4	7	20
THEORETICAL				
LITERARY	5	1	2	8
NON-LITERARY		2	1	3
literary + non-lit	4	1	4	9
CORPUS	3	2	4	9
CORPUS+mod.ed.	1		1	2
MOD. ED.	2	2	2	6
CONT. ED.				
FACSIMILE				
FACSIMILE +mod.ed	1			1

Table 2: Discourse markers, etc.

	Historical Pragmatics (1995)	Historical Dialogue Analysis	Historical Pragmatics (1998)	Journal of Historical Pragmatics	TOTAL
PAPERS	1	16	2	3	22
THEORETICAL		1			1
LITERARY		5	1	2	8
NON-LIT		6	1	1	8
literary+ non-lit	1	4			5
CORPUS		1			1
MOD.ED.		10	1	2	13
CONT.ED.		3			3
editions cont.+mod.				1	1
FACSIMILE		1			1
facs +mod. ed.	1				1
facs+cont. ed.			1		1

Table 3: Dialogue analysis

	Historical Pragmatics (1995)	*Journal of Historical Pragmatics*	TOTAL
PAPERS	2	2	4
THEORETICAL			
LITERARY	1	1	2
NON-LIT	1	1	2
literary+ non-lit			
CORPUS	1		1
corpus+ mod.ed.			
MOD.ED.	1	2	3
CONT.ED.			
FACSIMILE			

Table 4: Politeness and forms of address

	Journal of Historical Pragmatics
PAPERS	9[1]
THEORETICAL	3
LITERARY	3
NON-LITERARY	3
CORPUS	
MOD.ED.	3
corpus+ mod.ed	2
CONT.ED.	
FACSIMILE	

Table 5: Ritual

	Historical Pragmatics (1995)	*Historical Pragmatics* (1997)	*Journal of Historical Pragmatics*	TOTAL
PAPERS	1	1	11	13
THEORETICAL			4	4
LITERARY		1	3	4
NON-LITERARY	1		4	5
CORPUS	1		2	3
MOD.ED.		1	4	5
CONT.ED.				
FACSIMILE			1	1

Table 6: Discourse strategies; semantics

	Historical Pragmatics (1997)	*Journal of Historical Pragmatics*	TOTAL
PAPERS	1	4	5
THEORETICAL			
LITERARY			
NON-LITERARY	1	4	5
CORPUS			
corpus+mod.ed.		1	1
MOD.ED.		1	1
CONT.ED.			
editions cont. +mod.		1	1
FACSIMILE			
facs. + cont.ed.	1		1
facs. + mod. ed. +corpus		1	1

Table 7: Genre studies

Bibliography

Source texts

Furnivall, Frederick J. (ed.)
1897 *Child marriages and divorces in the diocese of Chester, A.D. 1561-6. Depositions in trials in the Bishop's Court, Chester.* (Early English Text Society. Original Series 108) London: Kegan Paul.

Hargrave, Francis (ed.)
1776-1781 *A complete collection of state-trials and proceedings for high-treason and other crimes and misdeamenours; the fourth edition.* London: T. Wright.

Holinshed, Raphael
1577 *The laste volume of the Chronicles of England, Scotlande, and Irelande, with their defcriptions. Conteyning the Chronicles of Englande from William Conqueror untill this prefent tyme. Faithfully gathered and compiled by Raphael Holinshed.* [no indication of publisher]

1554 "The order of the araignemente of Sir Nicholas Throckemorton Knight, in the Guild Hall of London the seuenteenth day of April, 1554. expressed in a Dialogue for the better vnderftanding of euery mans parte." [Manuscript indexed in the British Library as MSS Stowe 280], 75-103. [Also in: Raphael Holinshed 1577, 1737-1754.]

1576-1581 "The Trial of Sir Nicholas Throckmorton* Knight, in the Guildhall of London, for High-Treafon, the 17th of Aprill, 1554", in: Francis Hargrave (ed.), 63-78.

1776-1781 "The Triall of Thomas Howard Duke of Norfolk, before the Lords at Weftminfter, for Highe-Treafon, January 16. 1571", in: Francis Hargrave (ed.), 81-116.

1572 "The trial of Thomas Howard, Duke of Norfolk, before the lords at Westminster for high treason, 26 Jan. 1571", [Manuscript indexed in the British Library as MSS Sloane 1417], 32-81.

Secondary sources

Aczel, Richard
1998 "Hearing voices in narrative texts", *New Literary History* 29, 3: 467-500. (http://muse.jhu.edu/journals/new_literary_history/v029/29.3aczel.html) DOA 01/2005.
Adelmann, Kent
2004 "Dialogism and reported listening: students listening repertory and listening types in educational settings". (http://www.lut.mah.se/nms/NMS_Konferens/Adelmann.pdf) DOA 01/2005.
Aijmer, Karin
1996 *Conversational routines in English: Convention and creativity*. London – New York: Longman.
1997 "*I think* – an English modal particle", in: Toril Swan – Olaf Jansen Westvik (eds.), 1-47.
2002 *English discourse particles: Evidence from a corpus*. Amsterdam – Philadelphia: John Benjamins.
Aikhenvald, Alexandra Y. – R. M. W. Dixon (eds.)
2003 *Studies in evidentiality*. Amsterdam – Philadelphia: John Benjamins.
Akimoto, Monoji
2000 "The grammaticalisation of the verb 'pray'", in: Olga Fischer – Anette Rosenbach – Dieter Stein (eds.), 67-84.
Allen, Cynthia L.
1995 "On doing as you please", in: Andreas H. Jucker (ed.), 295-308.
Allibone, Samuel Austin
1859-71 *A critical dictionary of English literature, and British and American authors, living and deceased, from the earliest accounts to the middle of the nineteenth century. Containing thirty thousand biographies and literary notices, with forty indexes of subjects*. Philadelphia: J. B. Lippincott & co. (http://www.hti.umich.edu/cgi/ t/text/ textidx?c= moa;idno= AHN90 11.0 001.001) DOA 04/2005.
Álvarez-Cáccamo, Celso
1996 "The power of reflexive language(s): Code displacement in reported speech", *Journal of Pragmatics* 25, 1: 33-59.
Andersen, Gisle
2001 *Pragmatic markers and sociolinguistic variation: A relevance-theoretic approach to the language of adolescents*. Amsterdam – Philadelphia: John Benjamins.
Antaki, Charles – Ivan Leudar
2001 "Recruiting the record: Using opponents' exact words in parliamentary argumentation", *Text* 21, 4: 467-488.
Archer, Dawn
2002 ""Can innocent people be guilty?" A sociopragmatic analysis of examination transcripts from the Salem witchcraft trials", *Journal of Historical Pragmatics* 3, 1: 1-30.
2003 The role of the question in Early Modern English trial proceedings: A corpus-based approach. (Unpublished Ph.D. dissertation, Lancaster University, Lancaster).

Archer, Dawn – Jonathan Culpeper
2003   "Sociopragmatic annotation: new directions and possibilities in historical corpus linguistics", in: Andrew Wilson – Paul Rayson – Tony McEnery (eds.), 37-58.
Arnold, Jennifer – Renée Blake – Brad Davidson – Scott Schwenter – Julie Solomon (eds.)
1996   *Sociolinguistic variation. Data, theory and analysis. Selected papers from NWAV 23 at Stanford.* Stanford: CSLI Publications.
Arnovick, Leslie K.
1999   *Diachronic pragmatics: seven case studies in English illocutionary development.* Amsterdam – Philadelphia: John Benjamins.
Bach, Urlich
1998   "Early mass communication: political pamphlets from 1642 to 1647", in: Raimund Borgmeier – Herbert Grabes – Andreas H. Jucker (eds.), 97-111.
Baker, J.H.
2002   *An introduction to English legal history.* London: Butterworths.
Bakhtin, Mikhail
1981   *The dialogic imagination. Four essays.* Edited by Michael Holquist. Translated by Caryl Emerson and Michael Holquist. Austin: University of Texas Press.
Bally, Charles
1930   "Antiphrase et style indirect libre", in: N. Bøgholm – Aage Brusendorf – C. Bodelsen (eds.), 331-340.
Bamgbose, Ayọ
1986   "Reported speech in Yoruba", in: Florian Coulmas (ed.), 77-96.
Banfield, Ann
1993   "Where epistemology, style, and grammar meet literary history: the development of represented speech and thought", in: John Lucy (ed.), 339-364.
Barber, Charles
1997   *Early Modern English.* Edinburgh: Edinburgh University Press.
Barrell, John
1992   *The birth of Pandora and the division of knowledge.* Philadelphia: University of Pennsylvania Press.
Bauman, Richard
1992   "Contextualisation, tradition and the dialogue of genres: Icelandic legends of the *kraftaskáld*", in: Alessandro Duranti – Charles Goodwin (eds.), 125-145.
Bax, Marcel
1981   "Rules for ritual challenges; a speech convention among mediaeval knights", *Journal of Pragmatics* 5, 5: 423-444.
1983   "Die lebendige Dimension toter Sprachen. Zur pragmatischen Analyse von Sprachgebrauch in historischen Kontexten", *Zeitschrift für Germanistische Linguistik* 11: 1-21.
1991   "Historische Pragmatik: Eine Herausforderung für die Zukunft. Diachrone Untersuchungen zu pragmatischen Aspekten ritueller Herausforderungen in mittelalterlicher Literatur", in: Dietrich Busse (ed.), 197-215.
1999   "Ritual leveling: the balance between the eristic and the contractual motive in hostile verbal encounters in medieval romance and Early Modern drama", in: Andreas H. Jucker – Gerd Fritz – Franz Lebsanft (eds.), 35-80.
2001   "Historical frame analysis. Hoaxing and make-believe in seventeenth century Dutch play", *Journal of Historical Pragmatics* 2, 1: 33-67.

Bayley, Paul (ed.)
　　2004　　*Cross-cultural perspectives on parliamentary discourse.* Amsterdam – Philadelphia: John Benjamins.
Baynham, Mike
　　1996　　"Direct speech: What is it doing in non-narrative discourse?", *Journal of Pragmatics* 25, 1: 61-81.
　　1999　　"Double-voicing and the scholarly 'I': On incorporating the voice of others in academic discourse", *Text* 19, 4: 485-504.
Baynham, Mike – Stef Slembrouck
　　1999　　"Speech representation and institutional discourse", *Text* 19, 4: 439-457.
Becker, Monika
　　2002　　""'Yf ye wyll bergayne wullen cloth or othir marchandise... ": Bargaining in early modern language teaching textbooks", *Journal of Historical Pragmatics* 3, 2: 273-297.
Bellamy, John
　　1989　　*The Tudor law of treason.* London: Routledge and Kegan Paul.
Berger, Peter L. – Thomas Luckmann
　　1981　　*The social construction of reality. A treatise in the sociology of knowledge.* London: Penguin Press.
Berman, Ruth A.
　　2005　　"Introduction: developing discourse stance in different text-types and languages", *Journal of Pragmatics* 37, 2: 105-124.
Bernárdez, Enrique – Paloma Tejada
　　1995　　"Pragmatic constraints to word order, and word-order change in English", in: Andreas H. Jucker (ed.), 218-241.
Besnier, Niko
　　1993　　"Reported speech and affect on Nukulaelae atoll", in: Jane H. Hill –Judith T. Irvine (eds.), 161-181.
Biber, Douglas
　　1988　　*Variation across speech and writing.* Cambridge: Cambridge University Press.
　　2004　　"Historical patterns for the grammatical marking of stance. A cross-register comparison", *Journal of Historical Pragmatics* 5, 1: 107-136.
Biber, Douglas – Edward Finegan
　　1989　　"Drift and evolution of English style: a history of three genres", *Language* 65, 3: 487-517.
　　1992　　"The linguistic evolution of five written genres and speech-based English genres from the 17th to the 20th centuries", in: Matti Rissanen – Ossi Ihalainen – Terttu Nevalainen – Irma Taavitsainen (eds.), 688-704.
Biber, Douglas – Stig Johansson – Geoffrey Leech – Susan Conrad – Edward Finegan
　　1999　　*Longman grammar of spoken and written English.* Harlow – Essex: Pearson Education.
Bierwisch Manfred – Karl Erich Heidolph (eds.)
　　1970　　*Progress in linguistics. A collection of papers.* The Hague – Paris: Mouton.
Black, J. B.
　　1959　　*The reign of Elizabeth 1558-1603. Second edition.* Oxford: Clarendon Press.
Blakemore, Diane
　　2002　　*The semantics and pragmatics of discourse markers.* New York: Cambridge University Press.
　　2005　　"*and*-parentheticals", *Journal of Pragmatics* 37, 8: 1165-1181.

Borgmeier, Raimund – Herbert Grabes – Andreas H. Jucker (eds.)
1998 *Historical pragmatics. Reprinted from: Anglistentag 1997 Giessen. Proceedings.* Wissenschaftlicher Verlag Trier.
Bøgholm, N. – Aage Brusendorf – C. Bodelsen (eds.)
1930 *A grammatical miscellany offered to Otto Jespersen on his seventeenth birthday.* London: Allen and Unwin.
Bredel, Ursula
2003 "Polyphonic constructions in everyday speech", in: Titus Ensink – Christopher Sauer (eds.), 147-170.
Brinton, Laurel J.
1996 *Pragmatic markers in English. Grammaticalization and discourse functions.* Berlin – New York: Mouton de Gruyter.
1998 "'The flowers are lovely; only, they have no scent': The evolution of a pragmatic marker", in: Raimund Borgmeier – Herbert Grabes – Andreas H. Jucker (eds.), 9-33.
British Library Online Catalogue
2005 (http://www.bl.uk/catalogues/manuscripts) DOA 06/2005.
Brown, Penelope – Stephen C. Levinson
1987 *Politeness. Some universals in language usage.* Cambridge: Cambridge University Press.
Brown, Roger – Albert Gilman
1989 "Politeness theory in Shakespeare's four major tragedies", *Language in Society* 18, 2: 159-212.
Busse, Dietrich
1991 *Diachrone Semantik und Pragmatik. Untersuchungen zur Erklärung und Beschreibung des Sprachwandels.* Tübingen: Niemeyer.
Busse, Ulrich
2002 *Linguistic variation in the Shakespeare corpus. Morpho-syntactic variability of second person pronouns.* Amsterdam – Philadelphia: John Benjamins.
Buttny, Richard
1998 "Putting prior talk into context: Reported speech and the reporting context", *Research on Language and Social Interaction* 31, 1: 45-58.
Caldas-Coulthard, Carmen Rosa
1994 "On reporting reporting: the representation of speech in factual and factional narratives", in: Malcolm Coulthard (ed.), 295-308.
Camden, William
2001 *Annales Rerum Gestarum Angliae et Hiberniae Regnante Elizabetha (1615 and notations of Sir Francis Bacon. A hypertext edition by Dana F. Sutton. Posted March 27, 2000. Revised February 1, 2001.* (http: //www.philological.bham. ac.uk/camden) DOA 03/2005.
Cappelen, Herman – Ernie Lepore
1997 "Varieties of quotation", *Mind* 106: 429-450.
Carroll, Ruth – Janne Skaffari
2002 "Historical perspectives on text, discourse and pragmatics", *The European English Messenger* XI, 2: 48-52.
Carroll, Ruth – Risto Hiltunen – Matti Peikola – Janne Skaffari – Sanna-Kaisa Tanskanen – Ellen Valle – Brita Wårvik
2003 "Introduction", in: Risto Hiltunen – Janne Skaffari (eds.), 1-12.

Cate, ten Abraham P.
1996 "Modality of verb forms in German reported speech", in: Theo Janssen – Wim van der Wurff (eds.), 189-211.
Caton, Steve C.
1993 "The importance of reflexive language in George H. Mead's theory of self and communication", in: John Lucy (ed.), 315-337.
Chafe, Wallace
2001 "The analysis of discourse flow", in: Deborah Schiffrin – Deborah Tannen – Heidi E. Hamilton (eds.), 673-687.
Chambers, J.K – Peter Trudgill – Natalie Schilling-Estes (eds.)
2002 *Handbook of language variation and change.* Oxford – Malden: Blackwell Publishers.
Cicourel, Aaron V.
1992 "The interpretation of communicative contexts: examples from medical encounters", in: Alessandro Duranti – Charles Goodwin (eds.), 291-310.
Clark, Herbert H. – Richard J. Gerrig
1990 "Quotations as demonstrations", *Language* 66, 4: 764-805.
Coates, Jennifer
2003 "The role of epistemic modality in women's talk", in: Roberta Facchinetti – Manfred Krug – Frank Palmer (eds.), 331-348.
Collins, Daniel E.
2001 *Reanimated voices. Speech reporting in a historical-pragmatic perspective.* Amsterdam – Philadelphia: John Benjamins.
Coulmas, Florian
1986a "Nobody dies in Shangri-la: Direct and indirect speech across languages", in: Deborah Tannen – James E. Alatis (eds.), 140-154.
1986b "Reported speech: Some general issues", in: Florian Coulmas (ed.), 1-29.
Coulmas, Florian (ed.)
1986 *Direct and indirect speech.* Berlin: Mouton de Gruyter.
Coulthard, Malcolm (ed.)
1994 *Advances in written text analysis.* London – New York: Routledge.
Couper-Kuhlen, Elizabeth
1998 "Coherent voicing. On prosody in conversational reported speech", *Interaction and linguistic structures* 1. (http://www.uni-potsdam.de/u/ inlist/issues/1/inlist1 .pdf) DOA 12/2004.
Coupland, Nikolas – Srikant Sarangi – Christopher N. Candlin (eds.)
2001 *Sociolinguistics and social theory.* London: Longman – Pearson Education.
Cukor-Avila, Patricia
2002 "*She say, she go, she be like*: Verbs of quotation in African American", *American Speech* 77, 1: 3-21.
Culpeper, Jonathan – Merja Kytö
1999a "Modifying pragmatic force: hedges in Early Modern English dialogues", in: Andreas H. Jucker – Gerd Fritz – Franz Lebsanft (eds.), 293-312.
1999b "Investigating nonstandard language in a corpus of Early Modern English dialogues: Methodological considerations and problems", in: Irma Taavitsainen – Gunnel Melchers – Päivi Pahta (eds.), 171-187.
2000a "Data in historical pragmatics: Spoken interaction (re)cast as writing", *Journal of Historical Pragmatics* 1, 2: 175-199.

2000b "Lexical bundles in Early Modern English dialogues. A window into the speech-related language of the past", in: Teresa Fanego – Belén Méndez-Naya – Elena Seoane (eds.), 45-63.

2000c "Gender voices in the spoken interaction of the past: A pilot study based on Early Modern English trial records", in: Dieter Kastovsky – Arthur Mettinger (eds.), 53-89.

Culpeper, Jonathan – Elena Semino
2000 "Constructing witches and spells: Speech acts and activity types in Early Modern England", *Journal of Historical Pragmatics* 1, 1: 97-116.

Danet, Brenda – Bryna Bogoch
1992 "'Whoever alters this may God turn his face from him on the day of judgement'. Curses in Anglo-Saxon legal documents", *Journal of American Folklore* 105: 132-165.

Dendale, Patrick – Liliane Tasmowski
2001 "Introduction: evidentiality and related notions", *Journal of Pragmatics* 33, 3: 339-348.

Denison, David
1993 *English historical syntax: verbal constructions*. London – New York: Longman.

Derleck, Renaat
1999 "Remarks on Salkie and Reed's (1997) 'pragmatic hypothesis' of tense in reported speech", *English Language and Linguistics* 3, 1: 83-116.

Di Martino, Gabriella – Maria Lima (eds.)
2000 *English diachronic pragmatics*. Napoli: CUEN.

Di Luzio, Aldo – Günthner Susanne – Franca Orletti (eds.)
2001 *Culture in communication. Analyses of intercultural situations*. Amsterdam – Philadelphia: John Benjamins.

Dimmendaal, Gerrit J.
2001 "Logophoric marking and represented speech in African languages as evidential hedging strategies", *Australian Journal of Linguistics* 21, 1: 131-157.

Discourse Perspectives on Early English
2004 (www.utu.fi/hum/engfil/dpee.html) DOA 08/2004.

Dons, Ute
2004 *Descriptive adequacy of Early Modern English grammars*. Berlin – New York: Mouton de Gruyter

Doty, Kathleen L. – Risto Hiltunen
2002 "'I will tell, I will tell: confessional patterns in the Salem Witchcraft Trials, 1692", *Journal of Historical Pragmatics* 3, 2: 299-335.

Dömötör, Adrienne
2001 "Tendencies in the development of Old and Early Middle Hungarian main clauses of reported speech", *Acta Linguistica Hungarica* 48, 4: 337-369.

Duranti, Alessandro
1993 "Intentions, self and responsibility: an essay in Samoan ethnopragmatics", in: Jane H. Hill –Judith T. Irvine (eds.), 24-47.

Duranti, Alessandro – Charles Goodwin (eds.)
1992 *Rethinking context. Language as an interactive phenomenon*. Cambridge: Cambridge University Press.

Dylewski, Radosław – Piotr Cap (eds.)
2004 *History and present-day pragmatics of the English language*. Łódź: Wydawnictwo Wyższej Szkoły Humanistyczno-Ekonomicznej.

Ebert, Karen
1986 "Reported speech in some languages of Nepal", in: Florian Coulmas (ed.), 145-159.
Edward de Vere Newsletter No 14
1990 (http://drk.sd23.bc.ca/DeVere/Oldcastle_Norf_1_of_4-14.pdf) DOA 04/2005.
Emlyn, Solom
1730 "Preface to the second edition", in: Francis Hargrave (ed.), i-xvi.
Engberg-Pedersen, Elisabeth – Lisbeth Falster Jakobsen – Lone Schack Rasmussen (eds.)
1994 *Function and expression in functional grammar*. Berlin – New York: Mouton de Gruyter.
Ensink, Titus – Christoph Sauer
2003 "Social-functional and cognitive approaches to discourse interpretation: The role of frame and perspective", in: Titus Ensink – Christoph Sauer (eds.), 1-21.
Ensink, Titus – Christoph Sauer (eds.)
2003 *Framing and perspectivising in discourse*. Amstedam – Philadephia: John Benjamins.
Facchinetti, Roberta – Manfred Krug – Frank Palmer (eds.)
2003 *Modality in contemporary English*. Berlin – New York: Mouton de Gruyter.
Fairclough, Norman
2003 *Analysing discourse. Textual analysis for social research*. London – New York: Routledge.
Fanego, Teresa – Belén Méndez-Naya – Elena Seoane (eds.)
2000 *Sounds, words, texts and change*. Amsterdam – Philadelphia: John Benjamins.
Field, Margaret
1997 "The role of factive predicates in the indexicalisation of stance: A discourse perspective", *Journal of Pragmatics* 27, 6: 799-814.
Fischer, Kerstin
2000 *From cognitive semantics to lexical pragmatics. The functional polysemy of discourse particles*. Berlin – New York: Mouton de Gruyter.
Fischer, Olga – Frederike van der Leek
1983 "The demise of the Old English impersonal construction", *Journal of Linguistics* 19: 337-368.
Fischer, Olga – Anette Rosenbach – Dieter Stein (eds.)
2000 *Pathways of change: Grammaticalisation in English*. Amsterdam – Philadelphia: John Benjamins.
Fisiak, Jacek
2000 *An outline history of English. Third edition.* Poznań: Wydawnictwo Poznańskie.
Fludernik, Monika
1993 *The fictions of language and the languages of fiction*. London: Routledge.
2000 "Narrative discourse markers in Malory's Morte D'Arthur", *Journal of Historical Pragmatics* 1, 2: 231-262.
Friedman, Maurice
2004 "Martin Buber and Mikhail Bakhtin. The dialogue of voices and the word that is spoken", in: Patrick M. Jenlink – Bela H. Banathy (eds.), 29-39.
Fritz, Gerd
1995 "Topics in the history of dialogue forms", in: Andreas H. Jucker (ed.), 469-498.
Fritz, Gerd – Franz Hundsnurscher (eds.)
1994 *Handbuch der Dialoganalyse*. Tübingen: Niemayer.

Fuller, Janet M.
2003 "The influence of speaker roles on discourse marker use", *Journal of Pragmatics* 35, 1: 23-45.
Gerritsen, Marinel – Dieter Stein (eds.)
1992 *Internal and external factors in syntactic change*. Berlin: Mouton de Gruyter.
Gloning, Thomas
1999 "The pragmatic form of religious controversies around 1600", in: Andreas H. Jucker – Gerd Fritz – Franz Lebsanft (eds.), 81-110.
Goffman, Erving
1974 *Frame analysis. An essay on the organisation of experience*. New York: Harper and Row.
1981 *Forms of talk*. Philadelphia: University of Pennsylvania Press.
Golato, Andrea
2000 "An innovative German quotative for reporting on embodied actions: *Und ich so/ und er so* 'and I'm like and he's like'", *Journal of Pragmatics* 32, 1: 29-54.
2002 "Self-quotation in German: Reporting on past decisions", in: Tom Güldemann – Manfred von Roncador (eds.), 49-70.
Goodrich, Peter
1990 *Legal discourse: studies in linguistics, rhetoric and legal analysis*. London: Macmillan.
Goodwin, Charles
2003 "Embedded context", *Research on Language and Social Interaction* 36, 4: 323-350.
Goodwin, Charles – Alessandro Duranti
1992 "Rethinking context: an introduction", in: Alessandro Duranti – Charles Goodwin (eds.), 1-43.
Goodwin, Charles – Marjorie Harness Goodwin
1992 "Assessments and the construction of context", in: Alessandro Duranti – Charles Goodwin (eds.), 147-189.
Görlach, Manfred
1991 *Introduction to Early Modern English*. Cambridge: Cambridge University Press.
Green, Georgia M.
1990 "Linguistic analysis of conversation as evidence regarding the interpretation of speech events", in: Levi, Judith N. – Anne Graffam Walker (eds.), 247-278.
Green, Thomas Andrew
1985 *Verdict according to conscience. Perspectives on the English criminal trial jury 1200-1800*. Chicago – London: University of Chicago Press.
Grenoble, Lenore A.
2004 "Parentheticals in Russian", *Journal of Pragmatics* 36, 11: 1953-1974.
Grund, Peter – Merja Kytö – Matti Rissanen
2004 "Editing the Salem witchcraft records: exploration of a linguistic treasury", *American Speech* 79, 2: 146-166.
Gumperz, John J.
1982 *Discourse strategies*. Cambridge: Cambridge University Press.
1992 "Contextualisation and understanding", in: Alessandro Duranti – Charles Goodwin (eds.), 229-252.
Gumperz, John J. – Dell Hymes (eds.)
1972 *Directions in sociolinguistics: The ethnography of communication*. New York: Holt, Reinhard and Winston.

Güldemann, Tom – Manfred von Roncador (eds.)
    2002   *Reported discourse: A meeting ground for different linguistic domains.* Amsterdam – Philadelphia: John Benjamins.
Güldemann, Tom – Manfred von Roncador
    2002   "Preface", in: Tom Güldemann – Manfred von Roncador (eds.), vii-ix.
Güldemann, Tom – Manfred von Roncador – Wim van der Wurff
    2002   "A comprehensive bibliography of reported discourse", in: Tom Güldemann – Manfred von Roncador (eds.), 363-416.
Günthner, Susanne
    1999   "Polyphony and the layering of voices in reported dialogues: An analysis of the use of prosodic devices in everyday reported speech", *Journal of Pragmatics* 31, 5: 685-708.
Halliday, M.A.K.
    1985   *An introduction to functional grammar.* London: Edward Arnold.
The Handbook of Pragmatics Online
    2003   (http://www.benjamins.com/online/hop) DOA 08/2004.
Hanks, William F.
    1992   "The indexical ground of deictic reference", in: Alessandro Duranti – Charles Goodwin (eds.), 43-76.
    1993   "Metalanguage and pragmatics of deixis", in: John Lucy (ed.), 127-157.
Hansen, Maj-Britt Mosegaard
    2000   "The syntactic and semiotic status of direct quotes, with reference to French", *Transactions of the Philological Society* 98, 2: 281-322.
Harding, Alan
    1973   *The law courts of medieval England.* London: Allen and Unwin.
Harding, Alan
    1966 [1973]   *A social history of English law.* Reprint. Gloucester, Mass: Peter Smith.
Hargrave, Francis
    1775   "Preface to the present edition", in: Francis Hargrave (ed.) [unpaginated]
Harris, Sandra
    2003   "Politeness and power: Making and responding to 'requests' in institutional settings", *Text* 23, 1: 27-52.
Helmholtz, R.H.
    2003   "Judges and trials in the English ecclesiastical courts", in: Maureen Mullholand – Brian Pullan (eds), 102-116.
Hewlett, Nigel – Cherry Kelsey – Robin Lickley
    2003   "Children's perception of direct and indirect reported speech", in: M.J. Solé, D. Recasens & J. Romero (eds.), *Proceedings of the 15th International Congress of Phonetic Sciences*, 1313-1316: (http://sls.qmuc.ac.uk/PUBS/03ICPhS_1247.pdf) DOA 01/2005.
Hill, Jane H. – Judith T. Irvine
    1993a   "Introduction", in: Jane H. Hill –Judith T. Irvine (eds.), 1-23.
Hill, Jane H. – Judith T. Irvine (eds.)
    1993b   *Responsibility and evidence in oral discourse.* Cambridge: Cambridge University Press.
Hiltunen, Risto
    1990   *Chapters on legal English. Aspects past and present of the language of the law.* Helsinki: Suomalainen Tiedakademia.

2004 "Salem, 1692: A case of courtroom discourse in a historical perspective", in: Risto Hiltunen – Shinichiro Watanabe (eds.), 3-26.
Hiltunen, Risto – Janne Skaffari (eds.)
2003 *Discourse perspectives on English: Medieval to modern.* Amsterdam – Philadelphia: John Benjamins.
Hiltunen, Risto – Shinichiro Watanabe (eds.)
2004 *Approaches to style and discourse in English.* Osaka: Osaka University Press.
Holquist, Michael
1981 "Introduction", in: Mikhail Bakhtin, xiv-xxxiii.
Holt, Elizabeth
1996 "Reporting on talk: The use of direct reported speech in conversation", *Research on Language and Social Interaction* 29, 3: 219-245.
1999 "Just gassing: An analysis of direct reported speech in a conversation between employees of a gas supply company", *Text* 19, 4: 505-537.
2000 "Reporting and reacting: Concurrent responses to reported speech", *Research on Language and Social Interaction* 33, 4: 425-454.
Hope, Jonathan
1994 "The use of thou and you in Early Modern spoken English", in: Dieter Kastovsky (ed.), 141-151.
Huddleston, Rodney D. – Geoffrey K. Pullum (eds.)
2002 *The Cambridge grammar of the English language.* Cambridge: Cambridge University Press.
Hüllen, Werner
1995 "A close reading of William Caxton's *Dialogues*: "... to lerne shortly frenssh and englyssh"", in: Andreas H. Jucker (ed.), 99-125.
Hume, David
1778 [1983] *The History of England from the Invasion of Julius Caesar to the Revolution in 1688, Foreword by William B. Todd, 6 vols.* Indianapolis: Liberty Fund. (http://oll.libertyfund.org/Texts/ Hume0129 /History /0011-4_Bk.html) DOA 04/2005.
Hymes, Dell
1967 [1972] "Models of the interaction of language and social life", in: John J. Gumperz – Dell Hymes (eds.), 35-75.
Ilieva, Gabriela Nik.
2003 "The Rg Vedic hymn as a ritual speech event: About some grammatical rhetorical features of 10.39 from a pragmatic perspective", *Journal of Historical Pragmatics* 4, 2: 171-193.
Jacobs, Andreas – Andreas H. Jucker
1995 "The historical perspective in pragmatics", in: Andreas H. Jucker (ed.), 3-33.
Jacobs, Geert
2003 "Reporting annual results: A single-case analysis", in: Titus Ensink – Christopher Sauer (eds.), 91-108.
Jaconelli, Joseph
2003 "What is a trial?", in: Maureen Mullholand – Brian Pullan (eds), 18-36.
Jakobs, Eva-Maria
2003 "Reproductive writing – writing from sources", *Journal of Pragmatics* 35, 2: 893-906.
James Stuart, Earl of Moray
2005 *Wikipedia.* (http://en.wikipedia.org/wiki) DOA 04/2005.

Janssen, Theo A.J.M – Wim van der Wurff
  1996   "Introductory remarks on reported speech and thought", in: Theo Janssen – Wim van der Wurff (eds.), 1-15.
Janssen, Theo A.J.M – Wim van der Wurff (eds.)
  1996   *Reported speech: Forms and functions of the verb.* Amsterdam – Philadelphia: John Benjamins.
Jenlink, Patrick M. – Bela H. Banathy (eds.)
  2004   *Dialogue as a means of collective communication.* New York: Kluwer Academic Publishers.
Johnstone, Barbara
  1987   "'He says ... so I said': verb tense alternation and narrative depictions of authority in American English", *Linguistics* 25, 1: 33-52.
Joseph, Brian D.
  2003   "Evidentials", in: Alexandra Y. Aikhenvald – R. M. W. Dixon (eds.), 307-327.
Jucker, H. Andreas
  2000   "English historical pragmatics: Problems of data and methodology", in: Gabriella di Martino – Maria Lima (eds.), 17-55.
  2002   "Discourse markers in Early Modern English", in: Richard Watts – Peter Trudgill (eds.), 210-230.
Jucker, H. Andreas (ed.)
  1995   *Historical pragmatics. Pragmatic developments in the history of English.* Amsterdam – Philadelphia: John Benjamins.
  1998   "Historical pragmatics: An interdisciplinary approach", in: Raimund Borgmeier – Herbert Grabes – Andreas H. Jucker (eds.), 3-7.
Jucker, H. Andreas – Gerd Fritz – Franz Lebsanft
  1999   "Historical dialogue analysis. Roots and traditions in the study of Romance languages, German and English", in: Andreas H. Jucker – Gerd Fritz – Franz Lebsanft (eds.), 1-33.
Jucker, H. Andreas – Gerd Fritz – Franz Lebsanft (eds.)
  1999   *Historical dialogue analysis.* Amsterdam: John Benjamins.
Jucker, H. Andreas – Irma Taavitsainen
  2000   "Diachronic speech act analysis: Insults from flyting to flaming", *Journal of Historical Pragmatics* 1, 1: 67-95.
Kahlas-Tarkka, Leena – Matti Rissanen
  forthcoming "The talkative and the sullen: discourse strategies in the Salem witchcraft examinations".
Kalisz, Roman
  1993   *Pragmatyka językowa.* Gdańsk: Wydawnictwo Uniwersytetu Gdańskiego.
Kammerzell, Frank – Carsten Peust
  2002   "Reported speech in Egyptian. Forms, types and history", in: Tom Güldemann – Manfred von Roncador (eds.), 289-322.
Kastovsky, Dieter (ed.)
  1994   *Studies in Early Modern English.* Berlin – New York: Mouton de Gruyter.
Kastovsky, Dieter – Arthur Mettinger (eds.)
  2000   *The history of English in a social context. A contribution to historical sociolinguistics.* Berlin – New York: Mouton de Gruyter.
Kay, Christian J. – Jeremy J. Smith (eds.)
  2004   *Categorization in the history of English.* Amsterdam – Philadelphia: John Benjamins.

Kärkkäinen, Elise
    2003   *Epistemic stance in English conversation. A description of its interactional functions, with a focus on I think.* Amsterdam – Philadelphia: John Benjamins.

Kenny, Anthony
    1982   *The computation of style. An introduction to statistics for students of literature and humanities.* Oxford: Pergamon Press.

King, Ruth – Terry Nadasdi
    1999   "The expression of evidentiality in French-English bilingual discourse", *Language in Society* 28, 3: 355-365.

Kiparsky, Paul – Carol Kiparsky
    1970   "Fact", in: Manfred Bierwisch – Karl Erich Heidoph (eds.), 143-173.

Klewitz, Gabriele – Elizabeth Couper-Kuhlen
    1999   "QUOTE - UNQUOTE? The role of prosody in the contextualization of reported speech sequences", *Interaction and linguistic structures* 12. (http://www.ub.uni-konstanz.de/v13/volltexte/2000/464//pdf/464_1.pdf) DOA 12/2004.

Knoblauch, Hubert
    2001   "Communication, contexts and culture. A communicative constructivist approach to intercultural communication", in: Aldo Di Luzio – Günthner Susanne – Franca Orletti (eds.), 3-33.

Knowles, John
    1980   "The tag as a parenthetical", *Studies in Language* 4, 3: 379-409.

Koch, Peter
    1999   "Court records and cartoons. Reflections of spontaneous dialogue in early romance texts", in: Andreas H. Jucker – Gerd Fritz – Franz Lebsanft (eds.), 399-429.

Kopytko, Roman
    1993   *Polite discourse in Shakespeare's English.* Poznań: Wydawnictwo Naukowe UAM.
    2003   *The mental aspects of pragmatic theory. An integrative view.* Poznań: Motivex.

Koven, Michèle
    2001   "Comparing bilinguals' quoted performances of self and others in tellings of the same experience in two languages", *Language in Society* 30, 4: 513-558.
    2004   "Getting 'emotional' in two languages: Bilinguals' verbal performance of affect in narratives of personal experience", *Text* 24, 4: 471-515.

Kryk-Kastovsky, Barbara
    1998   "Pragmatic particles in Early Modern English court trials", in: Raimund Borgmeier – Herbert Grabes – Andreas H. Jucker (eds.), 47-56.
    2000   "Representations of orality in Early Modern English trial records", *Journal of Historical Pragmatics* 1, 2: 201-230.
    2002   *Synchronic and diachronic investigations in pragmatics.* Poznań: Motivex.

Kvavik, Karen H.
    1986   "Characteristics of direct and reported speech prosody: Evidence from Spanish", in: Florian Coulmas (ed.), 333-360.

Kytö, Merja – Matti Rissanen
    1983   "The syntactic study of early American English: the variationist at the mercy of his corpus?", *Neuphilologische Mitteilungen* 84, 2: 470-490.

Kytö, Merja – Terry Walker
    2003   "The linguistic study of Early Modern English speech- related texts. How "bad" can "bad" data be?", *Journal of English Linguistics* 31, 3: 221-248.

Labov, William
  1972   *Sociolinguistic patterns*. Philadelphia: University of Philadelphia Press.
  1994   *Principles of linguistic change: Internal factors*. Oxford: Blackwell Publishers.
Lass, Roger
  2004   "Texts as linguistic objects", in: Christian J. Kay – Jeremy J. Smith (eds.), 147-157.
Lass, Roger (ed.)
  2000   *Cambridge history of the English language. Volume III.* 1476-1776. Cambridge: Cambridge University Press.
Lebsanft, Franz
  1999   "A late medieval French bargain dialogue (Pahetlin II), or: further remarks on the history of dialogue forms", in: Andreas H. Jucker – Gerd Fritz – Franz Lebsanft (eds.), 269-292.
Leech, Geoffrey N.
  1983   *Principles of pragmatics*. London: Longman.
Leech, Geoffrey N. – Mick Short
  1981   *Style in fiction. A linguistic introduction to English fictional prose*. London – New York: Longman.
Lehrstuhl fuer Romanische Philologie I
  2004   (http://www.zv.uni-wuerzburg.de/forschungsbericht/FOBE-akt/LS-50003010b/xB-Frank%20-%20F1-E.htm) DOA 09/2004.
Lemert, Charles – Ann Branaman (eds.)
  1997   *The Goffman reader. Edited with introductory essays by Charles Lemert and Ann Branaman*. Malden – Oxford: Blackwell Publishers.
Levey, Stephen
  2003   "Reported dialogue and pragmatic particles in the narratives of preadolescents", *World Englishes* 22, 3: 305-321.
Levi, Judith N.
  1990   "The study of language in the judicial process", in: Judith N. Levi - Anne Graffam Walker (eds.), 3-31.
Levi, Judith N. – Anne Graffam Walker (eds.)
  1990   *Language in the judicial process*. New York – London: Plenum Press.
Levinson, Stephen C.
  1983   *Pragmatics*. Cambridge – New York: Cambridge University Press.
Lindstrom, Lamont
  1992   "Context contests: debatable truth statements on Tanna (Vanuatu)", in: Alessandro Duranti – Charles Goodwin (eds.), 101-122.
Linell, Per
  2001   "Dynamics of discourse or stability of structure: Sociolinguistics and the legacy from linguistics", in: Nikolas Coupland – Srikant Sarangi – Christopher N. Candlin (eds.), 107-126.
Loades, David M.
  1999   *Politics and nation England 1450-1660. Fifth edition*. Oxford: Blackwell.
Lowndes, William Thomas
  1864   *The bibliographer's manual of English literature. Containing an account of rare, curious, and useful books, published in or relating to Great Britain and Ireland...with bibliographical and critical notices...new edition, revised, corrected and enlarged*. London: Henry G. Bohn.

Lucy, John
1993a "General introduction", in: John Lucy (ed.), 1-4.
1993b "Metapragmatic presentationals: reporting speech with quotatives in Yucatec Maya", in: John Lucy (ed.), 91-125.
Lucy, John (ed.)
1993 *Reflexive language: Reported speech and metapragmatics*. Cambridge: Cambridge University Press.
Lunde, Ingunn
2004 "Rhetorical *enargeia* and linguistic pragmatics: On speech reporting strategies in East Slavic medieval hagiography and homiletics", *Journal of Historical Pragmatics* 5, 1: 49-80.
McGregor, William
1990 "The metafunctional hypothesis and syntagmatic relations", *Occasional Papers in Systemic Linguistics* 4: 5-50.
McHalle, Brian
1978 "Free indirect discourse: A survey of recent accounts", *Journal for Descriptive Poetics and Theory of Literature* 3: 249-287.
McIntosh, Angus
1956 "The analysis of written Middle English", *Transactions of the Philological Society*, 26-55.
[1989] [Reprinted in: Angus McIntosh – M. L. Samuels – Margaret Laing (eds.), 1-21.]
1963 "A new approach to Middle English dialectology", *English Studies* 44: 1-11.
[1989] [Reprinted in: Angus McIntosh – M. L. Samuels – Margaret Laing (eds.), 22-31.]
McIntosh, Angus – Michael L. Samuels – Margaret Laing (eds.)
1989 *Middle English dialectology: Essays on some principles and problems*. Aberdeen: Aberdeen University Press.
McIntyre, Dan – Carol Bellard-Thomson – John Heywood – Tony McEnery – Elena Semino – Mick Short
2004 "Investigating the presentation of speech, writing and thought in spoken British English: A corpus-based approach", *ICAME Journal* 28: 49-76.
Maingueneau, Dominique
1999 "Analysing self-constituting discourses", *Discourse Studies* 1, 2: 175-199.
Mäkinen, Martti
2002 "On interaction in herbals from Middle English to Early Modern English", *Journal of Historical Pragmatics* 3, 2: 229-251.
Marnette, Sophie
2001 "The French *theorie de l'énonciation* and the study of speech and thought presentation", *Language and Literature* 10, 3: 243-262.
Massamba, David P. B.
1986 "Reported speech in Swahili", in: Florian Coulmas (ed.), 99-119.
Matoesian, Greg
1999 "The grammaticalisation of participant roles in the constitution of expert identity", *Language in Society* 28, 4: 491-521.
2000 "Intertextual authority in reported speech: Production media in the Kennedy Smith rape trial", *Journal of Pragmatics* 32, 7: 879-914.
Maybin, Janet
1996 "Story voices: the use of reported speech in 10-12 years olds' spontaneous narratives", *Current Issues in Language & Society* 3, 1: 36-48.

1999 "Framing and evaluation in ten- to twelve-year-old school children's use of repeated, appropriated and reported speech in relation to their induction into educational procedures and practices", *Text* 19, 4: 459-484.

Mayes, Patricia
1990 "Quotation in spoken English", *Studies in Language* 14, 2: 325-363.

Maynard, Senko K.
1996 "Multivoicedness in speech and thought representation. The case of self-quotation in Japanese", *Journal of Pragmatics* 25, 2: 207-226.

Mazzon, Gabriela
1997 *"The study of language varieties in diachrony and synchrony, or: on methodological cross-fertilization.*
(http://www.univie.ac.at/Anglistik/hoe/mazzon.htm) DOA 08/2004.

Mellinkoff, David
1963 *The language of the law.* Boston, Toronto: Little, Brown and Company.

Moon, Rosamund
1994 "The analysis of fixed expressions in text", in: Malcolm Coulthard (ed.), 117-135.

Moore, Colette
2003 "Reporting direct speech in early Modern slander depositions", in: Robert Stockwell – Donka Minkova (eds.), 399-416.

Moore, Robert E.
1993 "Performance form and the voices of characters in five versions of the Wasco Coyote Cycle", in: John Lucy (ed.), 213-240.

Mullholand, Maureen
2003 "Introduction", in: Maureen Mullholand – Brian Pullan (eds.), 1-18.

Mullholand, Maureen – Brian Pullan (eds.)
2003 *Judicial tribunals in England and Europe, 1200-1700. The trial in history, volume I.* Manchester – New York: Manchester University Press.

Mushin, Ilana
2001a "Japanese reportive evidentiality and the pragmatics of retelling", *Journal of Pragmatics* 33, 9: 1361-1390.
2001b *Evidentiality and epistemological stance: narrative retelling.* Amsterdam – Philadelphia: John Benjamins.

Myers, Greg
1999a "Functions of reported speech in group discussions", *Applied Linguistics* 20, 3: 376-401.
1999b "Unspoken speech: Hypothetical reported discourse and the rhetoric of everyday talk", *Text* 19, 4: 571-590.

Nakayasu, Minako
2005 Modals in Shakespeare: a reappraisal. (Unpublished Ph.D. dissertation, Adama Mickiewicz University, Poznań).

Nevalainen, Terttu
1999 "Making the best use of 'bad' data", *Neuphilologische Mitteilungen* 100, 4: 499-533.

Nevalainen, Terttu – Helena Raumolin-Brunberg
1995 "Constraints on politeness: the pragmatics of address formulae in early English correspondence", in: Andreas H. Jucker (ed.), 541-601.
2003 *Historical sociolinguistics: Language change in Tudor and Stuart England.* London – New York: Pearson Education.

Nevalainen, Terttu – Helena Raumolin-Brunberg (eds.)
1996 *Sociolingustics and language history. Studies based on the Corpus of the Early English Correspondence.* Amsterdam – Atlanta: Rodopi.
Nurmi, Arja
1999 *A social history of periphrastic DO.* Helsinki: Société Néophilologique.
Nuyts, Jan
2001a *Epistemic modality, language and conceptualisation. A cognitive-pragmatic perspective.* Amsterdam – Philadelphia: John Benjamins.
2001b "Subjectivity as an evidential dimension in epistemic modal expressions", *Journal of Pragmatics* 33, 3: 383-400.
OED Online
2005 *Oxford English Dictionary. New edition, revised.* Oxford: Oxford University Press. (http://bu169.bu.amu.edu.pl/han/Oxford English Dictionary/dictionary.oed.Com/entrance.dtl) DOA 05/2005.
Oesterreicher, Wulf
1999 "Dialogue and violence: The Inca Atahualpa meets Fray Vincente de Valverde (Cajamarca, Peru, 16 November, 1532)", in: Andreas H. Jucker – Gerd Fritz – Franz Lebsanft (eds.), 431-463.
Onodera, Noriko
1995 "Diachronic analysis of Japanese discourse markers", in: Andreas H. Jucker (ed.), 393-437.
2000 "Development of demo type connectives and na elements: Two extremes of Japanese discourse markers", *Journal of Historical Pragmatics* 1, 1: 27-55.
Ormrod, W.M.
2003 "The use of English: language, law, and political culture in fourteenth century England", *Speculum* 78, 3: 750-787.
Overstreet, Maryann – George Yule
2002 "The metapragmatics of *and everything*", *Journal of Pragmatics* 34, 6: 785-794.
Palander-Collin, Minna
1996 "The rise and fall of METHINKS", in: Terttu Nevalainen and Helena Raumolin-Brunberg (eds.), 131-149.
1999 "I think, methinks: register variation, stratification, education and non-standard language", in: Irma Taavitsainen – Gunnel Melchers – Päivi Pahta (eds.), 243-262.
Palmer, Frank R.
2001 *Mood and modality. Second edition.* Cambridge: Cambridge University Press.
2003 "Modality in English: Theoretical, descriptive and typological issues", in: Roberta Facchinetti – Manfred Krug – Frank Palmer (eds.), 1-17.
Parmentier, Richard J.
1993 "The political function of reported speech: a Belauan example", in: John Lucy (ed.), 261-286.
Pateman, Trevor
1989 "Pragmatics in semiotic: Bakhtin/Volosinov" (Revised version of the article under the same title: *Journal of Literary Semantics* 18, 3: 203-216). (http://www.selectedworks.co.uk/pragmatics.rtf) DOA 09/2004.
Patterson, Annabel (ed.)
1998 *The trial of Nicholas Throckmorton. A modernised edition.* Toronto: Centre for Reformation and Renaissance Studies.

Precht, Kirsten
2003 "Stance moods in spoken English: Evidentiality and affect in British and American conversation", *Text* 23, 2: 239-257.
Preface to the first edition
1719 In: Francis Hargrave (ed.) [unpaginated]
Public Record Office
2005 (http://www.catalogue.nationalarchives.gov.uk) DOA 06/2005.
Quirk, Randolf – Sidney Greenbaum – Geoffrey Leech – Jan Svartvik
1985 *A comprehensive grammar of the English language.* London – New York: Longman.
Radcliffe, G.R.Y – Geoffrey Cross
1927 [1946] *The English legal system.* London: Butterworth and Co.
Ramge, Hans
1999 "Dialoge im Rechtsprotokoll: Ein Wetzlarer Erbstreit a. 1309 und die Entstehung einen neuen Textsorte", in: Andreas H. Jucker – Gerd Fritz – Franz Lebsanft (eds.), 371-398.
Recanati, François
2002 "Does linguistic communication rest on inference?", *Mind & Language* 17: 105-126.
Reilly, Judy – Anita Zamora – Robert F. McGivern
2005 "Acquiring perspective in English: the development of stance", *Journal of Pragmatics* 37, 3: 285-308.
Renouf, Antoinette (ed.)
1998 *Explorations in corpus linguistics.* Amsterdam – Atlanta: Rodopi.
Rice, Keren D.
1986 "Some remarks on direct and indirect speech in Slave (Northern Athapaskan)", in: Florian Coulmas (ed.), 161-178.
Rissanen, Matti
1985 "Periphrastic *do* in affirmative statements in early American English", *Journal of English Linguistics* 18, 2: 163-183.
[1998] [Reprinted in: in: Mats Rydén – Ingrid Tieken-Boon van Ostade – Merja Kytö (eds.), 201-219.]
1985 "Variation and the study of English historical syntax", in: David Sankoff (ed.), 97-110.
2000 "Syntax", in: Roger Lass (ed.), 187-331.
Rissanen, Matti – Ossi Ihalainen – Terttu Nevalainen – Irma Taavitsainen (eds.)
1992 *History of Englishes: New methods and interpretations in historical linguistics.* Berlin: Mouton the Gruyter.
Roeck, Marijke de
1994 "A functional typology of speech reports", in: Elisabeth Engberg-Pedersen – Lisbeth Falster Jakobsen – Lone Schack Rasmussen (eds.), 331-351.
Romaine, Suzanne
1982 *Socio-historical linguistics.* Cambridge: Cambridge University Press.
Ross, Richard J.
1998 "The commoning of the common law: The Renaissance debate over printing English law, 1520-1640", *University of Pennsylvania Law Review* 146, 2: 323-461.
Rowse, Alfred Leslie
1976 *Anglia w epoce Elżbietańskiej.* Warszawa: Państwowy Instytut Wydawniczy.

Rydén, Mats
1970 *Coordination of relative clauses in sixteenth century English.* Uppsala: Almqvist & Wiksells.
Rydén, Mats – Ingrid Tieken-Boon van Ostade – Merja Kytö (eds.)
1998 *A reader in Early Modern English.* Frankfurt am Main – New York: Peter Lang Verlag.
Sakita, Tomoko I.
2002 "Dialogue-internal and external features representing mental imagery of speaker attitudes", *Text* 22, 1: 83-105.
Salkie, Raphael – Susan Reed
1997 "Time reference in reported speech", *English Language and Linguistics* 1, 2: 319-348.
Sankoff, David (ed.)
1986 *Diversity and diachrony.* Amsterdam – Philadelphia: John Benjamins.
Schegloff, Emanuel A.
1992 "In another context", in: Alessandro Duranti – Charles Goodwin (eds.), 191-227.
Schiffrin, Deborah
1987 "Discovering the context of an utterance", *Linguistics* 25, 1: 11-32.
2002 "Mother and friends in a Holocaust life story", *Language in Society* 31, 3: 309-353.
Schiffrin, Deborah – Deborah Tannen – Heidi E. Hamilton (eds.)
2001 *The handbook of discourse analysis.* Malden: Blackwell Publishers.
Schlieben-Lange, Brigitte
1983 *Traditionen des Sprechens. Elemente einer pragmatischen Sprachgeschichtsschreibung,* Stuttgart: Kohlnammer.
1992 "The history of subordinating conjunctions in some Romance languages", in: Gerritsen, Marinel – Dieter Stein (eds.), 341-354.
Schneider, Edgar W.
2002 "Investigating language variation and change in written documents", in: J.K. Chambers – Peter Trudgill – Natalie Schilling-Estes (eds.), 67-96.
Schrott, Angela
1999 "Que fais, Adam?: Questions and seduction in the Jeu d'Adam", in: Andreas H. Jucker – Gerd Fritz – Franz Lebsanft (eds.), 331-370.
2000 "¿Qui los podrié contar? Interrogative acts in the Cantar de mio Cid: Some examples from Old Spanish on asking questions", *Journal of Historical Pragmatics* 1, 2: 263-299.
Schwenter, Scott, A. – Elizabeth Closs Traugott
1995 "The semantic and pragmatic development of substitutive complex prepositions in English", in: Andreas H. Jucker (ed.), 243-273.
Schwitalla, Johannes
1999 "The use of dialogue in early German pamphlets", in: Andreas H. Jucker – Gerd Fritz – Franz Lebsanft (eds.), 111-137.
Scott, Mike
1998 *WordSmith Tools 3.0.* Oxford: Oxford University Press.
Sell, Roger
1985 "Politeness in Chaucer: suggestions towards a methodology for pragmatic stylistics", *Studia Neophilologica* 57: 175-185.
Sell, Roger (ed.)
1991 *Literary pragmatics.* London – New York: Routledge.

Semino, Elena – Mick Short
2004   *Corpus stylistics: speech, writing and thought presentation in a corpus of English writing.* London – New York: Routledge.

Seoane Posse, Elena
2000   "Impersonalising strategies in Early Modern English", *English Studies* 81, 2: 102-116.

Shepard, Alexandra
2004   "Litigation and locality: the Cambridge university courts, 1560-1640", *Urban History* 31, 1: 5-28.

Shinzato, Rumiko
2004   "Some observations concerning mental verbs and speech act verbs", *Journal of Pragmatics* 36, 5: 861-882.

Short, Mick
2003   "A corpus-based approach to speech, thought and writing presentation", in: Andrew Wilson – Paul Rayson – Tony McEnery (eds.), 241-271.

Short, Mick – Elena Semino – Jonathan Culpeper
1996   "Using a corpus for stylistic research: speech and thought presentation", in: Jenny Thomas – Mick Short (eds.), 110-131.

Short, Mick – Elena Semino – Martin Wynne
2002   "Revisiting the notion of faithfulness in discourse report/(re)presentation using a corpus approach", *Language and Literature* 11, 4: 325-355.

Shuman, Amy
1993   ""Get outa my face": entitlement and authoritative discourse", in: Jane H. Hill – Judith T. Irvine (eds.), 135-160.

Shuy, Roger W.
2001   "Discourse analysis in the legal context", in: Deborah Schiffrin – Deborah Tannen – Heidi E. Hamilton (eds.), 437-452.

Slembrouck, Stef
1992   "The parliamentary Hansard 'verbatim' report: the written construction of spoken discourse", *Language and Literature* 1, 2: 101-119.

Sleurs, Kim – Geert Jacobs – Luuk van Waes
2003   "Constructing press releases, constructing quotations: A case study", *Journal of Sociolinguistics* 7, 2: 192-212.

Stein, Dieter
1985   "Perspectives on historical pragmatics", *Folia Linguistica Historica* VI, 2: 347-355.

1990   *The semantics of syntactic change: aspects of the evolution of do in English.* Berlin – New York: Mouton de Gruyter.

Sternberg, Meir
1982   "Proteus in quotation-land. Mimesis and the forms of reported discourse", *Poetics Today* 3, 2: 107-156.

1991   "How indirect discourse means. Syntax, semantics, poetics, pragmatics", in: Roger Sell (ed.), 62-93.

Stockwell, Robert – Donka Minkova (eds.)
2003   *Studies in the history of the English language. A millennial perspective.* Berlin – New York: Mouton de Gruyter.

Swan, Toril – Olaf Jansen Westvik (eds.)
1997   *Modality in Germanic languages. Historical and comparative perspectives.* Berlin – New York: Mouton de Gruyter.

Taavitsainen, Irma
1995 "Interjections in Early Modern English", in: Andreas H. Jucker (ed.), 439-465.
1999 "Dialogues in English medical writing", in: Andreas H. Jucker – Gerd Fritz – Franz Lebsanft (eds.), 242-268.
2001 "Middle English recipes: Genre characteristics, text type features and underlying traditions of writing", *Journal of Historical Pragmatics* 2, 1: 85-113.
Taavitsainen, Irma – Gunnel Melchers – Päivi Pahta (eds.)
1999 *Writing in nonstandard English*. Amsterdam – Philadelphia: John Benjamins.
Tannen, Deborah
1986 "Introducing constructed dialogue in Greek and American conversation and literary narrative", in: Florian Coulmas (ed.), 311-332.
1989 *Talking voices: Repetition, dialogue and imagery in conversational discourse*. Cambridge: Cambridge University Press.
Tannen, Deborah – James E. Alatis (eds.)
1986 *Languages and linguistics: The interdependence of theory, data, and application*. Washington, D.C.: Georgetown University Press.
Thomas, Jenny – Mick Short (eds.)
1996 *Using corpora for language research*. London: Longman.
Thompson, Geoff
1996 "Voices in the text: Discourse perspectives on language reports", *Applied Linguistics* 17, 4: 500-530.
Tieken-Boon van Ostade, Ingrid
1985 "Do support in the writings of Lady Mary Worley Montagu: a change in progress", *Folia Linguistica Historica* IV, 2: 127-151.
2000 "Sociohistorical linguistics and the observer's paradox", in: Dieter Kastovsky – Arthur Mettinger (eds.), 441-461.
Tiersma, Peter M.
1999 *Legal language*. Chicago – London: University of Chicago Press.
Tomasik, Wojciech
1992 *Sześć rozpraw o „mowie pozornie zależnej"*. Bydgoszcz: Wydawnictwo Uczelniane Wyższej Szkoły Pedagogicznej.
Traugott, Elizabeth Closs
1972 *The history of English syntax. A transformational approach to the history of English sentence structure*. New York – London: Holt, Rinehart and Winston, Inc.
Traugott, Elizabeth Closs – Richard Dasher
2002 *Regularity in semantic change*. Cambridge: Cambridge University Press.
Tree, Jean A. Fox – Josef C. Schrock
2002 "Basic meanings of *you know* and *I mean*", *Journal of Pragmatics* 34, 6: 727-747.
Turnbull, William – Karen L. Saxton
1997 "Modal expressions as facework in refusals to comply with requests: I think I should say 'no' right now", *Journal of Pragmatics* 27, 2: 145-181.
Uchida, Seiji
1997 "Immediate contexts and reported speech", *UCL Working Papers in Linguistics* 9, (http://www.phon.ucl.ac.uk/home/PUB/WPL/97papers/ uchida.pdf) DOA 01/2005.
Urban, Greg
1993 "The represented functions of speech in Shockleng myth", in: John Lucy (ed.), 241-260.

Van der Wurff, Wim
    2002   "Direct, indirect and other discourse in Bengali newspapers", in: Tom Güldemann – Manfred von Roncador (eds.), 121-139.
Van Dijk, Teun A.
    2004   "Text and context of parliamentary debates", in: Paul Bayley (ed.), 339-372.
Vandelanotte, Lieven
    2003   "Dependency, framing, scope? The syntagmatic structure of sentences of speech or thought representation" (provisional version – November 2003). (http://lieven.studentenweb.org/pdf/syntagmaticstructure.pdf) DOA 01/2005.
    2004a   "Deixis and grounding in speech and thought representation", *Journal of Pragmatics* 36, 5: 489-520.
    2004b   "From representational to scopal 'distancing indirect speech or thought': A cline of subjectification", *Text* 24, 4: 547-585.
Verschueren, Jef
    1995   "Metapragmatics", in: Jef Verschueren – Jan-Ola Östman – Jan Blomaert (eds.), 367-371.
    2003   "Introduction – The pragmatic perspective", in: *The Handbook of Pragmatics Online* DOA 08/2004.
Verschueren, Jef – Jan-Ola Östman – Jan Blomaert (eds.)
    1995   *Handbook of pragmatics: Manual.* Amsterdam – Philadelphia: John Benjamins.
Vincent, Diane – Sylvie Dubois
    1996   "A study of the use of reported speech in spoken language", in: Jennifer Arnold – Renée Blake – Brad Davidson – Scott Schwenter – Julie Solomon (eds.), 361-374.
Vincent, Diane – Laurent Perrin
    1999   "On the narrative vs. non-narrative functions of reported speech: a socio-pragmatic study", *Journal of Sociolinguistics* 3, 3: 291-313.
Volosinov, Valentin N.
    1929 [1973] *Marxism and the philosophy of language.* Translated by Ladislav Matejka and I. R. Titunik. New York – London: Seminar Press.
Watts, Richard J.
    1981   *The pragmalinguistic analysis of narrative texts. Narrative cooperation in Charles Dickens' Hard Times.* Tübingen: Gunter Narr.
    1995   "A socio-pragmatic foray into the discourse community of early English grammarians", in: Andreas H. Jucker (ed.), 145-185.
    1999   "*Refugiate in a strange countrey*: Learning English through dialogues in the 16th Century", in: Andreas Jucker – Gerd Fritz – Franz Lebsanft (eds.), 215-241.
Watts, Richard J. – Peter Trudgill (eds.)
    2001   *Alternative histories of English.* London – New York: Routledge.
Waugh, Linda
    1995   "Reported speech in journalistic discourse: The relation of function and text", *Text* 15, 1: 129-173.
White, P. R. R.
    2003   "Beyond modality and hedging: A dialogic view of the language of intersubjective stance", *Text* 23, 2: 259-284.
Wierzbicka, Anna
    1987   *English speech act verbs: a semantic dictionary.* Orlando – London: Academic Press.

Willet, Thomas
　　1988　　"A cross-linguistic survey of the grammaticalisation of evidentiality", *Studies in Language* 12, 1: 51-97.
Wilson, Andrew – Paul Rayson – Tony McEnery (eds.)
　　2003　　*Corpus linguistics by the lune. A festschrift for Geoffrey Leech.* Frankfurt am Main – New York: Peter Lang.
Wischer, Ilse
　　2000　　"'Methinks' there is some confusion", in: Olga Fischer – Anette Rosenbach – Dieter Stein (eds.), 355-370.
Włodarczyk-Golka, Matylda
　　2004　　"A costly compromise? – The 'bad' data problem in historical pragmatics", in: Radosław Dylewski – Piotr Cap (eds.), 75-110.
Wortham, Stanton – Michael Locher
　　1999　　"Embedded metapragmatics and lying politicians", *Language and Communication* 19, 2: 109-125.
Wright, Laura
　　1995　　"Syntactic structure of the witnesses' narratives from the sixteenth century Court Minute Books of the Royal Hospitals of Bridewell and Bedlam", *Neuphilologische Mitteilungen* 96, 1: 93-105.
Wynne, Martin – Mick Short – Elena Semino
　　1998　　"A corpus-based investigation of speech, thought and writing presentation in English narrative texts", in: Antoinette Renouf (ed.), 233-247.
Yule, George – Terrie Mathis
　　1992　　"The role of staging and constructed dialogue in establishing speaker's topic", *Linguistics* 30: 199-215.

Studies in English Medieval Language and Literature

Edited by Jacek Fisiak

Vol. 1 Dieter Kastovsky / Arthur Mettinger (eds.): Language Contact in the History of English. 2nd, revised edition. 2003.

Vol. 2 Studies in English Historical Linguistics and Philology. A Festschrift for Akio Oizumi. Edited by Jacek Fisiak. 2002.

Vol. 3 Liliana Sikorska: *In a Manner Morall Playe*: Social Ideologies in English Moralities and Interludes (1350-1517). 2002.

Vol. 4 Peter J. Lucas / Angela M. Lucas (eds.): Middle English from Tongue to Text. Selected Papers from the Third International Conference on Middle English: Language and Text, held at Dublin, Ireland, 1-4 July 1999. 2002.

Vol. 5 Chaucer and the Challenges of Medievalism. Studies in Honor of H. A. Kelly. Edited by Donka Minkova and Theresa Tinkle. 2003.

Vol. 6 Hanna Rutkowska: Graphemics and Morphosyntax in the *Cely Letters* (1472-88). 2003.

Vol. 7 The *Ancrene Wisse*. A Four-Manuscript Parallel Text. Preface and Parts 1-4. Edited by Tadao Kubouchi and Keiko Ikegami with John Scahill, Shoko Ono, Harumi Tanabe, Yoshiko Ota, Ayako Kobayashi and Koichi Nakamura. 2003.

Vol. 8 Joanna Bugaj: Middle Scots Inflectional System in the South-west of Scotland. 2004.

Vol. 9 Rafal Boryslawski: The Old English Riddles and the Riddlic Elements of Old English Poetry. 2004.

Vol. 10 Nikolaus Ritt / Herbert Schendl (eds.): Rethinking Middle English. Linguistic and Literary Approaches. 2005.

Vol. 11 The *Ancrene Wisse*. A Four-Manuscript Parallel Text. Parts 5–8 with Wordlists. Edited by Tadao Kubouchi and Keiko Ikegami with John Scahill, Shoko Ono, Harumi Tanabe, Yoshiko Ota, Ayako Kobayashi, Koichi Nakamura. 2005.

Vol. 12 Text and Language in Medieval English Prose. A Festschrift for Tadao Kubouchi. Edited by Akio Oizumi, Jacek Fisiak and John Scahill. 2005.

Vol. 13 Michiko Ogura (ed.): Textual and Contextual Studies in Medieval English. Towards the Reunion of Linguistics and Philology. 2006.

Vol. 14 Keiko Hamaguchi: Non-European Women in Chaucer. A Postcolonial Study. 2006.

Vol. 15 Ursula Schaefer (ed.): The Beginnings of Standardization. Language and Culture in Fourteenth-Century England. 2006.

Vol. 16 Nikolaus Ritt / Herbert Schendl / Christiane Dalton-Puffer / Dieter Kastovsky (eds): Medieval English and its Heritage. Structure, Meaning and Mechanisms of Change. 2006.

Vol. 17 Matylda Włodarczyk: Pragmatic Aspects of Reported Speech. The Case of Early Modern English Courtroom Discourse. 2007.

Vol. 18 Hans Sauer / Renate Bauer (eds.): *Beowulf* and Beyond. 2007.

www.peterlang.de

Melanie Brüngel-Dittrich

Speech Presentation in the British and German Press

Frankfurt am Main, Berlin, Bern, Bruxelles, New York, Oxford, Wien, 2006.
266 pp., 37 tab., 47 graf.
European University Studies: Series 21, Linguistics. Vol. 297
ISBN 3-631-54948-2 / US-ISBN 0-8204-9858-0 · pb. € 45.50*

This book is a comparative linguistic study analysing the phenomenon of speech presentation or *Redewiedergabe* in a corpus of British and German newspaper articles. By applying a modified speech presentation model to a corpus of 143 articles – originally, the prototype had been designed for the analysis of English literary texts – the author shows that it is possible to examine journalistic texts stylistically and to compare texts written in different languages. The analysis, divided into a qualitative and a quantitative part, reveals that the genre of a text or paper influences the use of speech presentation to a high extent. Differences between the German and English texts in terms of language structure and also newspaper culture are highlighted, involving an examination of the use of reporting verbs, the subjunctive and *berichtete Rede* in the German articles.

Contents: Speech presentation – models for the English and the German language · Newspapers on the Internet · Qualitative and quantitative analysis of speech presentation in British and German newspaper articles · Reporting verbs in British and German newspapers articles · Comparison of results with existing studies and theories · The use of the subjunctive in German news texts · *Berichtete Rede* · Speech presentation in headlines

Frankfurt am Main · Berlin · Bern · Bruxelles · New York · Oxford · Wien
Distribution: Verlag Peter Lang AG
Moosstr. 1, CH-2542 Pieterlen
Telefax 00 41 (0) 32 / 376 17 27

*The €-price includes German tax rate
Prices are subject to change without notice
Homepage http://www.peterlang.de